Prose Keys to Modern Poetry

Prose Keys to Modern Poetry

Edited by

KARL SHAPIRO
University of Nebraska

HARPER & ROW, PUBLISHERS
New York, Evanston, and London

ACKNOWLEDGMENTS

The editor wishes to express his thanks to the following publishers and individuals for granting permission to reprint the selections listed below:

"The Artist as Don Quixote" from *The Enchafed Flood*, by W. H. Auden. Copyright 1950 by the Rector and Visitors of the University of Virginia. Reprinted by permission of Random House, Inc.

"Three Drafts of a Preface" from *The Flowers of Evil* by Charles Baudelaire, edited by Marthiel and Jackson Mathews (translated by Jackson Mathews). Copyright 1955 by New Directions. Reprinted by permission of New Directions, Publishers.

Excerpts from *Intimate Journals* by Charles Baudelaire (translated by Christopher Isherwood). Copyright 1947 by Christopher Isherwood and reprinted by his permission.

Excerpt from *The Analects of Confucius* (translated by Arthur Waley). Reprinted by permission of The Macmillan Company. Canadian permission granted by George Allen & Unwin, Ltd.

"General Aims and Theories" by Hart Crane, as reprinted in Philip Horton, *Hart Crane* (New York: W. W. Norton & Company, 1937). Reprinted by permission of Samuel Loveman, executor of the Crane estate.

Introduction to *Poems 1923–1954* by E. E. Cummings. Copyright, 1938, by E. E. Cummings. Reprinted from *Poems 1923–1954* by E. E. Cummings by permission of Harcourt, Brace & World, Inc.

"The Metaphysical Poets" and "Tradition and the Individual Talent" from *Selected Essays* by T. S. Eliot, copyright, 1932, 1936, 1950, by Harcourt, Brace & World, Inc.; copyright, 1960, by T. S. Eliot. Reprinted by permission of the publishers. Canadian permission granted by Faber and Faber Ltd.

"The Chinese Written Character as a Medium for Poetry" by Ernest Fenollosa, from *Instigations of Ezra Pound*. Published by Arrow Editions and reprinted by permission of Ezra Pound.

"The King of the Wood" from *The Golden Bough* by Sir James Frazer. Copyright by Trinity College, Cambridge, England. Reprinted by permission of Trinity College, Macmillan & Co. Ltd., and St. Martin's Press, Inc.

Excerpts from "Inscape and Instress" in *Gerard Manley Hopkins: A Selection of His Poems and Prose*, edited by W. H. Gardner. Reprinted by permission of Oxford University Press, London.

Author's Preface to *Poems of Gerard Manley Hopkins*. Reprinted by permission of Oxford University Press, London.

"Romanticism and Classicism" from *Speculations* by T. E. Hulme. Reprinted by permission of Harcourt, Brace & World, Inc. Canadian permission granted by Routledge & Kegan Paul Ltd.

"Notice" from *Against the Grain* by J. K. Huysmans. Reprinted by courtesy of Random House, Inc.

Foreword to *Selected Poetry of Robinson Jeffers*. Copyright 1938 by Robinson Jeffers. Reprinted from *Selected Poetry of Robinson Jeffers* by permission of Random House, Inc.

FOREWORD

The key to understanding modern poetry lies not in the poems but in the prose foundation of the poems. Modern poetry is a structure of attitudes, carefully and rationally built up into a towering world view of life and art. To some readers this world view resembles the Tower of Babel; to others it represents the reality of modern life.

Ours is perhaps the only poetry in history which must be approached over the heavy causeways of prose. The very landscape of modern poetry is that of the prosaic. It is city poetry, and the city has always fallen or is about to fall. Whether it is the Dublin of Joyce or of Yeats, the London of Eliot, the New York of Lorca, or the Paris of Baudelaire, the centers of modern civilization are shown in dreary decline or under a state of siege. And the poet dwells in this city as an outcast or a "subterranean."

The complex social, political, and religious views implicit in modern literature must somehow be assimilated if the student is to master the literature itself. T. S. Eliot's *The Waste Land,* the central poem of the modern canon, has appended to it a series of scholarly notes without which the poem would be a considerable enigma. These notes cover in time and space nearly the whole history of Western culture. Ezra Pound's *Cantos* have had to be explained by a special dictionary of more than 17,000 scholarly references. Joyce's *Finnegans Wake* is written in a special language all its own.

The essays collected in the following pages bring together most of the chief prose documents upon which modern poetry is based and without which the poetry is all but meaningless. (The original texts were followed in all cases; no stylistic changes have been introduced.) The essays divide naturally into those of the "Classical" school and those of the "Romantic." Modern Classicist is the dominant poetry of the twentieth century, and it prides itself on its adherence to tradition, ritual, metaphysical wit, learned irony, and the need for discipline in art and in society. The Classicists identify themselves in their prose, and both define and elaborate their position. The Romantics are equally sweeping in their claims and objectives.

There is no attempt of any kind in this book to advocate one or another of the main philosophies of contemporary poetry. The sole object of this handbook is to provide the instructor and the student with those prose documents that have given modern poetry its special character. It has been my experience for many years that modern poetry cannot be taught or even surveyed without constant reference to these prose essays, notes, studies, and theories upon which it rests. Each essay or excerpt, therefore, will be introduced by a brief explanation of its place in the canon of modern poetry.

The sequence of chapters in this book presents certain problems. A purely chronological order would throw little light on the ideological background of modern Classicism or Romanticism. (We have appended a detailed chronological guide to the main literary events of the period.) The order of selections is based on *tendency*. For instance, the first chapters deal with the Symbolist tendency from Poe through Mallarmé. This section is followed by essays dealing with the Metaphysical tendency, and is succeeded by essays dealing with theories of myth and myth-making as they apply to modern poetry. In this way the reader can trace the intellectual roots of the Classical or the Romantic tree. It is the belief of the editor that most of the exotic blooms and graftings of modern poetry, especially those usually referred to as "obscure," can best be appreciated by a study of these prose documents.

Modern criticism is a vast field, and we have had to omit many relevant selections. Works such as Irving Babbitt's *Rousseau and Romanticism,* for example, should have a place here, but it was felt that limits had to be placed upon a handbook of this size. The object of the anthology is to lead the student to the poetry and to detain him among the critical documents no longer than necessary.

KARL SHAPIRO

viii

TABLE OF CONTENTS

PART I   KEYS TO MODERN CLASSICISM

✍ The Formation of Classical Doctrine

𝒽 Classical Uses of the Past

𝒽 Systems and Techniques

𝒻 Romantic Self-Criticism

Keys to Modern Classicism

THE FORMATION OF CLASSICAL DOCTRINE

EDGAR ALLAN POE

The Philosophy of Composition

This essay, written over a century ago, says more about modern poetry than anything written before or since. Poe's reputation as critic has never been high in this country, but it has been a major influence in Europe since the middle of the nineteenth century. Poe captivated Charles Baudelaire, who translated many of the major works of the American and used them as ballast for his own poetics. Thus Poe revolutionized modern literature indirectly and gave the impetus to the Symbolist Movement which, in France at least, has dominated poetry for generations. The magic of the French or Parisian *savoir-faire* in letters has electrified European and American writers generation after generation. Baudelaire, Rimbaud, Verlaine, Mallarmé, Laforgue, Valéry, Perse are all children of Poe. And although Eliot repudiates Poe, he is deeply in his debt.

"The Philosophy of Composition" is a classic analysis of one's own poem—in this case the famous "The Raven." But it is a great deal more. It states the doctrine of "the effect" as a primary motive of the work of art. It was Poe's theory of the "effect" (as against the didactic and the emotional in poetry) that started certain French poets of the nineteenth century on the road to "suggestion," "association," and "nuance."

Poe's essay also speaks out against the "fine frenzy" of the poet, against poetry written in passion. It legislates against the "long poem" such as *Paradise Lost*. The twentieth-century prejudice

3

against the "long" poem undoubtedly dates back to Poe, who conceived of a "mathematical" relationship of the length of the poem to its merit.

Perhaps the most sweeping doctrine of Poe's in this essay is his assertion that "Beauty is the sole legitimate province of the poem." In making Beauty the supreme ideal of poetry, he rules out both didacticism and personal feeling, or passion. The far-reaching consequences of this theory have come back to us in later theories of depersonalization of art, variously stated by Mallarmé, Eliot, Yeats, and Pound, and in the idea of a poetic priesthood which may provide a leadership for civilization.

Poe's account of the composition of "The Raven" is a tribute to his ingeniousness as a poet, a critic, and an intellectual.

*C*harles Dickens, in a note now lying before me, alluding to an examination I once made of the mechanism of "Barnaby Rudge," says—"By the way, are you aware that Godwin wrote his 'Caleb Williams' backwards? He first involved his hero in a web of difficulties, forming the second volume, and then, for the first, cast about him for some mode of accounting for what had been done."

I cannot think this the *precise* mode of procedure on the part of Godwin—and indeed what he himself acknowledges, is not altogether in accordance with Mr. Dickens' idea—but the author of "Caleb Williams" was too good an artist not to perceive the advantage derivable from at least a somewhat similar process. Nothing is more clear than that every plot, worth the name, must be elaborated to its *dénouement* before any thing be attempted with the men. It is only with the *dénouement* constantly in view that we can give a plot its indispensable air of consequence, or causation, by making the incidents, and especially the tone at all points, tend to the development of the intention.

There is a radical error, I think, in the usual mode of constructing a story. Either history affords a thesis—or one is suggested by an incident of the day—or, at best, the author sets himself to work in the combination of striking events to form merely the basis of his narrative—designing, generally, to fill in with description, dialogue, or autorial * comment, whatever crevices of fact, or action, may, from page to page, render themselves apparent.

I prefer commencing with the consideration of an *effect*. Keeping originality *always* in view—for he is false to himself who ventures to dispense with so obvious and so easily attainable a source of interest—I say to myself, in the first place, "Of the innumerable effects, or impressions, of which the heart, the intellect, or (more generally) the soul is susceptible, what one shall I, on the present occasion, select?" Having chosen a novel, first, and secondly a vivid effect, I consider whether it can be best wrought by incident or tone—whether by ordinary incidents and peculiar tone, or the converse, or by peculiarity both of

---

* [Obsolete variant of "authorial."—Ed.]

incident and tone—afterward looking about me (or rather within) for such combinations of event, or tone, as shall best aid me in the construction of the effect.

I have often thought how interesting a magazine paper might be written by any author who would—that is to say, who could—detail, step by step, the processes by which any one of his compositions attained its ultimate point of completion. Why such a paper has never been given to the world, I am much at a loss to say—but, perhaps, the autorial vanity has had more to do with the omission than any one other cause. Most writers—poets in especial—prefer having it understood that they compose by a species of fine frenzy—an ecstatic intuition—and would positively shudder at letting the public take a peep behind the scenes, at the elaborate and vacillating crudities of thought—at the true purposes seized only at the last moment—at the innumerable glimpses of idea that arrived not at the maturity of full view—at the fully matured fancies discarded in despair as unmanageable—at the cautious selections and rejections—at the painful erasures and interpolations—in a word, at the wheels and pinions—the tackle for scene-shifting—the step-ladders and demon-traps—the cock's feathers, the red paint and the black patches, which, in ninety-nine cases out of the hundred, constitute the properties of the literary *histrio*.

I am aware, on the other hand, that the case is by no means common, in which an author is at all in condition to retrace the steps by which his conclusions have been attained. In general, suggestions, having arisen pell-mell, are pursued and forgotten in a similar manner.

For my own part, I have neither sympathy with the repugnance alluded to, nor, at any time, the least difficulty in recalling to mind the progressive steps of any of my compositions; and, since the interest of an analysis, or reconstruction, such as I have considered a *desideratum,* is quite independent of any real or fancied interest in the thing analyzed, it will not be regarded as a breach of decorum on my part to show the *modus operandi* by which some one of my own works was put together. I select "The Raven" as most generally known. It is my design to render it manifest that no one point in its composition is referable either to accident or intuition—that the work proceeded, step by step, to its completion with the precision and rigid consequence of a mathematical problem.

Let us dismiss, as irrelevant to the poem, *per se,* the circumstance—or say the necessity—which, in the first place, gave rise to the intention of composing *a* poem that should suit at once the popular and the critical taste.

We commence, then, with this intention.

The initial consideration was that of extent. If any literary work is too long to be read at one sitting, we must be content to dispense with the immensely important effect derivable from unity of impression—for, if two sittings be required, the affairs of the world interfere, and every thing like totality is at once destroyed. But since, *ceteris paribus,* no poet can afford to dispense with *any thing* that may advance his design, it but remains to be seen whether there is, in extent, any advantage to counterbalance the loss of unity which attends it. Here I say no, at once. What we term a long poem, is, in fact, merely a succession of brief ones—that is to say, of brief poetical effects. It is needless to demonstrate that a poem is such, only inasmuch as it intensely excites, by elevating, the soul; and all intense excitements are, through a psychal necessity, brief. For this reason, at least one half of the "Paradise Lost" is essentially prose—a succession of poetical excitements interspersed, *inevitably,* with corresponding depressions—the whole being deprived, through the extremeness of its length, of the vastly important artistic element, or unity, of effect.

It appears evident, then, that there is a distinct limit, as regards length, to all works of literary art—the limit of a single sitting—and that, although in certain classes of prose composition, such as "Robinson Crusoe," (demanding no unity,) this limit may be advantageously overpassed, it can never properly be overpassed in a poem. Within this limit, the extent of a poem may be made to bear mathematical relation to its merit—in other words, to the excitement or elevation—again, in other words, to the degree of the true poetical effect which it is capable of inducing; for it is clear that the brevity must be in direct ratio of the intensity of the intended effect:—this, with one proviso—that a certain degree of duration is absolutely requisite for the production of any effect at all.

Holding in view these considerations, as well as that degree of excitement which I deemed not above the popular, while not below the critical, taste, I reached at once what I conceived the proper *length* for my intended poem—a length of about one hundred lines. It is, in fact, a hundred and eight.

My next thought concerned the choice of an impression, or effect, to be conveyed: and here I may as well observe that, throughout the construction, I kept steadily in view the design of rendering the work *universally* appreciable. I should be carried too far out of my immediate topic were I to demonstrate a point upon which I have repeatedly insisted, and which, with the poetical, stands not in the slightest need of demonstration—the point, I mean, that Beauty is the sole legitimate province of the poem. A few words, however, in elucidation of my real meaning, which some of my friends have evinced a disposition to misrepresent. That pleasure which is at once the most intense, the most elevating, and the most pure, is, I believe, found in the contemplation of the beautiful. When, indeed, men speak of Beauty, they mean, precisely, not a quality, as is supposed, but an effect—they refer, in short, just to that intense and pure elevation of *soul*—not of intellect, or of heart—upon which I have commented, and which is experienced in consequence of contemplating "the beautiful." Now I designate Beauty as the province of the poem, merely because it is an obvious rule of Art that effects should be made to spring from direct causes—that objects should be attained through means best adapted for their attainment—no one as yet having been weak enough to deny that the peculiar elevation alluded to, is *most readily* attained in the poem. Now the object Truth, or the satisfaction of the intellect, and the object Passion, or the excitement of the heart, are, although attainable, to a certain extent, in poetry, far more readily attainable in prose. Truth, in fact, demands a precision, and Passion a *homeliness* (the truly passionate will comprehend me) which are absolutely antagonistic to that Beauty which, I maintain, is the excitement, or pleasurable elevation, of the soul. It by no means follows from any thing here said, that passion, or even truth, may not be introduced, and even profitably introduced, into a poem—for they may serve in elucidation, or aid the general effect, as do discords in music, by contrast—but the true artist will always contrive, first, to tone them into proper subservience to the predominant aim, and, secondly, to enveil them, as far as possible, in that Beauty which is the atmosphere and the essence of the poem.

Regarding, then, Beauty as my province, my next question referred to the *tone* of its highest manifestation—and all experience has shown that this tone is one of *sadness*. Beauty of whatever kind, in its supreme development, invariably excites the sensitive soul to tears. Melancholy is thus the most legitimate of all the poetical tones.

The length, the province, and the tone, being thus determined, I betook myself to ordinary induction, with the view of obtaining some artistic piquancy which might serve me as a key-note in the construction of the poem—some pivot upon which the whole structure might turn. In carefully thinking over all the usual artistic effects—or more properly *points*, in the theatrical sense—I did not fail to perceive immediately that no one had been so universally employed as that of the *refrain*. The universality of its employment sufficed to assure me of its intrinsic value, and spared me the necessity of submitting it to analysis. I considered it, however, with regard to its susceptibility of improvements, and soon saw it to be in a primitive condition. As commonly used, the *refrain,* or burden, not only is limited to lyric verse, but depends for its impression upon the force of monotone—both in sound and thought. The pleasure is deduced solely from the sense of identity—of repetition. I resolved to diversify, and so heighten, the effect, by adhering, in general, to the monotone of sound, while I continually varied that of thought: that is to say, I determined to produce continuously novel effects, by the variation of *the application* of the *refrain*—the *refrain* itself remaining, for the most part, unvaried.

These points being settled, I next bethought me of the *nature* of my *refrain.* Since its application was to be repeatedly varied, it was clear that the *refrain* itself must be brief, for there would have been an insurmountable difficulty in frequent variations of application in any sentence of length. In proportion to the brevity of the sentence, would, of course, be the facility of the variation. This led me at once to a single word as the best *refrain.*

The question now arose as to the *character* of the word. Having made up my mind to a *refrain,* the division of the poem into stanzas was, of course, a corollary: the *refrain* forming the close to each stanza. That such a close, to have force, must be sonorous and susceptible of protracted emphasis, admitted no doubt: and these considerations, inevitably led me to the long *o* as the most sonorous vowel, in connection with *r* as the most producible consonant.

The sound of the *refrain* being thus determined, it became necessary to select a word embodying this sound, and at the same time in the fullest possible keeping with that melancholy which I had predetermined as the tone of the poem. In such a search it would have been absolutely impossible to overlook the word "Nevermore." In fact, it was the very first which presented itself.

The next *desideratum* was a pretext for the continuous use of the one word "nevermore." In observing the difficulty which I at once found in inventing a sufficiently plausible reason for its continuous repetition, I did not fail to perceive that this difficulty arose solely from the pre-assumption that the word was to be so continuously or monotonously spoken by *a human* being—I did not fail to perceive, in short, that the difficulty lay in the reconciliation of this monotony with the exercise of reason on the part of the creature repeating the word. Here, then, immediately arose the idea of a *non*-reasoning creature capable of speech; and, very naturally, a parrot, in the first instance, suggested itself, but was superseded forthwith by a Raven, as equally capable of speech, and infinitely more in keeping with the intended *tone.*

I had now gone so far as the conception of a Raven—the bird of ill omen—monotonously repeating the one word, "Nevermore," at the conclusion of each stanza, in a poem of melancholy tone, and in length about one hundred lines. Now, never losing sight of the object *supremeness,* or perfection, at all points, I asked myself—"Of all melancholy topics, what, according to the *universal* understanding of mankind, is the *most* melancholy?" Death—was the obvious reply. "And when," I said, "is this most melancholy of topics most poetical?" From what I have already explained at some length, the answer, here also, is obvious—"When it most closely allies itself to *Beauty*: the death, then, of a beautiful woman is, unquestionably, the most poetical topic in the world—and equally is it beyond doubt that the lips best suited for such topic are those of a bereaved lover."

I had now to combine the two ideas, of a lover lamenting his deceased mistress and a Raven continuously repeating the word "Nevermore."—I had to combine these, bearing in mind my design of varying, at every turn, the *application* of the word repeated; but the only intelligible mode of such combination is that of imagining the Raven employing the word in answer to the queries of the lover. And here it was that I saw at once the opportunity afforded for the effect on which I had been depending —that is to say, the effect of the *variation of application.* I saw that I could make the first query propounded by the lover—the first query to

which the Raven should reply "Nevermore"—that I could make this first
query a commonplace one—the second less so—the third still less, and so
on—until at length the lover, startled from his original *nonchalance* by the
melancholy character of the word itself—by its frequent repetition—and
by a consideration of the ominous reputation of the fowl that uttered it—
is at length excited to superstition, and wildly propounds queries of a
far different character—queries whose solution he has passionately at
heart—propounds them half in superstition and half in that species of
despair which delights in self-torture—propounds them not altogether
because he believes in the prophetic or demoniac character of the bird
(which, reason assures him, is merely repeating a lesson learned by
rote) but because he experiences a frenzied pleasure in so modeling his
questions as to receive from the *expected* "Nevermore" the most delicious because the most intolerable of sorrow. Perceiving the opportunity thus afforded me—or, more strictly, thus forced upon me in the
progress of the construction—I first established in mind the climax, or
concluding query—that query to which "Nevermore" should be in the
last place an answer—that query in reply to which this word "Nevermore" should involve the uttermost conceivable amount of sorrow and
despair.

Here then the poem may be said to have its beginning—at the end,
where all works of art should begin—for it was here, at this point of my
preconsiderations, that I first put pen to paper in the composition of the
stanza:

> "Prophet," said I, "thing of evil! prophet still if bird or devil!
> By that heaven that bends above us—by that God we both
>   adore,
> Tell this soul with sorrow laden, if within the distant Aidenn,
> It shall clasp a sainted maiden whom the angels name Le-
>   nore—
> Clasp a rare and radiant maiden whom the angels name Le-
>   nore."
>   Quoth the raven "Nevermore."

I composed this stanza, at this point, first that, by establishing the
climax, I might the better vary and graduate, as regards seriousness and
importance, the preceding queries of the lover—and, secondly, that I
might definitely settle the rhythm, the metre, and the length and
general arrangement of the stanza—as well as graduate the stanzas
which were to precede, so that none of them might surpass this in
rhythmical effect. Had I been able, in the subsequent composition, to
construct more vigorous stanzas, I should, without scruple, have pur-
posely enfeebled them, so as not to interfere with the climacteric effect.

And here I may as well say a few words of the versification. My first
object (as usual) was originality. The extent to which this has been
neglected, in versification, is one of the most unaccountable things in
the world. Admitting that there is little possibility of variety in mere

rhythm, it is still clear that the possible varieties of metre and stanza are absolutely infinite—and yet, *for centuries, no man, in verse, has ever done, or ever seemed to think of doing, an original thing.* The fact is, that originality (unless in minds of very unusual force) is by no means a matter, as some suppose, of impulse or intuition. In general, to be found, it must be elaborately sought, and although a positive merit of the highest class, demands in its attainment less of invention than negation.

Of course, I pretend to no originality in either the rhythm or metre of the "Raven." The former is trochaic—the latter is octameter acatalectic, alternating with heptameter catalectic repeated in the *refrain* of the fifth verse, and terminating with tetrameter catalectic. Less pedantically —the feet employed throughout (trochees) consist of a long syllable followed by a short: the first line of the stanza consists of eight of these feet—the second of seven and a half (in effect two-thirds)—the third of eight—the fourth of seven and a half—the fifth the same—the sixth three and a half. Now, each of these lines, taken individually, has been employed before, and what originality the "Raven" has, is in their combination *into stanza;* nothing even remotely approaching this combination has ever been attempted. The effect of this originality of combination is aided by other unusual, and some altogether novel effects, arising from an extension of the application of the principles of rhyme and alliteration.

The next point to be considered was the mode of bringing together the lover and the Raven—and the first branch of this consideration was the *locale.* For this the most natural suggestion might seem to be a forest, or the fields—but it has always appeared to me that a close *circumscription of space* is absolutely necessary to the effect of insulated incident:—it has the force of a frame to a picture. It has an indisputable moral power in keeping concentrated the attention, and, of course, must not be confounded with mere unity of place.

I determined, then, to place the lover in his chamber—in a chamber rendered sacred to him by memories of her who had frequented it. The room is represented as richly furnished—this in mere pursuance of the ideas I have already explained on the subject of Beauty, as the sole true poetical thesis.

The *locale* being thus determined, I had now to introduce the bird —and the thought of introducing him through the window was inevitable. The idea of making the lover suppose, in the first instance, that the flapping of the wings of the bird against the shutter, is a "tapping" at the door, originated in a wish to increase, by prolonging, the reader's curiosity, and in a desire to admit the incidental effect arising from the lover's throwing open the door, finding all dark, and thence adopting the half-fancy that it was the spirit of his mistress that knocked.

I made the night tempestuous, first, to account for the Raven's seeking admission, and secondly, for the effect of contrast with the (physical) serenity within the chamber.

I made the bird alight on the bust of Pallas, also for the effect of contrast between the marble and the plumage—it being understood that the bust was absolutely *suggested* by the bird—the bust of *Pallas* being chosen, first, as most in keeping with the scholarship of the lover, and, secondly, for the sonorousness of the word Pallas, itself.

About the middle of the poem, also, I have availed myself of the force of contrast, with a view of deepening the ultimate impression. For example, an air of the fantastic—approaching as nearly to the ludicrous as was admissible—is given to the Raven's entrance. He comes in "with many a flirt and flutter."

> Not the *least obeisance made he*—not a moment stopped or
>   stayed he.
> *But with mien of lord or lady*, perched above my chamber
>   door.

In the two stanzas which follow, the design is more obviously carried out:—

> Then this ebony bird beguiling my sad fancy into smiling
> By the *grave and stern decorum of the countenance it wore,*
> "Though thy *crest be shorn and shaven* thou," I said, "art
>   sure no craven.
> Ghastly grim and ancient Raven wandering from the nightly
>   shore—
> Tell me what thy lordly name is on the Night's Plutonian
>   shore?"
>   Quoth the Raven "Nevermore."
>
> Much I marvelled *this ungainly fowl* to hear discourse so
>   plainly,
> Though its answer little meaning—little relevancy bore;
> For we cannot help agreeing that no living human being
> *Ever yet was blessed with seeing bird above his chamber
>   door—*
> *Bird or beast upon the sculptured bust above his chamber
>   door,*
>   With such name as "Nevermore."

The effect of the *dénouement* being thus provided for, I immediately drop the fantastic for a tone of the most profound seriousness:—this tone commencing in the stanza directly following the one last quoted, with the line,

> But the Raven, sitting lonely on that placid bust, spoke only,
>   etc.

From this epoch the lover no longer jests—no longer sees any thing even of the fantastic in the Raven's demeanor. He speaks of him as a "grim, ungainly, ghastly, gaunt, and ominous bird of yore," and feels the "fiery eyes" burning into his "bosom's core." This revolution of thought, or fancy, on the lover's part, is intended to induce a similar one on the part of the reader—to bring the mind into a proper frame for the *dénouement*—which is now brought about as rapidly and as *directly* as possible.

With the *dénouement* proper—with the Raven's reply, "Nevermore," to the lover's final demand if he shall meet his mistress in another world—the poem, in its obvious phase, that of a simple narrative, may be said to have its completion. So far, every thing is within the limits of the accountable—of the real. A raven, having learned by rote the single word "Nevermore," and having escaped from the custody of its owner, is driven at midnight, through the violence of a storm, to seek admission at a window from which a light still gleams—the chamber-window of a student, occupied half in poring over a volume, half in dreaming of a beloved mistress deceased. The casement being thrown open at the fluttering of the bird's wings, the bird itself perches on the most convenient seat out of the immediate reach of the student, who, amused by the incident and the oddity of the visitor's demeanor, demands of it, in jest and without looking for a reply, its name. The raven addressed, answers with its customary word, "Nevermore"—a word which finds immediate echo in the melancholy heart of the student, who, giving utterance aloud to certain thoughts suggested by the occasion, is again startled by the fowl's repetition of "Nevermore." The student now guesses the state of the case, but is impelled, as I have before explained, by the human thirst for self-torture, and in part by superstition, to pro-pound such queries to the bird as will bring him, the lover, the most of the luxury of sorrow, through the anticipated answer "Nevermore." With the indulgence, to the extreme, of this self-torture, the narration, in what I have termed its first or obvious phase, has a natural termination, and so far there has been no overstepping of the limits of the real.

But in subjects so handled, however skilfully, or with however vivid an array of incident, there is always a certain hardness or nakedness, which repels the artistical eye. Two things are invariably required—first, some amount of complexity, or more properly, adaptation; and, secondly, some amount of suggestiveness—some under current, however indefinite, of meaning. It is this latter, in especial, which imparts to a work of art so much of that *richness* (to borrow from colloquy a forcible term) which we are too fond of confounding with *the ideal*. It is the *excess* of the suggested meaning—it is the rendering this the upper instead of the under current of the theme—which turns into prose (and that of the very flattest kind) the so-called poetry of the so-called transcendentalists.

Holding these opinions, I added the two concluding stanzas of the poem—their suggestiveness being thus made to pervade all the narrative which has preceded them. The under current of meaning is rendered first apparent in the lines—

"Take thy beak from out *my heart,* and take thy form from
        off my door!"
            Quoth the Raven "Nevermore!"

It will be observed that the words, "from out my heart," involve the first metaphorical expression in the poem. They, with the answer, "Nevermore," dispose the mind to seek a moral in all that has been previously narrated. The reader begins now to regard the Raven as emblematical —but it is not until the very last line of the very last stanza, that the intention of making him emblematical of *Mournful and Never-ending Remembrance* is permitted distinctly to be seen:

> And the Raven, never flitting, still is sitting, still is sitting,
> On the pallid bust of Pallas just above my chamber door;
> And his eyes have all the seeming of a demon's that is
>   dreaming,
> And the lamplight o'er him streaming throws his shadow on
>   the floor;
> And my soul *from out that shadow* that lies floating on the
>   floor
>   Shall be lifted—nevermore.

EDGAR ALLAN POE

The Poetic Principle

The Poe aesthetic has had far-reaching consequences in the twentieth century. It is quite probable, for instance, that the modern prejudice against the "long poem" may be traced to Poe's criticism of the great epics (the *Iliad* and *Paradise Lost*) as a series of short poems strung together without real unity. Almost scientifically Poe discusses the value of the poem in terms of its power to elevate the soul. A long poem loses such power. "I hold," says Poe, "that a long poem does not exist."

More important, however, is Poe's isolation of Beauty from Intellect and Conscience in the true poem. Here we find stated the modern aesthetic doctrine of Beauty as the Ideal and the poet's struggle to apprehend "the supernal Loveliness." Poe was aware that his aesthetic bordered on the mystical; subsequently the Beautiful developed into a mystique in the hands of the Symbolists which bore many characteristics of a religion.

Poe's illustrations from the poems of his contemporaries may strike the reader as quaint, yet the force of his ideas overshadows the examples he uses.

*I*n speaking of the Poetic Principle, I have no design to be either thorough or profound. While discussing, very much at random, the essentiality of what we call Poetry, my principal purpose will be to cite for consideration some few of those minor English or American poems which best suit my own taste, or which, upon my own fancy, have left the most definite impression. By "minor poems" I mean, of course, poems of little length. And here, in the beginning, permit me to say a few words in regard to a somewhat peculiar principle, which, whether rightfully or wrongfully, has always had its influence in my own critical estimate of the poem. I hold that a long poem does not exist. I maintain that the phrase, "a long poem," is simply a flat contradiction in terms.

I need scarcely observe that a poem deserves its title only inasmuch as it excites, by elevating the soul. The value of the poem is in the ratio of this elevating excitement. But all excitements are, through a psychal necessity, transient. That degree of excitement which would entitle a poem to be so called at all cannot be sustained throughout a composition of any great length. After the lapse of half an hour, at the very utmost, it flags—fails—a revulsion ensues—and then the poem is, in effect, and in fact, no longer such.

There are, no doubt, many who have found difficulty in reconciling the critical dictum that the *Paradise Lost* is to be devoutly admired throughout, with the absolute impossibility of maintaining for it, during perusal, the amount of enthusiasm which that critical dictum would demand. This great work, in fact, is to be regarded as poetical, only when, losing sight of that vital requisite in all works of Art, Unity, we view it merely as a series of minor poems. If, to preserve its Unity—its totality of effect or impression—we read it (as would be necessary) at a single sitting, the result is but a constant alternation of excitement and depression. After a passage of what we feel to be true poetry, there follows, inevitably, a passage of platitude which no critical pre-judgment can force us to admire; but if, upon completing the work, we read it again omitting the first book—that is to say, commencing with the second —we shall be surprised at now finding that admirable which we before condemned—that damnable which we had previously so much admired. It follows from all this that the ultimate, aggregate, or absolute effect of even the best epic under the sun, is a nullity:—and this is precisely the fact.

In regard to the *Iliad*, we have, if not positive proof, at least very good reason, for believing it intended as a series of lyrics; but, granting the epic intention, I can say only that the work is based in an imperfect sense of Art. The modern epic is, of the supposititious ancient model, but an inconsiderate and blindfold imitation. But the day of these artistic anomalies is over. If, at any time, any very long poem *were* popular in reality, which I doubt, it is at least clear that no very long poem will ever be popular again.

That the extent of a poetical work is, *ceteris paribus*, the measure of its merit, seems undoubtedly, when we thus state it, a proposition sufficiently absurd—yet we are indebted for it to the Quarterly Reviews. Surely there can be nothing in mere *size*, abstractly considered—there can be nothing in mere *bulk*, so far as a volume is concerned, which has so continuously elicited admiration from these saturnine pamphlets! A mountain, to be sure, by the mere sentiment of physical magnitude which it conveys, *does* impress us with a sense of the sublime—but no man is impressed after *this* fashion by the material grandeur of even *The Columbiad*. Even the Quarterlies have not instructed us to be so impressed by it. *As yet,* they have not *insisted* on our estimating Lamartine by the cubic foot, or Pollok by the pound—but what else are we to *infer* from their continued prating about "sustained effort"? If, by "sustained effort," any little gentleman has accomplished an epic, let us frankly commend him for the effort—if this indeed be a thing commendable—but let us forbear praising the epic on the effort's account. It is to be hoped that common sense, in the time to come, will prefer deciding upon a work of art, rather by the impression it makes, by the effect it produces, than by the time it took to impress the effect or by the amount of "sustained effort" which had been found necessary in effecting the impression. The fact is, that perseverance is one thing, and genius quite another—nor can all the Quarterlies in Christendom confound them. By-and-by, this proposition, with many which I have been just urging, will be received as self-evident. In the mean time, by being generally condemned as falsities, they will not be essentially damaged as truths.

On the other hand, it is clear that a poem may be improperly brief. Undue brevity degenerates into mere epigrammatism. A *very* short poem, while now and then producing a brilliant or vivid, never produces a profound or enduring effect. There must be the steady pressing down of the stamp upon the wax. Béranger has wrought innumerable things, pungent and spirit-stirring; but, in general, they have been too imponderous to stamp themselves deeply into the public attention; and thus, as so many feathers of fancy, have been blown aloft only to be whistled down the wind.

A remarkable instance of the effect of undue brevity in depressing a poem—in keeping it out of the popular view—is afforded by the following exquisite little serenade:

> I arise from dreams of thee
>   In the first sweet sleep of night,
> When the winds are breathing low,
>   And the stars are shining bright;
> I arise from dreams of thee,
>   And a spirit in my feet
> Hath led me—who knows how?—
>   To thy chamber-window, sweet!
>
> The wandering airs, they faint
>   On the dark, the silent stream;
> The champak odors fail
>   Like sweet thoughts in a dream;
> The nightingale's complaint,
>   It dies upon her heart,

As I must die on thine,
  Oh, beloved as thou art!

Oh, lift me from the grass!
  I die! I faint! I fail!
Let thy love in kisses rain
  On my lips and eyelids pale.
My cheek is cold and white, alas!
  My heart beats loud and fast:
Oh! press it close to thine again,
  Where it will break at last!

Very few, perhaps, are familiar with these lines—yet no less a poet than Shelley is their author. Their warm, yet delicate and ethereal imagination will be appreciated by all—but by none so thoroughly as by him who has himself arisen from sweet dreams of one beloved to bathe in the aromatic air of a southern midsummer night.

One of the finest poems by Willis—the very best in my opinion, which he has ever written—has, no doubt, through this same defect of undue brevity, been kept back from its proper position, not less in the critical than in the popular view.

The shadows lay along Broadway,
  'Twas near the twilight tide,
And slowly there a lady fair
  Was walking in her pride.
Alone walked she; but, viewlessly,
  Walked spirits at her side.

Peace charmed the street beneath her feet
  And Honor charmed the air;
And all astir looked kind on her,
  And called her good as fair,
For all God ever gave to her
  She kept with chary care.

She kept with care her beauties rare
  From lovers warm and true,
For her heart was cold to all but gold,
  And the rich came not to woo—
But honored well are charms to sell
  If priests the selling do.

Now walking there was one more fair—
  A slight girl, lily pale;
And she had unseen company
  To make the spirit quail:
'Twixt Want and Scorn she walked forlorn,
  And nothing could avail.

No mercy now can clear her brow
  For this world's peace to pray;

> For, as love's wild prayer dissolved in air,
> Her woman's heart gave way!—
> But the sin forgiven by Christ in heaven
> By man is cursed alway!

In this composition we find it difficult to recognize the Willis who has written so many mere "verses of society." The lines are not only richly ideal, but full of energy; while they breathe an earnestness—an evident sincerity of sentiment—for which we look in vain throughout all the other works of this author.

While the epic mania—while the idea that, to merit in poetry, prolixity is indispensable—has, for some years past, been gradually dying out of the public mind, by mere dint of its own absurdity—we find it succeeded by a heresy too palpably false to be long tolerated, but one which, in the brief period it has already endured, may be said to have accomplished more in the corruption of our Poetical Literature than all its other enemies combined. I allude to the heresy of *The Didactic*. It has been assumed, tacitly and avowedly, directly and indirectly, that the ultimate object of all Poetry is Truth. Every poem, it is said, should inculcate a moral; and by this moral is the poetical merit of the work to be adjudged. We Americans, especially, have patronized this happy idea; and we Bostonians, very especially, have developed it in full. We have taken it into our heads that to write a poem simply for the poem's sake, and to acknowledge such to have been our design, would be to confess ourselves radically wanting in the true Poetic dignity and force: —but the simple fact is, that, would we but permit ourselves to look into our own souls, we should immediately there discover that under the sun there neither exists nor *can* exist any work more thoroughly dignified —more supremely noble than this very poem—this poem *per se*—this poem which is a poem and nothing more—this poem written solely for the poem's sake.

With as deep a reverence for the True as ever inspired the bosom of man, I would, nevertheless, limit, in some measure, its modes of inculcation. I would limit to enforce them. I would not enfeeble them by dissipation. The demands of Truth are severe. She has no sympathy with the myrtles. All *that* which is so indispensable in Song, is precisely all *that* with which *she* has nothing whatever to do. It is but making her a flaunting paradox, to wreathe her in gems and flowers. In enforcing a truth, we need severity rather than efflorescence of language. We must be simple, precise, terse. We must be cool, calm, unimpassioned. In a word, we must be in that mood which, as nearly as possible, is the exact converse of the poetical. He must be blind, indeed, who does not perceive the radical and chasmal differences between the truthful and the poetical modes of inculcation. He must be theory-mad beyond redemption who, in spite of these differences, shall still persist in attempting to reconcile the obstinate oils and waters of Poetry and Truth.

Dividing the world of mind into its three most obvious distinctions, we have the Pure Intellect, Taste, and the Moral Sense. I place Taste in the middle, because it is just this position which in the mind it occupies. It holds intimate relations with either extreme; but from the Moral Sense is separated by so faint a difference that Aristotle has not hesitated to place some of its operations among the virtues themselves. Nevertheless, we find the *offices* of the trio marked with a sufficient distinction. Just as the Intellect concerns itself with Truth, so Taste informs us of the Beautiful, while the Moral Sense is regardful of Duty. Of this latter, while Conscience teaches the obligation, and Reason the expediency, Taste contents herself with displaying the charms:—waging war upon Vice solely on the ground of her deformity—her disproportion, her animosity to the fitting, to the appropriate, to the harmonious—in a word, to Beauty.

An immortal instinct, deep within the spirit of man, is thus, plainly, a sense of the Beautiful. This it is which administers to his delight in the manifold forms, and sounds, and odors, and sentiments amid which he exists. And just as the lily is repeated in the lake, or the eyes of Amaryllis in the mirror, so is the mere oral or written repetition of these forms, and sounds, and colors, and odors, and sentiments, a duplicate source of delight. But this mere repetition is not poetry. He who shall simply sing, with however glowing enthusiasm, or with however vivid a truth of description, of the sights, and sounds, and odors, and colors, and sentiments, which greet *him* in common with all mankind—he, I say, has yet failed to prove his divine title. There is still a something in the distance which he has been unable to attain. We have still a thirst unquenchable, to allay which he has not shown us the crystal springs. This thirst belongs to the immortality of Man. It is at once a consequence and an indication of his perennial existence. It is the desire of the moth for the star. It is no mere appreciation of the Beauty before us—but a wild effort to reach the Beauty above. Inspired by an ecstatic prescience of the glories beyond the grave, we struggle, by multiform combinations among the things and thoughts of Time, to attain a portion of that Loveliness whose very elements, perhaps, appertain to eternity alone. And thus when by Poetry—or when by Music, the most entrancing of the Poetic moods—we find ourselves melted into tears—not as the Abbaté Gravina supposes—through excess of pleasure, but through a certain, petulant, impatient sorrow at our inability to grasp *now*, wholly, here on earth, at once and forever, those divine and rapturous joys, of which *through* the poem, or *through* the music, we attain to but brief and indeterminate glimpses.

The struggle to apprehend the supernal Loveliness—this struggle, on the part of souls fittingly constituted—has given to the world all *that* which it (the world) has ever been enabled at once to understand and *to feel* as poetic.

The Poetic Sentiment, of course, may develop itself in various modes —in Painting, in Sculpture, in Architecture, in the Dance—very especially in Music—and very peculiarly, and with a wide field, in the composition of the Landscape Garden. Our present theme, however, has regard only

to its manifestation in words. And here let me speak briefly on the topic of rhythm. Contenting myself with the certainty that Music, in its various modes of metre, rhythm, and rhyme, is of so vast a moment in Poetry as never to be wisely rejected—is so vitally important an adjunct, that he is simply silly who declines its assistance—I will not now pause to maintain its absolute essentiality. It is in Music, perhaps, that the soul most nearly attains the great end for which, when inspired by the Poetic Sentiment, it struggles—the creation of supernal Beauty. It *may* be, indeed, that here this sublime end is, now and then, attained *in fact*. We are often made to feel, with a shivering delight, that from an earthly harp are stricken notes which *cannot* have been unfamiliar to the angels. And thus there can be little doubt that in the union of Poetry with Music in its popular sense, we shall find the widest field for the Poetic development. The old Bards and Minnesingers had advantages which we do not possess—and Thomas Moore, singing his own songs, was, in the most legitimate manner, perfecting them as poems.

To recapitulate, then:—I would define, in brief, the Poetry of words as *The Rhythmical Creation of Beauty*. Its sole arbiter is Taste. With the Intellect or with the Conscience, it has only collateral relations. Unless incidentally, it has no concern whatever either with Duty or with Truth.

A few words, however, in explanation. *That* pleasure which is at once the most pure, the most elevating, and the most intense, is derived, I maintain, from the contemplation of the Beautiful. In the contemplation of Beauty we alone find it possible to attain that pleasurable elevation, or excitement, *of the soul*, which we recognize as the Poetic Sentiment, and which is so easily distinguished from Truth, which is the satisfaction of the Reason, or from Passion, which is the excitement of the heart. I make Beauty, therefore—using the word as inclusive of the sublime—I make Beauty the province of the poem, simply because it is an obvious rule of Art that effects should be made to spring as directly as possible from their causes:—no one as yet having been weak enough to deny that the peculiar elevation in question is at least *most readily* attainable in the poem. It by no means follows, however, that the incitements of Passion, or the precepts of Duty, or even the lessons of Truth, may not be introduced into a poem, and with advantage; for they may subserve, incidentally, in various ways, the general purposes of the work:—but the true artist will always contrive to tone them down in proper subjection to that *Beauty* which is the atmosphere and the real essence of the poem.

I cannot better introduce the few poems, which I shall present for your consideration, than by the citation of the "Proem" to Mr. Longfellow's "Waif":

> The day is done, and the darkness
> Falls from the wings of Night,
> As a feather is wafted downward
> From an eagle in his flight.

I see the lights of the village
   Gleam through the rain and the mist,
And a feeling of sadness comes o'er me,
   That my soul cannot resist:

A feeling of sadness and longing,
   That is not akin to pain,
And resembles sorrow only
   As the mist resembles the rain.

Come, read to me some poem,
   Some simple and heartfelt lay,
That shall soothe this restless feeling,
   And banish the thoughts of day.

Not from the grand old masters,
   Not from the bards sublime,
Whose distant footsteps echo
   Through the corridors of Time.

For, like strains of martial music,
   Their mighty thoughts suggest
Life's endless toil and endeavor;
   And tonight I long for rest.

Read from some humbler poet,
   Whose songs gushed from his heart,
As showers from the clouds of summer,
   Or tears from the eyelids start;

Who, through long days of labor,
   And nights devoid of ease,
Still heard in his soul the music
   Of wonderful melodies.

Such songs have power to quiet
   The restless pulse of care,
And come like the benediction
   That follows after prayer.

Then read from the treasured volume
   The poem of thy choice,
And lend to the rhyme of the poet
   The beauty of thy voice.

And the night shall be filled with music,
   And the cares that infest the day,
Shall fold their tents, like the Arabs,
   And as silently steal away.

With no great range of imagination, these lines have been justly admired for their delicacy of expression. Some of the images are very effective. Nothing can be better than—

      the bards sublime
   Whose distant footsteps echo
      Through the corridors of Time.

The idea of the last quatrain is also very effective. The poem, on the whole, however, is chiefly to be admired for the graceful *insouciance* of its metre, so well in accordance with the character of the sentiments, and especially for the *ease* of the general manner. This "ease," or naturalness, in a literary style, it has long been the fashion to regard as ease in appearance alone—as a point of really difficult attainment. But not so:—a natural manner is difficult only to him who should never meddle with it—to the unnatural. It is but the result of writing with the understanding, or with the instinct, that *the tone,* in composition, should always be that which the mass of mankind would adopt—and must perpetually vary, of course, with the occasion. The author who, after the fashion of the "North American Review," should be, upon *all* occasions, merely "quiet," must necessarily, upon *many* occasions, be simply silly, or stupid; and has no more right to be considered "easy," or "natural," than a Cockney exquisite, or than the sleeping Beauty in the wax-works.

Among the minor poems of Bryant, none has so much impressed me as the one which he entitles "June." I quote only a portion of it:—

> There, through the long, long summer hours,
>   The golden light should lie,
> And thick young herbs and groups of flowers
>   Stand in their beauty by.
> The oriole should build and tell
> His love-tale, close beside my cell;
>   The idle butterfly
> Should rest him there, and there be heard
> The housewife-bee and humming-bird.
>
> And what if cheerful shouts at noon
>   Come, from the village sent,
> Or songs of maids, beneath the moon,
>   With fairy laughter blent?
> And what if, in the evening light,
> Betrothèd lovers walk in sight
>   Of my low monument?
> I would the lovely scene around
> Might know no sadder sight nor sound.
>
> I know that I no more should see
>   The season's glorious show,
> Nor would its brightness shine for me,
>   Nor its wild music flow;
> But if, around my place of sleep,
> The friends I love should come to weep,
>   They might not haste to go.
> Soft airs, and song, and light, and bloom
> Should keep them lingering by my tomb.
>
> These to their softened hearts should bear
>   The thought of what has been,
> And speak of one who cannot share
>   The gladness of the scene;

> Whose part, in all the pomp that fills
> The circuit of the summer hills,
> Is—that his grave is green;
> And deeply would their hearts rejoice
> To hear again his living voice.

The rhythmical flow, here, is even voluptuous—nothing could be more melodious. The poem has always affected me in a remarkable manner. The intense melancholy which seems to well up, perforce, to the surface of all the poet's cheerful sayings about his grave, we find thrilling us to the soul—while there is the truest poetic elevation in the thrill. The impression left is one of a pleasurable sadness. And if, in the remaining compositions which I shall introduce to you, there be more or less of a similar tone always apparent, let me remind you that (how or why we know not) this certain taint of sadness is inseparably connected with all the higher manifestations of true Beauty. It is, nevertheless,

> A feeling of sadness and longing
> That is not akin to pain,
> And resembles sorrow only
> As the mist resembles the rain.

The taint of which I speak is clearly perceptible even in a poem so full of brilliancy and spirit as the "Health" of Edward Coate Pinkney:

> I fill this cup to one made up
> Of loveliness alone,
> A woman, of her gentle sex
> The seeming paragon;
> To whom the better elements
> And kindly stars have given
> A form so fair, that, like the air,
> 'Tis less of earth than heaven.
>
> Her every tone is music's own,
> Like those of morning birds,
> And something more than melody
> Dwells ever in her words;
> The coinage of her heart are they,
> And from her lips each flows
> As one may see the burdened bee
> Forth issue from the rose.
>
> Affections are as thoughts to her,
> The measures of her hours;
> Her feelings have the fragrancy,
> The freshness of young flowers;
> And lovely passions, changing oft,
> So fill her, she appears
> The image of themselves by turns,—
> The idol of past years!

Of her bright face one glance will trace
   A picture on the brain,
And of her voice in echoing hearts
   A sound must long remain;
But memory, such as mine of her,
   So very much endears,
When death is nigh my latest sigh
   Will not be life's, but hers.

I fill this cup to one made up
   Of loveliness alone,
A woman, of her gentle sex
   The seeming paragon—
Her health! and would on earth there stood
   Some more of such a frame,
That life might be all poetry,
   And weariness a name.

It was the misfortune of Mr. Pinkney to have been born too far south. Had he been a New Englander, it is probable that he would have been ranked as the first of American lyrists, by that magnanimous cabal which has so long controlled the destinies of American Letters, in conducting the thing called the "North American Review." The poem just cited is especially beautiful; but the poetic elevation which it induces, we must refer chiefly to our sympathy in the poet's enthusiasm. We pardon his hyperboles for the evident earnestness with which they are uttered.

It was by no means my design, however, to expatiate upon the *merits* of what I should read you. These will necessarily speak for themselves. Boccalini, in his "Advertisements from Parnassus," tells us that Zoilus once presented Apollo a very caustic criticism upon a very admirable book:—whereupon the god asked him for the beauties of the work. He replied that he only busied himself about the errors. On hearing this, Apollo, handing him a sack of unwinnowed wheat, bade him pick out *all the chaff* for his reward.

Now this fable answers very well as a hit at the critics—but I am by no means sure that the god was in the right. I am by no means certain that the true limits of the critical duty are not grossly misunderstood. Excellence, in a poem especially, may be considered in the light of an axiom, which need only be properly *put*, to become self-evident. It is *not* excellence if it require to be demonstrated as such:—and thus, to point out too particularly the merits of a work of Art is to admit that they are *not* merits altogether.

Among the "Melodies" of Thomas Moore, is one whose distinguished character as a poem proper seems to have been singularly left out of view. I allude to his lines beginning—"Come, rest in this bosom." The intense energy of their expression is not surpassed by anything in Byron. There are two of the lines in which a sentiment is conveyed that embodies the *all in all* of the divine passion of love—a sentiment which, perhaps, has found its echo in more, and in more passionate, human hearts than any other single sentiment ever embodied in words:

> Come, rest in this bosom, my own stricken deer,
> Though the herd have fled from thee, thy home is still here;
> Here still is the smile, that no cloud can o'ercast,
> And a heart and a hand all thy own to the last.
>
> Oh! what was love made for, if 'tis not the same
> Through joy and through torment, through glory and shame?
> I know not, I ask not, if guilt's in that heart,
> I but know that I love thee, whatever thou art.
>
> Thou hast called me thy Angel in moments of bliss,
> And thy Angel I'll be, 'mid the horrors of this,—
> Through the furnace, unshrinking, thy steps to pursue,
> And shield thee, and save thee,—or perish there too!

It has been the fashion, of late days, to deny Moore imagination, while granting him fancy—a distinction originating with Coleridge—than whom no man more fully comprehended the great powers of Moore. The fact is, that the fancy of this poet so far predominates over all his other faculties, and over the fancy of all other men, as to have induced, very naturally, the idea that he is fanciful *only*. But never was there a greater mistake. Never was a grosser wrong done the fame of a true poet. In the compass of the English language I can call to mind no poem more profoundly—more weirdly *imaginative*, in the best sense, than the lines commencing—"I would I were by that dim lake"—which are the composition of Thomas Moore. I regret that I am unable to remember them.

One of the noblest—and, speaking of fancy, one of the most singularly fanciful of modern poets, was Thomas Hood. His "Fair Ines" had always, for me, an inexpressible charm:

> O saw ye not fair Ines?
>   She's gone into the West,
> To dazzle when the sun is down,
>   And rob the world of rest:
> She took our daylight with her,
>   The smiles that we love best,
> With morning blushes on her cheek,
>   And pearls upon her breast.
>
> O turn again, fair Ines,
>   Before the fall of night,
> For fear the Moon should shine alone,
>   And stars unrivalled bright;
> And blessèd will the lover be
>   That walks beneath their light,
> And breathes the love against thy cheek
>   I dare not even write!

Would I had been, fair Ines,
  That gallant cavalier,
Who rode so gaily by thy side,
  And whispered thee so near!
Were there no bonny dames at home,
  Or no true lovers here,
That he should cross the seas to win
  The dearest of the dear?

I saw thee, lovely Ines,
  Descend along the shore,
With bands of noble gentlemen,
  And banners waved before;
And gentle youth and maidens gay,
  And snowy plumes they wore;
It would have been a beauteous dream,
  If it had been no more!

Alas, alas, fair Ines,
  She went away with song,
With Music waiting on her steps,
  And shoutings of the throng;
But some were sad, and felt no mirth,
  But only Music's wrong,
In sounds that sang Farewell, Farewell,
  To her you've loved so long.

Farewell, farewell, fair Ines,
  That vessel never bore
So fair a lady on its deck,
  Nor danced so light before,—
Alas for pleasure on the sea,
  And sorrow on the shore!
The smile that blest one lover's heart
  Has broken many more!

"The Haunted House," by the same author, is one of the truest poems ever written—one of the *truest*—one of the most unexceptionable—one of the most thoroughly artistic, both in its theme and in its execution. It is, moreover, powerfully ideal—imaginative. I regret that its length renders it unsuitable for the purposes of this Lecture. In place of it, permit me to offer the universally appreciated "Bridge of Sighs."

One more Unfortunate,
Weary of breath,
Rashly importunate,
Gone to her death!

Take her up tenderly,
Lift her with care;—
Fashioned so slenderly,
Young, and so fair!

Look at her garments
Clinging like cerements;
Whilst the wave constantly
Drips from her clothing;
Take her up instantly,
Loving, not loathing.

Touch her not scornfully;
Think of her mournfully,
Gently and humanly;
Not of the stains of her,
All that remains of her
Now is pure womanly.

Make no deep scrutiny
Into her mutiny
Rash and undutiful;
Past all dishonor,
Death has left on her
Only the beautiful.

Still, for all slips of hers,
One of Eve's family—
Wipe those poor lips of hers
Oozing so clammily.
Loop up her tresses
Escaped from the comb,
Her fair auburn tresses;
Whilst wonderment guesses
Where was her home?

Who was her father?
Who was her mother?
Had she a sister?
Had she a brother?
Or was there a dearer one
Still, and a nearer one
Yet, than all other?

Alas! for the rarity
Of Christian charity
Under the sun!
Oh! it was pitiful!
Near a whole city full,
Home she had none.

Sisterly, brotherly,
Fatherly, motherly
Feelings had changed:
Love, by harsh evidence,
Thrown from its eminence;
Even God's providence
Seeming estranged.

Where the lamps quiver
So far in the river,
With many a light
From window and casement,
From garret to basement,
She stood, with amazement,
Houseless by night.

The bleak wind of March
Made her tremble and shiver;
But not the dark arch,
Or the black flowing river:
Mad from life's history,
Glad to death's mystery,
Swift to be hurled—
Anywhere, anywhere
Out of the world!

In she plunged boldly,
No matter how coldly
The rough river ran,—
Over the brink of it,
Picture it,—think of it,
Dissolute Man!
Lave in it, drink of it
Then, if you can!

Take her up tenderly
Lift her with care
Fashion'd so slenderly,
Young, and so fair!

Ere her limbs frigidly
Stiffen too rigidly,
Decently,—kindly,—
Smoothe, and compose them;
And her eyes, close them,
Staring so blindly!

Dreadfully staring
Through muddy impurity,
As when with the daring
Last look of despairing
Fixed on futurity.

Perishing gloomily,
Spurred by contumely,
Cold inhumanity,
Burning insanity,
Into her rest.—
Cross her hands humbly,
As if praying dumbly,
Over her breast!

> Owning her weakness,
> Her evil behavior,
> And leaving, with meekness,
> Her sins to her Savior!

The vigor of this poem is no less remarkable than its pathos. The versification, although carrying the fanciful to the very verge of the fantastic, is nevertheless admirably adapted to the wild insanity which is the thesis of the poem.

Among the minor poems of Lord Byron, is one which has never received from the critics the praise which it undoubtedly deserves:

> Though the day of my destiny's over,
> And the star of my fate hath declined,
> Thy soft heart refused to discover
> The faults which so many could find;
> Though thy soul with my grief was acquainted,
> It shrunk not to share it with me,
> And the love which my spirit hath painted
> It never hath found but in *thee.*
>
> Then when nature around me is smiling,
> The last smile which answers to mine,
> I do not believe it beguiling,
> Because it reminds me of thine;
> And when winds are at war with the ocean,
> As the breasts I believed in with me,
> If their billows excite an emotion,
> It is that they bear me from *thee.*
>
> Though the rock of my last hope is shivered,
> And its fragments are sunk in the wave,
> Though I feel that my soul is delivered
> To pain—it shall not be its slave.
> There is many a pang to pursue me:
> They may crush, but they shall not contemn—
> They may torture, but shall not subdue me—
> 'Tis of *thee* that I think—not of them.
>
> Though human, thou didst not deceive me,
> Though woman, thou didst not forsake,
> Though loved, thou forborest to grieve me,
> Though slandered, thou never couldst shake,—
> Though trusted, thou didst not disclaim me,
> Though parted, it was not to fly,
> Though watchful, 'twas not to defame me,
> Nor mute, that the world might belie.
>
> Yet I blame not the world, nor despise it,
> Nor the war of the many with one—
> If my soul was not fitted to prize it,
> 'Twas folly not sooner to shun:

And if dearly that error hath cost me,
  And more than I once could foresee,
I have found that whatever it lost me,
  It could not deprive me of *thee*.

From the wreck of the past, which hath perished,
  Thus much I at least may recall,
It hath taught me that which I most cherished,
  Deserved to be dearest of all:
In the desert a fountain is springing,
  In the wide waste there still is a tree,
And a bird in the solitude singing,
  Which speaks to my spirit of *thee*.

Although the rhythm here is one of the most difficult, the versification could scarcely be improved. No nobler *theme* ever engaged the pen of poet. It is the soul-elevating idea, that no man can consider himself entitled to complain of Fate while, in his adversity, he still retains the unwavering love of woman.

From Alfred Tennyson—although in perfect sincerity I regard him as the noblest poet that ever lived—I have left myself time to cite only a very brief specimen. I call him, and *think* him, the noblest of poets—*not* because the impressions he produces are, at *all* times, the most profound —*not* because the poetical excitement which he induces is, at *all* times, the most intense—but because it *is*, at all times, the most ethereal—in other words, the most elevating and the most pure. No poet is so little of the earth, earthy. What I am about to read is from his last long poem, "The Princess":

        Tears, idle tears, I know not what they mean,
        Tears from the depth of some divine despair
        Rise in the heart, and gather to the eyes,
        In looking on the happy autumn fields,
        And thinking of the days that are no more.

        Fresh as the first beam glittering on a sail
        That brings our friends up from the underworld,
        Sad as the last which reddens over one
        That sinks with all we love below the verge;
        So sad, so fresh, the days that are no more.

        Ah, sad and strange as in dark summer dawns
        The earliest pipe of half-awaken'd birds
        To dying ears, when unto dying eyes
        The casement slowly grows a glimmering square;
        So sad, so strange, the days that are no more.

        Dear as remembered kisses after death,
        And sweet as those by hopeless fancy feigned
        On lips that are for others; deep as love,
        Deep as first love, and wild with all regret;
        O Death in Life, the days that are no more.

Thus, although in a very cursory and imperfect manner, I have endeavored to convey to you my conception of the Poetic Principle. It has been my purpose to suggest that, while this Principle itself is, strictly and simply, the Human Aspiration for Supernal Beauty, the manifestation of the Principle is always found in *an elevating excitement of the Soul* —quite independent of that passion which is the intoxication of the Heart—or of that truth which is the satisfaction of the Reason. For, in regard to Passion, alas! its tendency is to degrade, rather than to elevate the Soul. Love, on the contrary—Love—the true, the divine Eros—the Uranian, as distinguished from the Dionæan Venus—is unquestionably the purest and truest of all poetical themes. And in regard to Truth —if, to be sure, through the attainment of a truth, we are led to perceive a harmony where none was apparent before, we experience, at once, the true poetical effect—but this effect is referable to the harmony alone, and not in the least degree to the truth which merely served to render the harmony manifest.

We shall reach, however, more immediately a distinct conception of what the true Poetry is, by mere reference to a few of the simple elements which induce in the Poet himself the true poetical effect. He recognizes the ambrosia which nourishes his soul, in the bright orbs that shine in Heaven—in the volutes of the flower—in the clustering of low shrubberies—in the waving of the grain-fields—in the slanting of tall, Eastern trees—in the blue distance of mountains—in the grouping of clouds—in the twinkling of half-hidden brooks—in the gleaming of silver rivers—in the repose of sequestered lakes—in the star-mirroring depths of lonely wells. He perceives it in the songs of birds—in the harp of Æolus—in the sighing of the night-wind—in the repining voice of the forest—in the surf that complains to the shore—in the fresh breath of the woods—in the scent of the violet—in the voluptuous perfume of the hyacinth—in the suggestive odor that comes to him, at eventide, from far-distant, undiscovered islands, over dim oceans, illimitable and un-explored. He owns it in all noble thoughts—in all unworldly motives—in all holy impulses—in all chivalrous, generous, and self-sacrificing deeds. He feels it in the beauty of woman—in the grace of her step—in the lustre of her eye—in the melody of her voice—in her soft laughter—in her sigh—in the harmony of the rustling of her robes. He deeply feels it in her winning endearments—in her burning enthusiasms—in her gentle charities—in her meek and devotional endurances—but above all —ah, far above all—he kneels to it—he worships it in the faith, in the purity, in the strength, in the altogether divine majesty—of her *love*.

Let me conclude—by the recitation of yet another brief poem—one very different in character from any that I have before quoted. It is by Motherwell, and is called "The Song of the Cavalier." With our modern and altogether rational ideas of the absurdity and impiety of warfare, we are not precisely in that frame of mind best adapted to sympathize with the sentiments, and thus to appreciate the real excellence of the poem.

To do this fully, we must identify ourselves, in fancy, with the soul of
the old cavalier.

> Then mounte! then mounte, brave gallants, all,
>   And don your helmes amaine:
> Death's couriers, Fame and Honor, call
>   Us to the field againe.
> No shrewish teares shall fill our eye
>   When the sword-hilt's in our hand,—
> Heart-whole we'll part, and no whit sighe
>   For the fayrest of the land;
> Let piping swaine, and craven wight,
>   Thus weepe and puling crye,
> Our business is like men to fight,
>   And hero-like to die!

CHARLES BAUDELAIRE

from THE FLOWERS OF EVIL

Three Drafts of a Preface

In all probability, the writings of Edgar Allan Poe would never
have become influential in Europe, and indirectly in modern
poetry, had it not been for Charles Baudelaire. It was Baudelaire
who discovered in Poe the doctrine of "the effect" in art and the
doctrine of Beauty as "the sole province of the poem." Baudelaire
translated virtually everything of importance of Poe's, thus laying
the groundwork for the later European Symbolists, who all acknowledge Poe as their master.

Philosophically, Baudelaire is a Classicist in the modern sense
which Hulme and Eliot define. At the center of Baudelaire's complex negations of modern life—the city as a modern Hell, and the
increasing meaninglessness of man's progress—lies the orthodox
doctrine of Original Sin. Baudelaire's prefaces to his collection of
poems and his notes from his intimate journals introduce many of
the intellectual themes of the modern poet, some of which (for
instance, contempt for the middle class) have become stock attitudes. Eliot's essay on Baudelaire acknowledges Baudelaire as a
precursor of Classicism.

I. Preface

*F*rance is passing through a period of vulgarity. Paris, a center
radiating universal stupidity. Despite Molière and Béranger, no one

would ever have believed that France would take to the road of progress at such a rate. Matters of art, *terrae incognitae.*

Great men are stupid.

My book may have done some good; I do not regret that. It may have done harm; I do not rejoice at that.

The aim of poetry. This book is not made for my wives, my daughters, or my sisters.

Every sin, every crime I have related has been imputed to me.

Hatred and contempt as forms of amusement. Elegists are vulgar scum. *Et verbum caro factum est.* The poet is of no party. Otherwise, he would be a mere mortal.

The Devil. Original sin. Man as good. If you would, you could be the Tyrant's favorite; it is more difficult to love God than to believe in Him. On the other hand, it is more difficult for people nowadays to believe in the Devil than to love him. Everyone smells him and no one believes in him. Sublime subtlety of the Devil.

A soul to my liking. The scene.—Thus, novelty.—The Epigraph.— D'Aurevilly.—The Renaissance.—Gérard de Nerval.—We are all hanged or hangable.

I have included a certain amount of filth to please the gentlemen of the press. They have proved ungrateful.

II. Preface to the Flowers

It is not for my wives, my daughters, or my sisters that this book has been written; nor for the wives, daughters, or sisters of my neighbors. I leave that to those who have some reason to confuse good deeds with fine language.

I know the passionate lover of fine style exposes himself to the hatred of the masses; but no respect for humanity, no false modesty, no conspiracy, no universal suffrage will ever force me to speak the unspeakable jargon of this age, or to confuse ink with virtue.

Certain illustrious poets have long since divided among themselves the more flowery provinces of the realm of poetry. I have found it amusing, and the more pleasant because the task was more difficult, to extract *beauty* from *Evil.* This book, which is quintessentially useless and absolutely innocent, was written with no other aim than to divert myself and to practice my passionate taste for the difficult.

Some have told me that these poems might do harm; I have not rejoiced at that. Others, good souls, that they might do good; and that has given me no regret. I was equally surprised at the former's fear and the latter's hope, which only served to prove once again that this age has unlearned all the classical notions of literature.

Despite the encouragement a few celebrated pedants have given to man's natural stupidity, I should never have believed our country could move with such speed along the road of *progress.* The world has taken on a thickness of vulgarity that raises a spiritual man's contempt to the violence of a passion. But there are those happy hides so thick that poison itself could not penetrate them.

I had intended, at first, to answer numerous criticisms and at the same time to explain a few quite simple questions that have been totally obscured by modern enlightenment: What is poetry? What is its aim? On the distinction between the Good and the Beautiful; on the Beauty of Evil; that rhythm and rhyme answer the immortal need in man for monotony, symmetry, and surprise; on adapting style to subject; on the vanity and danger of inspiration, etc., etc.; but this morning I was so rash as to read some of the public newspapers; suddenly an indolence of the weight of twenty atmospheres fell upon me, and I was stopped, faced by the appalling uselessness of explaining anything whatever to anyone whatever. Those who know can divine me, and for those who can not or will not understand, it would be fruitless to pile up explanations.

C.B.

How the artist, by a prescribed series of exercises, can proportionately increase his originality;

How poetry is related to music through prosody, whose roots go deeper into the human soul than any classical theory indicates;

That French poetry possesses a mysterious and unrecognized prosody, like the Latin and English languages;

Why any poet who does not know exactly how many rhymes each word has is incapable of expressing any idea whatever;

That the poetic phrase can imitate (and in this, it is like the art of music and the science of mathematics) a horizontal line, an ascending or descending vertical line; that it can rise straight up to heaven without losing its breath, or go perpendicularly to hell with the velocity of any weight; that it can follow a spiral, describe a parabola, or zigzag, making a series of superimposed angles;

That poetry is like the arts of painting, cooking, and cosmetics in its ability to express every sensation of sweetness or bitterness, beatitude or horror, by coupling a certain noun with a certain adjective, in analogy or contrast;

How, by relying on my principles and using the knowledge which I guarantee to teach him in twenty lessons, any man can learn to compose a tragedy that will be no more hooted at than another, or line up a poem long enough to be as dull as any epic known.

A difficult matter, to rise to that divine callousness! For, despite my most commendable efforts, even I have not been able to resist the desire to please my contemporaries, as witness in several places, laid on like make-up, certain patches of base flattery aimed at democracy, and even a certain amount of filth meant to excuse the dreariness of my subject. But the gentlemen of the press having proved ungrateful for tender attentions of this kind, I have eliminated every trace of both, so far as possible, from this new edition.

I propose, in order to prove again the excellence of my method, to apply it in the near future to celebrating the pleasures of devotion and the raptures of military glory, though I have never known either.

Notes on plagiarisms.—Thomas Gray. Edgar Poe (2 passages). Longfellow (2 passages). Statius. Virgil (the whole of Andromache). Aeschylus. Victor Hugo.

III. Draft of a Preface for the *Flowers of Evil*

If there is any glory in not being understood, or in being only very slightly so, I may without boasting say that with this little book I have at a single stroke both won and deserved that glory. Submitted several times over to various publishers who rejected it with disgust, put on trial and mutilated in 1857 as a result of a quite bizarre misapprehension, then gradually revived, augmented, and fortified during several years' silence, only to disappear again thanks to my losing interest, this discordant product of the *Muse of modern times,* again enlivened with a few violent new touches, dares today for the third time to face the sun of stupidity.

This is not my fault, but that of an insistent publisher who thinks he is strong enough to brave the public distaste. "This book will remain a stain on your whole life," one of my friends, a great poet, predicted from the beginning. And indeed all my misadventures have so far justified him. But I have one of those happy characters that enjoy hatred and feel glorified by contempt. My diabolically passionate taste for stupidity makes me take peculiar pleasure in the falsifications of calumny. Being as chaste as paper, as sober as water, as devout as a woman at communion, as harmless as a sacrificial lamb, it would not displease me to be taken for a debauchee, a drunkard, an infidel, a murderer. My publisher insists that it might be of some use, to me and to him, to explain why and how I have written this book, what were my means and aim, my plan and method. Such a critical task might well have the luck to interest those minds that love profound rhetoric. For those I shall perhaps write it later on and have it printed in ten copies. But, on second thought, doesn't it seem obvious that this would be a quite superfluous undertaking for everyone concerned since those are the minds that already know or guess and the rest will never understand? I have too much fear of being ridiculous to wish to breathe into the mass of humanity the understanding of an art object; in doing so, I should fear to resemble those Utopians who by decree wish to make all Frenchmen rich and virtuous at a single stroke. And moreover, my best, my supreme reason is that it annoys and bores me. Do we invite the crowd, the audience, behind the scenes, into the workshops of the costume and scene designers; into the actress's dressingroom? Do we show the public (enthusiastic today, tomorrow indifferent) the mechanism behind our effects? Do we explain to them the revisions, the improvisations adopted in rehearsal, and even to what extent instinct and sincerity are mixed with artifice and charlatanry, all indispensable to the amalgam that is the work itself? Do we display all the rags, the rouge, the pulleys, the chains, the alterations, the scribbled-over proof sheets, in short all the horrors that make up the sanctuary of art?

In any case, such is not my mood today. I have no desire either to demonstrate, to astonish, to amuse, or to persuade. I have my nerves and my vertigo. I aspire to absolute rest and continuous night. Though I have sung the mad pleasures of wine and opium, I thirst only for a liquor unknown on earth, which the pharmaceutics of heaven itself could not afford me; a liquor that contains neither vitality nor death, neither excitation nor extinction. To know nothing, to teach nothing, to will nothing, to feel nothing, to sleep and still to sleep, this today is my only wish. A base and loathsome wish, but sincere.

Nevertheless, since the best of taste teaches us not to fear contradicting ourselves a bit, I have collected at the end of this abominable book certain testimonials of sympathy from a few of the men I prize most, so that an impartial reader may infer from them that I am not absolutely deserving of excommunication, and that since I have managed to make myself loved of some, my heart, whatever a certain printed rag may have said of it, is perhaps not "as frightfully hideous as my face."

Finally, the uncommon generosity which those gentlemen, the critics . . .

Since ignorance is increasing . . .

I take it on myself to denounce imitations . . .

CHARLES BAUDELAIRE

notes from

INTIMATE JOURNALS

XXXVII

*B*elief in Progress is a doctrine of idlers and Belgians. It is the individual relying upon his neighbours to do his work.

There cannot be any Progress (true progress, that is to say, moral) except within the individual and by the individual himself.

But the world is composed of people who can think only in common, in the herd. Like the *Sociétés belges.*

There are also people who can only take their pleasures in a flock. The true hero takes his pleasure alone.

LI

I am sick of France; chiefly because everybody is like Voltaire.

Emerson has forgotten Voltaire in his *Representative Men*. He could have written a fine chapter entitled *Voltaire, or the Anti-Poet*, the king of loungers, the prince of triflers, the anti-artist, the preacher to concierges, the Father Gigogne of the Editors of Le Siècle.

LXX

There are no great men save the poet, the priest, and the soldier.

The man who sings, the man who offers up sacrifice, and the man who sacrifices himself.

The rest are born for the whip.

Let us beware of the rabble, of common-sense, good-nature, inspiration, and evidence.

LXXII

Woman cannot distinguish between her soul and her body. She simplifies things, like an animal. A cynic would say that it is because she has nothing but a body.

A chapter on *The Toilet*.

Morality of the toilet, the delights of the toilet.

LXXIV

To be a great man and a saint by *one's own standards*, that is all that matters.

LXXXI

Theory of the true civilization. It is not to be found in gas or steam or table-turning. It consists in the diminution of the traces of original sin.

Nomad peoples, shepherds, hunters, farmers and even cannibals, may all, by virtue of energy and personal dignity, be the superiors of our races of the West.

These will perhaps be destroyed.

Theocracy and communism.

XCIII

The more a man cultivates the arts the less he fornicates. A more and more apparent cleavage occurs between the spirit and the brute.

Only the brute is really potent. Sexuality is the lyricism of the masses.

To fornicate is to aspire to enter into another; the artist never emerges from himself.

I have forgotten the name of that slut. Bah! I shall remember it at the last judgment.

Music conveys the idea of space.

So do all the arts, more or less; since they are *number* and since number is a translation of space.

To will every day to be the greatest of men!

XCIV

When I was a child I wanted sometimes to be pope, but a military pope, and sometimes to be an actor.

The pleasures that I derived from these two phantasies.

XCVII

Commerce is, in its very essence, *satanic*. Commerce is return of the loan, a loan in which there is the understanding: *give me more than I give you.*

The spirit of every business-man is completely depraved.

Commerce is *natural,* therefore *shameful.*

The least vile of all merchants is he who says: "Let us be virtuous, since, thus, we shall gain much more money than the fools who are dishonest."

For the merchant, even honesty is a financial speculation.

Commerce is satanic, because it is the basest and vilest form of egoism.

J. K. HUYSMANS

from

AGAINST THE GRAIN

Against the Grain (*A Rebours*) means against the grain of Nature. In this strange novel (1884) Huysmans depicted the modern man whose sensibilities have been destroyed by modern life and who is revolted by progress, industrialism, middle-class mores, and the literary school of Naturalism. The hero of the novel, Des Esseintes, a neurotic aristocrat, withdraws entirely from the world and barricades himself in a house where he is attended by two servants whom he has trained as nurses to care for him.

He surrounds himself with every refinement of intellect, discarding all works of art that have been tainted with popularity or common approval. In poetry he discovers only the Decadent writers as suitable to his taste. Des Esseintes himself is supposed to be modeled upon the supreme poet of the Symbolists, Stéphane Mallarmé. (Mallarmé responded favorably to the compliment by writing a poem called "Prose for Des Esseintes.")

Huysmans' novel is an analysis and a commentary upon the modern poetic sensibility, and, as in the case of Oscar Wilde, it is difficult to say whether he intended the work as a satire of or a eulogy for the Mallarmé-Poe type of artist.

*T*o judge by such family portraits as were preserved in the Château de Lourps, the race of the Floressas des Esseintes had been composed in olden days of stalwart veterans of the wars, grim knights with scowling visages. Imprisoned in the old-fashioned picture frames that seemed all too narrow to contain their broad shoulders, they glared out alarmingly at the spectator, who was equally impressed by the fixed stare in the eyes, the martial curl of the mustaches and the noble development of the chests encased in enormous steel cuirasses.

These were ancestral portraits; those representing subsequent generations were conspicuous by their absence. There was a gap in the series, a gap which one face alone served to fill and so connect the past and present—a mysterious, world-weary countenance. The features were heavy and drawn, the prominent cheekbones touched with a spot of rouge, the hair plastered to the head and entwined with a string of pearls, the slender neck rising from amid the pleatings of a stiff ruff.

Already in this picture of one of the most intimate friends of the Duc d'Epernon and the Marquis d'O, the vitiation of an exhausted race, the excess of lymph in the blood were plainly to be traced.

No doubt the gradual degeneration of this ancient house had followed a regular and unbroken course; the progressive effemination of the men had gone on continuously from bad to worse. Moreover, to complete the deteriorating effect of time, the Des Esseintes had for centuries been in the habit of intermarrying among themselves, thus wasting the small remains of their original vigor and energy.

Sole surviving descendant of this family, once so numerous that it covered nearly all the domains of the Ile-de-France and of La Brie, was the Duc Jean des Esseintes, a frail young man of thirty, anemic and nervous, with hollow cheeks, eyes of a cold, steely blue, a small but still straight nose, and long, slender hands.

By a curious accident of heredity, this last scion of a race bore a strong resemblance to the far-off ancestor, the mignon of princes, from whom he had got the pointed beard of the very palest possible blond and the ambiguous look of the eyes, at once languid and energetic in expression, which marked the portrait.

His childhood had been beset with perils. Threatened with scrofulous affections, worn out with persistent attacks of fever, he had nevertheless successfully weathered the breakers of puberty, after which critical period his nerves had recovered the mastery, vanquished the languors and depressions of chlorosis and permitted the constitution to reach its full and complete development.

The mother, a tall, silent, white-faced woman, died of general debility; then the father succumbed to a vague and mysterious malady. At the time Des Esseintes was approaching his seventeenth birthday.

The only recollection he retained of his parents was one of fear rather than of anything resembling gratitude or affection. His father, who generally resided in Paris, was almost a total stranger; his mother he only remembered as a chronic invalid, who never left the precincts of a shuttered bedroom in the Château de Lourps. It was only on rare occasions that husband and wife met, and of these meetings all he recalled was the drab, colorless dullness—his father and mother seated on either side of a table lighted only by a deeply shaded lamp, for the Duchess could not endure light and noise without suffering from nervous attacks. In the semidarkness, they would exchange two or three sentences at most; then the Duke would slip away with a yawn and take his departure by the first available train.

At the Jesuit College to which Jean was sent to be educated, his life proved pleasanter and less trying. The Fathers made much of the lad, whose intelligence amazed them; yet, in spite of all their efforts, they failed entirely to induce him to pursue any definite and disciplined course of study. He devoted himself eagerly to certain tasks, acquired a precocious mastery of the Latin tongue; but on the other hand, he was absolutely incapable of construing three words of Greek; displayed no aptitude whatever for living languages and showed himself a perfect fool directly any attempt was made to teach him the merest rudiments of the physical sciences.

His family pretty much washed their hands of him; occasionally his father would pay him a visit at the College, but, "Good day, good evening, be a good boy and work hard," was about all he ever said to him. His summer holidays he used to spend at the Château de Lourps, where his presence quite failed to rouse his mother from her reveries; she hardly seemed to see him, or, if she did, would gaze at him for a few moments with a painful smile, then sink back again into the artificial night in which the heavy curtains drawn across the windows wrapped the apartment.

The domestics were old and tiresome. The boy, left to himself, would turn over the books in the library on wet days, or on fine afternoons take long walks in the country.

It was his great delight to make his way down into the valley to Jutigny, a village standing at the foot of the hills—a little cluster of cottages with thatched roofs tufted with moss. He would lie out in the meadows under the lee of the tall hayricks, listening to the dull rumble of the water-mills, filling his lungs with the fresh air of the Voulzie.

Sometimes he would wander as far as the peat-workings, to the hamlet of Longueville with its hovels painted green and black; at another time climb the wind-swept hills and gaze out over the vast prospect. There he had below him on one side the valley of the Seine, losing itself in immensity and melting into the blue haze of the far distance; on the other, high on the horizon line, the churches and Castle keep of Provins that seemed to shake and shiver in a sunlit dust-cloud.

He spent the hours in reading or dreaming, drinking his fill of solitude till nightfall. By dint of constantly brooding over the same thoughts, his mind gained concentration and his still undeveloped ideas ripened towards maturity. After each vacation, he went back more thoughtful and more stubborn to his masters. These changes did not escape their notice; clear-sighted and shrewd, taught by their profession to sound the deepest depths of the human soul, they were well aware of the qualities and limitations of this alert but indocile intelligence; they realized that this pupil of theirs would never enhance the fame of the House, and as his family was wealthy and appeared to take little interest in his future, they soon abandoned all idea of directing his energies towards any of the lucrative careers open to the successful student. Though he was ready enough to enter with them into those theological disputations that attracted him by their subtleties and casuistical distinctions, they never even thought of preparing him for Holy Orders, for despite their efforts, his faith remained feeble. In the last resort, out of prudence and a fear of the unknown, they left him to himself to work at such studies as he chose and neglect the rest, unwilling to alienate this independent spirit by petty restrictions such as lay ushers are so fond of imposing.

So he lived a perfectly contented life, scarcely conscious of the priests' fatherly yoke. He pursued his Latin and French studies after his own fashion, and, albeit Theology found no place in the curriculum of his classes, he completed the apprenticeship to that science which he had begun at the Château de Lourps in the library of books left by his great great-uncle Dom Prosper, erstwhile Prior of the Canons Regular of Saint-Ruf.

The time, however, arrived when he must quit the Jesuit College; he was coming of age and would be master of his fortune; his cousin and guardian, the Comte de Montchevrel, gave him an account of his stewardship. The intimacy thus established was of short duration, for what point of contact could there be between the two, one of whom was an old man, the other a young one? Out of curiosity, lack of occupation, courtesy, Des Esseintes kept up relations with this family, and on several occasions, at his hotel in the Rue de la Chaise, endured evenings of a deadly dullness at which good ladies of his kin, as ancient as the hills, conversed about quarterings of nobility, heraldic scutcheons and ceremonial observances of years gone by.

Even more than these worthy dowagers, the men, gathered round a whist-table, betrayed their hopeless nullity; these descendants of the old *preux chevaliers,* last scions of the feudal houses, appeared to Des Esseintes under the guise of a parcel of snuffling, grotesque graybeards, repeating *ad nauseam* a wearisome string of insipid outworn platitudes. Just as when you cut the stalk of a fern, you can see the mark of a lily, really a fleur-de-lis seemed to be the one and only impress left on the softened pulp that took the place of brains in these poor old heads.

The young man was filled with an ineffable pity for these mummies buried in their rococo catafalques; for these crusty dandies who lived with eyes forever fixed on a vaguely defined land of promise, an imaginary Canaan of good hope.

After a few experiences of the kind, he firmly resolved, in spite of all invitations and reproaches, never again to set foot in this society.

Thereupon he began to spend his days among young men of his own age and rank. Some of these, who had been brought up like himself at religious seminaries, had retained from this training a special character of their own. They attended church, communicated at Easter, frequented Catholic clubs, and dropping their eyes in mock modesty, hid from each other, as if they had been crimes, their enterprises with women. For the most part they were witless fellows, with a sufficiency of good looks, but without a spark of mind or spirit; prime dunces who had exhausted their masters' patience, but had nevertheless fulfilled the latters' ambition to send out into the world obedient and pious sons of the Church.

Others, reared in the Colleges of the State or at *Lycées,* were more outspoken and less of hypocrites, but they were neither more interesting nor less narrow-minded. These were men of pleasure, devotees of operettas and races, playing lansquenet and baccarat, staking fortunes on horses and cards—all the diversions in fact that empty-headed folks love. After a year's trial of this life an enormous weariness resulted; he was sick and tired of these people whose indulgences struck him as paltry and commonplace, carried out without discrimination, without excitement, without any real stirring of blood or stimulation of nerves.

Little by little, he left off frequenting their society, and approached the men of letters, with whom his mind must surely find more points of sympathy and feel itself more at ease in their company. It was a fresh disappointment; he was revolted by their spiteful and petty judgments, their conversation that was as hackneyed as a church door, their nauseous discussions invariably appraising the merit of a work solely according to the number of editions and the amount of profit on the sales. At the same time, he discovered the apostles of freedom, the wiseacres of the bourgeoisie, the thinkers who clamored for entire liberty—liberty to strangle the opinions of other people—to be a set of greedy, shameless hypocrites, whom as men of education he rated below the level of the village cobbler.

His scorn of humanity grew by what it fed on; he realized in fact that the world is mostly made up of solemn humbugs and silly idiots. There was no room for doubt; he could entertain no hope of discovering in another the same aspirations and the same antipathies, no hope of joining forces with a mind that, like his own, should find its satisfaction in a life of studious idleness; no hope of uniting a keen and doctrinaire spirit such as his, with that of a writer and a man of learning.

His nerves were on edge, he was ill at ease; disgusted at the triviality of the ideas exchanged and received, he was growing to be like the men Nicole speaks of, who are unhappy everywhere; he was continually being chafed almost beyond endurance by the patriotic and social exaggerations he read every morning in the papers, overrating the importance of the triumphs which an all-powerful public reserves always and under all circumstances for works equally devoid of ideas and of style.

Already he was dreaming of a refined Thebaïd, a desert hermitage combined with modern comfort, an ark on dry land and nicely warmed, whither he could fly for refuge from the incessant deluge of human folly.

One passion and one only, woman, might have arrested him in this universal disdain that was rising within him; but this too was exhausted. He had tasted the sweets of the flesh with the appetite of a sick man, an invalid debilitated and full of whimsies, whose palate quickly loses savor. In the days when he had consorted with the coarse and carnal-minded men of pleasure, he had participated like the rest in some of those unconventional supper parties where tipsy women bare their bosoms at dessert and beat the table with disheveled heads; he had been a visitor likewise behind the scenes, had had relations with actresses and popular singers, had endured, added to the natural and innate folly of the sex, the frantic vanity of women of the stage; then he had kept mistresses already famous for their gallantry, and contributed to swell the exchequer of those agencies that supply, for a price, highly dubious gratifications; last of all, sick and satiated with this pretense of pleasure, of these stale caresses that are all alike, he had plunged into the nether depths, hoping to revive his flagging passions by sheer force of contrast, thinking to stimulate his exhausted senses by the very foulness of the filth and beastliness of low-bred vice.

Try what he would, an overpowering sense of ennui weighed him down. But still he persisted, and presently had recourse to the perilous caresses of the experts in amorousness. But his health was unable to bear the strain and his nerves gave way; the back of the neck began to prick and the hands were tremulous—steady enough still when a heavy object had to be lifted, but uncertain if they held anything quite light such as a wine glass.

The physicians he consulted terrified him. It was indeed high time to change his way of life, to abandon these practices that were draining away his vitality. For a while, he led a quiet existence; but before long his passions awoke again and once more piped to arms. Like young girls who, under the stress of poverty, crave after highly spiced or even repulsive foods, he began to ponder and presently to practice abnormal indulgences, unnatural pleasures. This was the end; as if all possible delights of the flesh were exhausted, he felt sated, worn out with weariness; his senses fell into a lethargy, impotence was not far off.

So he found himself stranded, a lonely, disillusioned, sobered man, utterly and abominably tired, beseeching an end of it all—an end the cowardice of his flesh forbade his winning.

His projects of finding some retreat far from his fellows, of burying himself in a hermit's cell, of deadening, as they do the noise of the traffic for sick people by laying down straw in the streets, the inexorable turmoil of life, these projects more and more attracted him.

Besides, it was quite time to come to some definite decision for other reasons; he reckoned up the state of his finances and was appalled at the result. In reckless follies and riotous living generally, he had squandered the major part of his patrimony, while the balance, invested in land, brought him in only an insignificant revenue.

He determined to sell the Château de Lourps, which he never visited and where he would leave behind him no tender memories, no fond regrets; by this means he paid off all claims on the rest of his property, bought Government annuities and so secured himself an annual income of fifty thousand francs, while reserving, over and above, a round sum to buy and furnish the little house where he proposed to steep himself in a peace and quiet that should last his lifetime.

He searched the outer suburbs of the capital and presently discovered a cottage for sale, above Fontenay-aux-Roses, in a remote spot, far from all neighbors, near the Fort. His dream was fulfilled; in this district, still unspoiled by intruders from Paris, he was secure against all harassment; the very difficulties of communication—the place was wretchedly served by a grotesquely inefficient railway at the far end of the little town and a rustic tramway that went and came according to a self-appointed timetable—were a comfort to him.

As he thought over the new existence he meant to make for himself, he experienced a lively sense of relief, seeing himself just far enough withdrawn for the flood of Paris activity not to touch his retreat, yet near enough for the proximity of the metropolis to add a spice to his solitariness. Indeed, in view of the well-known fact that for a man to find himself in a situation where it is impossible for him to visit a particular spot is of itself quite enough to fill him with an instant wish to go there, he was really guarding himself, by thus not entirely barring the road, from any craving to renew intercourse with the world or any regret for having abandoned it.

He set the masons to work on the house he had bought; then suddenly one day, without telling a soul of his plans, he got rid of his former stock of furniture, dismissed his servants and disappeared without leaving any address with the concierge.

.   .   .   .   .   .

Of all forms of literature that of the prose poem was Des Esseintes' chosen favorite. Handled by an alchemist of genius, it should, according to him, store up in its small compass, like an extract of meat, so to say, the essence of the novel, while suppressing its long, tedious analytical passages and superfluous descriptions. Again and again Des Esseintes had pondered the distracting problem, how to write a novel concentrated in a few sentences, but which should yet contain the cohobated juice of the hundreds of pages always taken up in describing the setting, sketching the characters, gathering together the necessary incidental observations and minor details. In that case, so inevitable and unalterable would be the words selected that they must take the place of all others; in so ingenious and masterly a fashion would each adjective be chosen that it could not with any justice be robbed of its right to be there, and would open up such wide perspectives as would set the reader dreaming for weeks together of its meaning, at once precise and manifold, and enable him to know the present, reconstruct the past, divine the future of the spiritual history of the characters, all revealed by the flashlight of this single epithet.

The novel, thus conceived, thus condensed in a page or two, would become a communion, an interchange of thought between a magic-working author and an ideal reader, a mental collaboration by consent between half a score of persons of superior intellect scattered up and down the world, a delectable feast for epicures and appreciated by them only.

In a word, the prose poem represented in Des Esseintes' eyes the concrete juice, the osmazone of literature, the essential oil of art.

This succulence, developed and concentrated in a drop, already existed in Baudelaire, as also in those poems of Mallarmé's which he savored with so deep a delight.

When he had closed his anthology, Des Esseintes told himself, here was the last book of his library, which would probably never receive another addition.

In fact, the decadence of a literature, attacked by incurable organic disease, enfeebled by the decay of ideas, exhausted by the excess of grammatical subtlety, sensitive only to the whims of curiosity that torment a fever patient, and yet eager in its expiring hours to express every thought and fancy, frantic to make good all the omissions of the past, tortured on its deathbed by the craving to leave a record of the most subtle pangs of suffering, was incarnate in Mallarmé in the most consummate and exquisite perfection.

Here was to be found, pushed to its completest expression, the quintessence of Baudelaire and Poe; here was the same powerful and refined basis yet further distilled and giving off new savors, new intoxications.

It was the dying spasm of the old tongue which, after a progressive decay from century to century, was ending in a total dissolution, in the same deliquium the Latin language had suffered, as it expired finally in the mystic conceptions and enigmatic phases of St. Boniface and St. Adhelm.

For the rest, the decomposition of the French language had come about at a blow. In Latin, a lengthy period of transition, a pause of four hundred years, had intervened between the variegated and magnificent phraseology of Claudian and Rutilius and the dialect of the eighth century with its taint of decomposition. Not so in French; here no interval of time, no long-drawn series of ages, occurred; the variegated and magnificent style of the De Goncourts and the tainted style of Verlaine and Mallarmé rubbed elbows at Paris, dwelling together at the same time, in the same period, in the same century.

And Des Esseintes smiled to himself as he looked at one of the folios lying open on his church reading desk, thinking how the moment might come when a learned scholar would compile for the decadence of the French language a glossary like that in which the erudite Du Cange has noted down the last stammering accents, the last spasmodic efforts, the last flashes of brilliancy, of the Latin tongue as it perished of old age, the death rattle sounding through the recesses of monkish cloisters.

WALTER PATER

from

STUDIES IN THE HISTORY OF THE RENAISSANCE

Walter Pater, scholar and critic of Renaissance art in the latter years of the nineteenth century, helped mold the literary attitudes of the Pre-Raphaelites, the Aesthetes, and the modern Classicists as well. The single paragraph given below describes Leonardo's *Mona Lisa* in such a manner that, as W. B. Yeats said, to this day "men shrink from Leonardo's masterpiece as from an over-flattered woman." (Yeats used a sentence from this passage, broken into free verse, as the opening "poem" of his anthology of modern verse.)

In turning the *Mona Lisa* into a symbol of Woman, or the *femme fatale,* Pater provided an example of what Yeats called the *object without contour.* The object or character "without contour," which can fade into a different but related character, is a typical feature of the modern poem. The "protagonists" of such poems as *The Waste Land* or the *Cantos* are characters who change contour rapidly, very often to the confusion of the uninitiated reader.

*T*he presence that rose thus so strangely beside the waters, is expressive of what in the ways of a thousand years men had come to desire. Hers is the head upon which all "the ends of the world are come," and the eyelids are a little weary. It is a beauty wrought out from within upon the flesh, the deposit, little cell by cell, of strange thoughts and fantastic reveries and exquisite passions. Set it for a moment beside one of those white Greek goddesses or beautiful women of antiquity, and how would they be troubled by this beauty, into which the soul with all its maladies has passed! All the thoughts and experience of the world have etched and moulded there, in that which they have of power to refine and make expressive the outward form, the animalism of Greece, the lust of Rome, the mysticism of the Middle Age with its spiritual ambition and imaginative loves, the return of the Pagan world, the sins of the Borgias. She is older than the rocks among which she sits; like the vampire, she has been dead many times, and learned the secrets of the grave; and has been a diver in deep seas, and keeps their fallen day about her; and trafficked for strange webs with Eastern merchants; and, as Leda, was the mother of Helen of Troy, and, as Saint Anne, the mother of Mary; and all this has been to her but as the sound of lyres and flutes, and lives only in the delicacy with which it has moulded the changing lineaments, and tinged the eyelids and the hands. The fancy of a perpetual life, sweeping together ten thousand experiences, is an old one; and modern philosophy has conceived the idea of humanity as wrought upon by, and summing up in itself, all modes of thought and life. Certainly Lady Lisa might stand as the embodiment of the old fancy, the symbol of the modern idea.

ARTHUR SYMONS

from THE SYMBOLIST MOVEMENT IN LITERATURE

Stéphane Mallarmé

First published in 1899, Symons' *The Symbolist Movement in Literature* opened the door to French Symbolism for such poets as William Butler Yeats and T. S. Eliot. Eliot concedes that the book was a major influence upon his work. The Symons book, Eliot says, "is one of those which have affected the course of my life."

Mallarmé is usually regarded as the ultimate Symbolist poet, the one who provided the purest examples of Symbolist poetry.

I

*S*téphane Mallarmé was one of those who love literature too much to write it except by fragments; in whom the desire of perfection brings its own defeat. With either more or less ambition he would have done more to achieve himself; he was always divided between an absolute aim at the absolute, that is, the unattainable, and a too logical disdain for the compromise by which, after all, literature is literature. Carry the theories of Mallarmé to a practical conclusion, multiply his powers in a direct ratio, and you have Wagner. It is his failure not to be Wagner. And, Wagner having existed, it was for him to be something more, to complete Wagner. Well, not being able to be that, it was a matter of sincere indifference to him whether he left one or two little, limited masterpieces of formal verse and prose, the more or the less. It was "the work" that he dreamed of, the new art, more than a new religion, whose precise form in the world he was never quite able to settle.

Un auteur difficile, in the phrase of M. Catulle Mendès, it has always been to what he himself calls "a labyrinth illuminated by flowers" that Mallarmé has felt it due to their own dignity to invite his readers. To their own dignity, and also to his. Mallarmé was obscure, not so much because he wrote differently, as because he thought differently, from other people. His mind was elliptical, and, relying with undue confidence on the intelligence of his readers, he emphasised the effect of what was unlike other people in his mind by resolutely ignoring even the links of connection that existed between them. Never having aimed at popularity, he never needed, as most writers need, to make the first advances. He made neither intrusion upon nor concession to those who, after all, were not obliged to read him. And when he spoke, he considered it neither needful nor seemly to listen in order to hear whether he was heard. To the charge of obscurity he replied, with sufficient disdain, that there are many who do not know how to read—except the newspaper, he adds, in one of those disconcerting, oddly-printed parentheses, which makes his work, to those who rightly apprehend it, so full of wise limitations, so safe from hasty or seemingly final conclusions. No one in our time has more significantly vindicated the supreme right of the artist in the aristocracy of letters; wilfully, perhaps, not always wisely, but nobly, logically. Has not every artist shrunk from that making of himself "a motley to the view," that handing over of his naked soul to the laughter of the multitude? But who, in our time, has wrought so subtle a veil, shining on this side, where the few are, a thick cloud on the other, where are the many? The oracles have always had the wisdom to hide their secrets in the obscurity of many meanings, or of what has seemed meaningless; and might it not, after all, be the finest epitaph for a self-respecting man of letters to be able to say, even after the writing of many books: I have kept my secret, I have not betrayed myself to the multitude?

But to Mallarmé, certainly, there might be applied the significant warning of Rossetti:

> Yet woe to thee if once thou yield
> Unto the act of doing nought!

After a life of persistent devotion to literature, he has left enough poems to make a single small volume (less, certainly, than a hundred poems in all), a single volume of prose, a few pamphlets, and a prose translation of the poems of Poe. It is because among these there are masterpieces, poems which are among the most beautiful poems written in our time, prose which has all the subtlest qualities of prose, that, quitting the abstract point of view, we are forced to regret the fatal enchantments, fatal for him, of theories which are so greatly needed by others, so valuable for our instruction, if we are only a little careful in putting them into practice.

In estimating the significance of Stéphane Mallarmé, it is necessary to take into account not only his verse and prose, but, almost more than these, the Tuesdays of the Rue de Rome, in which he gave himself freely to more than one generation. No one who has ever climbed those four flights of stairs will have forgotten the narrow, homely interior, elegant with a sort of scrupulous Dutch comfort; the heavy, carved furniture, the tall clock, the portraits, Manet's, Whistler's, on the walls; the table on which the china bowl, odorous with tobacco, was pushed from hand to hand; above all, the rocking-chair, Mallarmé's, from which he would rise quietly, to stand leaning his elbow on the mantelpiece, while one hand, the hand which did not hold the cigarette, would sketch out one of those familiar gestures: *un peu de prêtre, un peu de danseuse* (in M. Rodenbach's admirable phrase), *avec lesquels il avait l'air chaque fois d'entrer dans la conversation, comme on entre en scène.** One of the best talkers of our time, he was, unlike most other fine talkers, harmonious with his own theories in giving no monologues, in allowing every liberty to his guests, to the conversation; in his perfect readiness to follow the slightest indication, to embroider upon any frame, with any material presented to him. There would have been something almost of the challenge of the improvisatore in this easily moved alertness of mental attitude, had it not been for the singular gentleness with which Mallarmé's intelligence moved, in these considerable feats, with the half-apologetic negligence of the perfect acrobat. He seemed to be no more than brushing the dust off your own ideas, settling, arranging them a little, before he gave them back to you, surprisingly luminous. It was only afterwards that you realised how small had been your own part in the matter, as well as what it meant to have enlightened without dazzling you. But there was always the feeling of comradeship, the comradeship of a master, whom, while you were there at least, you did not question, and that very feeling lifted you, in your own estimation, nearer to art.

Invaluable, it seems to me, those Tuesdays must have been to the young men of two generations who have been making French literature; they were unique, certainly, in the experience of the young Englishman

---

* ["something of the priest, something of the dancer, he shared their manner each time he entered the conversation, as one makes an entrance on stage." —Ed.]

who was always so cordially received there, with so flattering a cordiality. Here was a house in which art, literature, was the very atmosphere, a religious atmosphere; and the master of the house, in his just a little solemn simplicity, a priest. I never heard the price of a book mentioned, or the number of thousand francs which a popular author had been paid for his last volume; here, in this one literary house, literature was unknown as a trade. And, above all, the questions that were discussed were never, at least, in Mallarmé's treatment, in his guidance of them, other than essential questions, considerations of art in the abstract, of literature before it coagulates into a book, of life as its amusing and various web spins the stuff of art. When, indeed, the conversation, by some untimely hazard, drifted too near to one, became for a moment, perhaps inconveniently, practical, it was Mallarmé's solicitous politeness to wait, a little constrained, almost uneasy, rolling his cigarette in silence, until the disturbing moment had passed.

There were other disturbing moments, sometimes. I remember one night, rather late, the sudden irruption of M. de Heredia, coming on after a dinner-party, and seating himself, in his well-filled evening dress, precisely in Mallarmé's favourite chair. He was intensely amusing, voluble, floridly vehement; Mallarmé, I am sure, was delighted to see him; but the loud voice was a little trying to his nerves, and then he did not know what to do without his chair. He was like a cat that has been turned out of its favourite corner, as he roamed uneasily about the room, resting an unaccustomed elbow on the sideboard, visibly at a disadvantage.

For the attitude of those young men, some of them no longer exactly young, who frequented the Tuesdays, was certainly the attitude of the disciple. Mallarmé never exacted it, he seemed never to notice it; yet it meant to him, all the same, a good deal; as it meant, and in the best sense, a good deal to them. He loved art with a supreme disinterestedness, and it was for the sake of art that he wished to be really a master. For he knew that he had something to teach, that he had found out some secrets worth knowing, that he had discovered a point of view which he could to some degree perpetuate in those young men who listened to him. And to them this free kind of apprenticeship was, beyond all that it gave in direct counsels, in the pattern of work, a noble influence. Mallarmé's quiet, laborious life was for some of them the only counterpoise to the Bohemian example of the *d'Harcourt* or the *Taverne,* where art is loved, but with something of haste, in a very changing devotion. It was impossible to come away from Mallarmé's without some tranquillising influence from that quiet place, some impersonal ambition towards excellence, the resolve, at least, to write a sonnet, a page of prose, that should be in its own way as perfect as one could make it, worthy of Mallarmé.

II

"Poetry," said Mallarmé, "is the language of a state of crisis"; and all his poems are the evocation of a passing ecstasy, arrested in mid-flight.

This ecstasy is never the mere instinctive cry of the heart, the simple human joy or sorrow, which, like the Parnassians, but for not quite the same reason, he did not admit in poetry. It is a mental transposition of emotion or sensation, veiled with atmosphere, and becoming, as it becomes a poem, pure beauty. Here, for instance, in a poem which I have translated line for line, and almost word for word, a delicate emotion, a figure vaguely divined, a landscape magically evoked, blend in a single effect.

SIGH

My soul, calm sister, towards thy brow, whereon scarce grieves
An autumn strewn already with its russet leaves,
And towards the wandering sky of thine angelic eyes,
Mounts, as in melancholy gardens may arise
Some faithful fountain sighing whitely towards the blue!
—Towards the blue pale and pure that sad October knew,
When, in those depths, it mirrored languors infinite,
And agonising leaves upon the waters white,
Windily drifting, traced a furrow cold and dun,
Where, in one long last ray, lingered the yellow sun.

Another poem comes a little closer to nature, but with what exquisite precautions, and with what surprising novelty in its unhesitating touch on actual things!

SEA-WIND

The flesh is sad, alas! and all the books are read.
Flight, only flight! I feel that birds are wild to tread
The floor of unknown foam, and to attain the skies!
Nought, neither ancient gardens mirrored in the eyes,
Shall hold this heart that bathes in waters its delight,
O nights! nor yet my waking lamp, whose lonely light
Shadows the vacant paper, whiteness profits best,
Nor the young wife who rocks her baby on her breast.
I will depart. O steamer, swaying rope and spar,
Lift anchor for exotic lands that lie afar!
A weariness, outworn by cruel hopes, still clings
To the last farewell handkerchief's last beckonings!
And are not these, the masts inviting storms, not these
That an awakening wind bends over wrecking seas,
Lost, not a sail, a sail, a flowering isle, ere long?
But, O my heart, hear thou, hear thou the sailors' song!

These (need I say?) belong to the earlier period, in which Mallarmé had not yet withdrawn his light into the cloud; and to the same period belong the prose-poems, one of which, perhaps the most exquisite, I will translate here.

AUTUMN LAMENT

"Ever since Maria left me, for another star—which? Orion, Altair, or thou, green Venus?—I have always cherished solitude. How many long days I have passed, alone with my cat! By *alone,* I mean without a material being, and my cat is a mystical companion, a spirit. I may say, then, that I have passed long days alone with my cat, and alone, with one of the last writers of the Roman decadence; for since the white creature is no more, strangely and singularly, I have loved all that may be summed up in the word: fall. Thus, in the year, my favourite season is during those last languid summer days which come just before the autumn; and, in the day, the hour when I take my walk is the hour when the sun lingers before fading, with rays of copper-yellow on the grey walls, and of copper-red on the window-panes. And, just so, the literature from which my soul demands delight must be the poetry dying out of the last moments of Rome, provided, nevertheless, that it breathes nothing of the rejuvenating approach of the Barbarians, and does not stammer the infantile Latin of the first Christian prose.

"I read, then, one of those beloved poems (whose streaks of rouge have more charm for me than the fresh cheek of youth), and buried my hand in the fur of the pure animal, when a barrel-organ began to sing, languishingly and melancholy, under my window. It played in the long alley of poplars, whose leaves seem mournful to me even in spring, since Maria passed that way with the capers, for the last time. Yes, sad people's instrument, truly: the piano glitters, the violin brings one's torn fibres to the light, but the barrel-organ, in the twilight of memory, has set me despairingly dreaming. While it murmured a gaily vulgar air, such as puts mirth into the heart of the suburbs, an old-fashioned, an empty air, how came it that its refrain went to my very soul, and made me weep like a romantic ballad? I drank it in, and I did not throw a penny out of the window, for fear of disturbing my own impression, and of perceiving that the instrument was not singing by itself."

Between these characteristic, clear, and beautiful poems, in verse and in prose, and the opaque darkness of the later writings, come one or two poems, perhaps the finest of all, in which already clearness is "a secondary grace," but in which a subtle rapture finds incomparable expression. *L'Après-midi d'un Faune* and *Hérodiade* have already been introduced, in different ways, to English readers: the former by Mr. Gosse, in a detailed analysis; the latter by a translation into verse. And Debussy, in his new music, has taken *L'Après-midi d'un Faune* almost for his new point of departure, interpreting it, at all events, faultlessly. In these two poems I find Mallarmé at the moment when his own desire achieves itself; when he attains Wagner's ideal, that "the most complete work of the poet should be that which, in its final achievement, becomes a perfect music": every word is a jewel, scattering and recapturing sudden fire, every image is a symbol, and the whole poem is visible music. After this point began that fatal "last period" which comes to most artists who

have thought too curiously, or dreamed too remote dreams, or followed a
too wandering beauty. Mallarmé had long been too conscious that all
publication is "almost a speculation, on one's modesty, for one's silence";
that "to unclench the fists, breaking one's sedentary dream, for a ruffling
face to face with the idea," was after all unnecessary to his own conception of himself, a mere way of convincing the public that one exists;
and having achieved, as he thought, "the right to abstain from doing
anything exceptional," he devoted himself, doubly, to silence. Seldom
condescending to write, he wrote now only for himself, and in a manner
which certainly saved him from intrusion. Some of Meredith's poems,
and occasional passages of his prose, can alone give in English some
faint idea of the later prose and verse of Mallarmé. The verse could not,
I think, be translated; of the prose, in which an extreme lucidity of
thought comes to us but glimmeringly through the entanglements of a
construction, part Latin, part English, I shall endeavour to translate some
fragments, in speaking of the theoretic writings, contained in the two
volumes of *Vers et Prose* and *Divagations*.

III

It is the distinction of Mallarmé to have aspired after an impossible
liberation of the soul of literature from what is fretting and constraining
in "the body of that death," which is the mere literature of words. Words,
he has realised, are of value only as a notation of the free breath of the
spirit; words, therefore, must be employed with an extreme care, in their
choice and adjustment, in setting them to reflect and chime upon one
another; yet least of all for their own sake, for what they can never,
except by suggestion, express. "Every soul is a melody," he has said,
"which needs to be readjusted; and for that are the flute or viol of
each." The word, treated indeed with a kind of "adoration," as he says,
is so regarded in a magnificent sense, in which it is apprehended as a
living thing, itself the vision rather than the reality; at least the philtre of
the evocation. The word, chosen as he chooses it, is for him a liberating
principle, by which the spirit is extracted from matter; takes form, perhaps assumes immortality. Thus an artificiality, even, in the use of
words, that seeming artificiality which comes from using words as if they
had never been used before, that chimerical search after the virginity of
language, is but the paradoxical outward sign of an extreme discontent
with even the best of their service. Writers who use words fluently,
seeming to disregard their importance, do so from an unconscious confidence in their expressiveness, which the scrupulous thinker, the precise
dreamer, can never place in the most carefully chosen among them. To
evoke, by some elaborate, instantaneous magic of language, without the
formality of an after all impossible description; to be, rather than to
express: that is what Mallarmé has consistently, and from the first, sought
in verse and prose. And he has sought this wandering, illusive, beckon-
ing butterfly, the soul of dreams, over more and more entangled ground;

and it has led him into the depths of many forests, far from the sunlight. To say that he has found what he sought is impossible; but (is it possible to avoid saying?) how heroic a search, and what marvellous discoveries by the way!

I think I understand, though I cannot claim his own authority for my supposition, the way in which Mallarmé wrote verse, and the reason why it became more and more abstruse, more and more unintelligible. Remember his principle: that to name is to destroy, to suggest is to create. Note, further, that he condemns the inclusion in verse of anything but, "for example, the horror of the forest, or the silent thunder afloat in the leaves; not the intrinsic, dense wood of the trees." He has received, then, a mental sensation: let it be the horror of the forest. This sensation begins to form in his brain, at first probably no more than a rhythm, absolutely without words. Gradually thought begins to concentrate itself (but with an extreme care, lest it should break the tension on which all depends) upon the sensation, already struggling to find its own consciousness. Delicately, stealthily, with infinitely timid precaution, words present themselves, at first in silence. Every word seems like a desecration, seems, the clearer it is, to throw back the original sensation farther and farther into the darkness. But, guided always by the rhythm, which is the executive soul (as, in Aristotle's definition, the soul is the form of the body), words come slowly, one by one, shaping the message. Imagine the poem already written down, at least composed. In its very imperfection, it is clear, it shows the links by which it has been riveted together; the whole process of its construction can be studied. Now most writers would be content; but with Mallarmé the work has only begun. In the final result there must be no sign of the making, there must be only the thing made. He works over it, word by word, changing a word here, for its colour, which is not precisely the colour required, a word there, for the break it makes in the music. A new image occurs to him, rarer, subtler, than the one he has used; the image is transferred. By the time the poem has reached, as it seems to him, a flawless unity, the steps of the progress have been only too effectually effaced; and while the poet, who has seen the thing from the beginning, still sees the relation of point to point, the reader, who comes to it only in its final stage, finds himself in a not unnatural bewilderment. Pursue this manner of writing to its ultimate development; start with an enigma, and then withdraw the key of the enigma; and you arrive, easily, at the frozen impenetrability of those latest sonnets, in which the absence of all punctuation is scarcely a recognisable hindrance.

That, I fancy to myself, was his actual way of writing; here, in what I prefer to give as a corollary, is the theory. "Symbolist, Decadent, or Mystic, the schools thus called by themselves, or thus hastily labelled by our information-press, adopt, for meeting-place, the point of an Idealism which (similarly as in fugues, in sonatas) rejects the 'natural' materials, and, as brutal, a direct thought ordering them; to retain no more than suggestion. To be instituted, a relation between images, exact; and that therefrom should detach itself a third aspect, fusible and clear, offered to the divination. Abolished, the pretension, aesthetically an error, despite its dominion over almost all the masterpieces, to enclose within the subtle paper other than, for example, the horror of the forest, or the silent thunder afloat in the leaves; not the intrinsic, dense wood of the trees. Some few bursts of personal pride, veridically trumpeted, awaken the architecture of the palace, alone habitable; not of stone, on which the pages would close but ill." For example (it is his own): "I say: a flower! and out of the oblivion to which my voice consigns every contour, so far as anything save the known calyx, musically arises, idea, and exquisite, the one flower absent from all bouquets." "The pure work," then, "implies the elocutionary disappearance of the poet, who yields place to the words, immobilised by the shock of their inequality; they take light from mutual reflection, like an actual train of fire over precious stones, replacing the old lyric afflatus or the enthusiastic personal direction of the phrase." "The verse which out of many vocables remakes an entire word, new, unknown to the language, and as if magical, attains this isolation of speech." Whence, it being "music which rejoins verse, to form, since Wagner, Poetry," the final conclusion: "That we are now precisely at the moment of seeking, before that breaking up of the large rhythms of literature, and their scattering in articulate, almost instrumental, nervous waves, an art which shall complete the transposition, into the Book, of the symphony, or simply recapture our own: for, it is not in elementary sonorities of brass, strings, wood, unquestionably, but in the intellectual word at its utmost, that, fully and evidently, we should find, drawing to itself all the correspondences of the universe, the supreme Music."

Here, literally translated, in exactly the arrangement of the original, are some passages out of the theoretic writings, which I have brought together, to indicate what seem to me the main lines of Mallarmé's doctrine. It is the doctrine which, as I have already said, had been divined by Gérard de Nerval; but what, in Gérard, was pure vision, becomes in Mallarmé a logical sequence of meditation. Mallarmé was not a mystic, to whom anything came unconsciously; he was a thinker, in whom an extraordinary subtlety of mind was exercised on always explicit, though by no means the common, problems. "A seeker after something in the world, that is there in no satisfying measure, or not at all," he pursued his search with unwearying persistence, with a sharp mental division of dream and idea, certainly very lucid to himself, however he may have failed to render his expression clear to others. And I, for one, cannot doubt that he was, for the most part, entirely right in his statement and analysis of the new conditions under which we are now privileged or condemned to write. His obscurity was partly his failure to carry out the spirit of his own directions; but, apart from obscurity, which we may all be fortunate enough to escape, is it possible for a writer, at the present day, to be quite simple, with the old, objective simplicity, in either thought or expression? To be naïf, to be archaic, is not to be either natural or simple; I affirm that it is not natural to be what is called "natural" any longer. We have no longer the mental attitude of those to whom a story was but a story, and all stories good; we have realised, since it was proved to us by Poe, not merely that the age of epics is past, but that no long poem was ever written; the finest long poem in the world being but a series of short poems linked together by prose. And, naturally, we can no longer write what we can no longer accept. Symbolism, implicit in all literature from the beginning, as it is implicit in the very words we use, comes to us now, at last quite conscious of itself, offering us the only escape from our many imprisonments. We find a new, an older, sense in the so worn out forms of things; the world, which we can no longer believe in as the satisfying material object it was to our grandparents, becomes transfigured with a new light; words, which long usage had darkened almost out of recognition, take fresh lustre. And it is on the lines of that spiritualising of the word, that perfecting of form in its capacity for allusion and suggestion, that confidence in the eternal correspondences between the visible and the invisible universe, which Mallarmé taught, and too intermittently practised, that literature must now move, if it is in any sense to move forward.

OSCAR WILDE

from

The Decay of Lying

"Lying," according to the witty Oscar Wilde, meant poetry. It meant a conscious artificiality in one's behavior and in one's writing. Good poetry, he claimed, did not try for realism or for the imitation of Nature. On the contrary, Wilde contended, *Nature imitates Art.*

Wilde was satirized in his own time by Gilbert and Sullivan, among others, and by himself for his attitudinizing as an Aesthete. Whatever the seriousness of his intentions, he became in his own life the figurehead of the decadent and dandified artist, until his own downfall over a homosexual scandal that sent him to prison.

The British Aesthetic stance, exemplified by Wilde, was a counterpart or an imitation of the French Decadent movement, out of which grew such writings as those of Laforgue and Corbière, the masters of T. S. Eliot, and the poetry of the Symbolists, who exalted their wit above the banality of "middle-class" art.

Cyril. . . . I want you to tell me briefly the doctrines of the new æsthetics.

Vivian. Briefly, then, they are these. Art never expresses anything but itself. It has an independent life, just as Thought has, and develops purely on its own lines. It is not necessarily realistic in an age of realism, nor spiritual in an age of faith. So far from being the creation of its time, it is usually in direct opposition to it, and the only history that it preserves for us is the history of its own progress. Sometimes it returns upon its footsteps, and revives some antique form, as happened in the archaistic movement of late Greek Art, and in the pre-Raphaelite movement of our own day. At other times it entirely anticipates its age, and produces in one century work that it takes another century to understand, to appreciate, and to enjoy. In no case does it reproduce its age. To pass from the art of a time to the time itself is the great mistake that all historians commit.

The second doctrine is this. All bad art comes from returning to Life and Nature, and elevating them into ideals. Life and Nature may sometimes be used as part of Art's rough material, but before they are of any real service to art they must be translated into artistic conventions. The moment Art surrenders its imaginative medium it surrenders everything. As a method Realism is a complete failure, and the two things that every artist should avoid are modernity of form and modernity of subject-matter. To us, who live in the nineteenth century, any century is a suitable subject for art except our own. The only beautiful things are the things that do not concern us. It is, to have the pleasure of quoting myself, exactly because Hecuba is nothing to us that her sorrows are so suitable a motive for a tragedy. Besides, it is only the modern that ever becomes old-fashioned. M. Zola sits down to give us a picture of the Second Empire. Who cares for the Second Empire now? It is out of date. Life goes faster than Realism, but Romanticism is always in front of Life.

The third doctrine is that Life imitates Art far more than Art imitates Life. This results not merely from Life's imitative instinct, but from the fact that the self-conscious aim of Life is to find expression, and that Art offers it certain beautiful forms through which it may realize that energy. It is a theory that has never been put forward before, but it is extremely fruitful, and throws an entirely new light upon the history of Art.

It follows, as a corollary from this, that external Nature also imitates Art. The only effects that she can show us are effects that we have already seen through poetry, or in paintings. This is the secret of Nature's charm, as well as the explanation of Nature's weakness.

The final revelation is that Lying, the telling of beautiful untrue things, is the proper aim of Art. But of this I think I have spoken at sufficient length. And now let us go out on the terrace, where "droops the milk-white peacock like a ghost," while the evening star "washes the dusk with silver." At twilight nature becomes a wonderfully suggestive effect, and is not without loveliness, though perhaps its chief use is to illustrate quotations from the poets. Come! We have talked long enough.

2

CLASSICAL USES OF THE PAST

T. S. ELIOT

The Metaphysical Poets

The poetry called "Metaphysical" from seventeenth-century England was virtually unknown in English literature until its revival in our time. Eliot's part in its revival is paramount. In one of his most forceful essays—another of his book reviews—he argued for the unity of feeling and intellect, which he claimed had ceased to exist since the time of the Metaphysical poets. "A thought to Donne," says Eliot, "was an experience; it modified his sensibility." And Eliot follows this observation with one of the key theories of modern poetry: "In the seventeenth century a dissociation of sensibility set in, from which we have never recovered. . . ." The famous catch phrase "dissociation of sensibility" refers to a split between thought and feeling which, according to Eliot, calls for a reunion of the two by the poet.

In the same essay Eliot turns toward the French poets of the Symbolist school, Laforgue and Corbière, for a more recent illustration of a method for uniting the sophisticated intellect with the feelings. Thus Eliot attempts a fusion between the complex technique of the seventeenth-century poet and the rarified irony of the nineteenth-century French Symbolists, with Poe's theory of "the effect" playing a strong role in the background.

The "dissociation of sensibility" is dramatized in one of Eliot's finest poems, "The Love-Song of J. Alfred Prufrock," in which passion is played against reasoning to the point of stalemate.

$\mathscr{B}$y collecting these poems[1] from the work of a generation more often named than read, and more often read than profitably studied, Professor Grierson has rendered a service of some importance. Certainly the reader will meet with many poems already preserved in other anthologies, at the same time that he discovers poems such as those of Aurelian Townshend or Lord Herbert of Cherbury here included. But the function of such an anthology as this is neither that of Professor Saintsbury's admirable edition of Caroline poets nor that of the *Oxford Book of English Verse*. Mr. Grierson's book is in itself a piece of criticism and a provocation of criticism; and we think that he was right in including so many poems of Donne, elsewhere (though not in many editions) accessible, as documents in the case of "metaphysical poetry." The phrase has long done duty as a term of abuse or as the label of a quaint and pleasant taste. The question is to what extent the so-called metaphysicals formed a school (in our own time we should say a "movement"), and how far this so-called school or movement is a digression from the main current.

Not only is it extremely difficult to define metaphysical poetry, but difficult to decide what poets practise it and in which of their verses. The poetry of Donne (to whom Marvell and Bishop King are sometimes nearer than any of the other authors) is late Elizabethan, its feeling often very close to that of Chapman. The "courtly" poetry is derivative from Jonson, who borrowed liberally from the Latin; it expires in the next century with the sentiment and witticism of Prior. There is finally the devotional verse of Herbert, Vaughan, and Crashaw (echoed long after by Christina Rossetti and Francis Thompson); Crashaw, sometimes more profound and less sectarian than the others, has a quality which returns through the Elizabethan period to the early Italians. It is difficult to find any precise use of metaphor, simile, or other conceit, which is common to all the poets and at the same time important enough as an element of style to isolate these poets as a group. Donne, and often Cowley, employ a device which is sometimes considered characteristically "metaphysical"; the elaboration (contrasted with the condensation) of a figure of speech to the farthest stage to which ingenuity can carry it. Thus Cowley develops the commonplace comparison of the world to a chess-board through long stanzas (*To Destiny*), and Donne, with more grace, in *A Valediction*, the comparison of two lovers to a pair of compasses. But elsewhere we find, instead of the mere explication of the content of a comparison, a development by rapid association of thought which requires considerable agility on the part of the reader.

> On a round ball
> A workman that hath copies by, can lay
> An Europe, Afrique, and an Asia,

---

[1] *Metaphysical Lyrics and Poems of the Seventeenth Century*: Donne to Butler. Selected and edited, with an Essay, by Herbert J. C. Grierson (Oxford: Clarendon Press. London: Milford).

> And quickly make that, which was nothing, All,
> > So doth each teare,
> > Which thee doth weare,
> A globe, yea, world by that impression grow,
> Till thy teares mixt with mine doe overflow
> This world, by waters sent from thee, my heaven dissolved so.

Here we find at least two connexions which are not implicit in the first figure, but are forced upon it by the poet: from the geographer's globe to the tear, and the tear to the deluge. On the other hand, some of Donne's most successful and characteristic effects are secured by brief words and sudden contrasts:

> A bracelet of bright hair about the bone,

where the most powerful effect is produced by the sudden contrast of associations of "bright hair" and of "bone." This telescoping of images and multiplied associations is characteristic of the phrase of some of the dramatists of the period which Donne knew: not to mention Shakespeare, it is frequent in Middleton, Webster, and Tourneur, and is one of the sources of the vitality of their language.

Johnson, who employed the term "metaphysical poets," apparently having Donne, Cleveland, and Cowley chiefly in mind, remarks of them that "the most heterogeneous ideas are yoked by violence together." The force of this impeachment lies in the failure of the conjunction, the fact that often the ideas are yoked but not united; and if we are to judge of styles of poetry by their abuse, enough examples may be found in Cleveland to justify Johnson's condemnation. But a degree of heterogeneity of material compelled into unity by the operation of the poet's mind is omnipresent in poetry. We need not select for illustration such a line as:

> Notre âme est un trois-mâts cherchant son Icarie;*

we may find it in some of the best lines of Johnson himself (*The Vanity of Human Wishes*):

> His fate was destined to a barren strand,
> A petty fortress, and a dubious hand;
> He left a name at which the world grew pale,
> To point a moral, or adorn a tale.

where the effect is due to a contrast of ideas, different in degree but the same in principle, as that which Johnson mildly reprehended. And in one of the finest poems of the age (a poem which could not have been written in any other age), the *Exequy* of Bishop King, the extended comparison is used with perfect success: the idea and the simile become one, in the passage in which the Bishop illustrates his impatience to see his dead wife, under the figure of a journey:

---

* ["The soul is a three-master searching for its Icaria;"—Ed.]

Stay for me there; I will not faile
To meet thee in that hollow Vale.
And think not much of my delay;
I am already on the way,
And follow thee with all the speed
Desire can make, or sorrows breed.
Each minute is a short degree,
And ev'ry houre a step towards thee.
At night when I betake to rest,
Next morn I rise nearer my West
Of life, almost by eight houres sail,
Than when sleep breath'd his drowsy gale. . . .
But heark! My Pulse, like a soft Drum
Beats my approach, tells *Thee* I come;
And slow howere my marches be,
I shall at last sit down by *Thee*.

(In the last few lines there is that effect of terror which is several times
attained by one of Bishop King's admirers, Edgar Poe.) Again, we may
justly take these quatrains from Lord Herbert's Ode, stanzas which
would, we think, be immediately pronounced to be of the metaphysical
school:

So when from hence we shall be gone,
    And be no more, nor you, nor I,
    As one another's mystery,
Each shall be both, yet both but one.

This said, in her up-lifted face,
    Her eyes, which did that beauty crown,
    Were like two starrs, that having faln down,
Look up again to find their place:

While such a moveless silent peace
    Did seize on their becalmed sense,
    One would have thought some influence
Their ravished spirits did possess.

There is nothing in these lines (with the possible exception of the
stars, a simile not at once grasped, but lovely and justified) which fits
Johnson's general observations on the metaphysical poets in his essay
on Cowley. A good deal resides in the richness of association which is
at the same time borrowed from and given to the word "becalmed";
but the meaning is clear, the language simple and elegant. It is to be
observed that the language of these poets is as a rule simple and pure;
in the verse of George Herbert this simplicity is carried as far as it can
go—a simplicity emulated without success by numerous modern poets.
The *structure* of the sentences, on the other hand, is sometimes far from
simple, but this is not a vice; it is a fidelity to thought and feeling. The
effect, at its best, is far less artificial than that of an ode by Gray. And as

this fidelity induces variety of thought and feeling, so it induces variety of music. We doubt whether, in the eighteenth century, could be found two poems in nominally the same metre, so dissimilar as Marvell's *Coy Mistress* and Crashaw's *Saint Teresa;* the one producing an effect of great speed by the use of short syllables, and the other an ecclesiastical solemnity by the use of long ones:

> Love, thou art absolute sole lord
> Of life and death.

If so shrewd and sensitive (though so limited) a critic as Johnson failed to define metaphysical poetry by its faults, it is worth while to inquire whether we may not have more success by adopting the opposite method: by assuming that the poets of the seventeenth century (up to the Revolution) were the direct and normal development of the precedent age; and, without prejudicing their case by the adjective "metaphysical," consider whether their virtue was not something permanently valuable, which subsequently disappeared, but ought not to have disappeared. Johnson has hit, perhaps by accident, on one of their peculiarities, when he observes that "their attempts were always analytic"; he would not agree that, after the dissociation, they put the material together again in a new unity.

It is certain that the dramatic verse of the later Elizabethan and early Jacobean poets expresses a degree of development of sensibility which is not found in any of the prose, good as it often is. If we except Marlowe, a man of prodigious intelligence, these dramatists were directly or indirectly (it is at least a tenable theory) affected by Montaigne. Even if we except also Jonson and Chapman, these two were notably erudite, and were notably men who incorporated their erudition into their sensibility: their mode of feeling was directly and freshly altered by their reading and thought. In Chapman especially there is a direct sensuous apprehension of thought, or a recreation of thought into feeling, which is exactly what we find in Donne:

> in this one thing, all the discipline
> Of manners and of manhood is contained;
> A man to join himself with th' Universe
> In his main sway, and make in all things fit
> One with that All, and go on, round as it;
> Not plucking from the whole his wretched **part,**
> And into straits, or into nought revert,
> Wishing the complete Universe might **be**
> Subject to such a rag of it as he;
> But to consider great Necessity.

We compare this with some modern passage:

> No, when the fight begins within himself,
> A man's worth something. God stoops o'er his **head,**

> Satan looks up between his feet—both tug—
> He's left, himself, i' the middle; the soul wakes
> And grows. Prolong that battle through his life!

It is perhaps somewhat less fair, though very tempting (as both poets are concerned with the perpetuation of love by offspring), to compare with the stanzas already quoted from Lord Herbert's Ode the following from Tennyson:

> One walked between his wife and child,
> With measured footfall firm and mild,
> And now and then he gravely smiled.
> The prudent partner of his blood
> Leaned on him, faithful, gentle, good,
> Wearing the rose of womanhood.
> And in their double love secure,
> The little maiden walked demure,
> Pacing with downward eyelids pure.
> These three made unity so sweet,
> My frozen heart began to beat,
> Remembering its ancient heat.

The difference is not a simple difference of degree between poets. It is something which had happened to the mind of England between the time of Donne or Lord Herbert of Cherbury and the time of Tennyson and Browning; it is the difference between the intellectual poet and the reflective poet. Tennyson and Browning are poets, and they think; but they do not feel their thought as immediately as the odour of a rose. A thought to Donne was an experience; it modified his sensibility. When a poet's mind is perfectly equipped for its work, it is constantly amalgamating disparate experience; the ordinary man's experience is chaotic, irregular, fragmentary. The latter falls in love, or reads Spinoza, and these two experiences have nothing to do with each other, or with the noise of the typewriter or the smell of cooking; in the mind of the poet these experiences are always forming new wholes.

We may express the difference by the following theory: The poets of the seventeenth century, the successors of the dramatists of the sixteenth, possessed a mechanism of sensibility which could devour any kind of experience. They are simple, artificial, difficult, or fantastic, as their predecessors were; no less nor more than Dante, Guido Cavalcanti, Guinizelli, or Cino. In the seventeenth century a dissociation of sensibility set in, from which we have never recovered; and this dissociation, as is natural, was aggravated by the influence of the two most powerful poets of the century, Milton and Dryden. Each of these men performed certain poetic functions so magnificently well that the magnitude of the effect concealed the absence of others. The language went on and in some respects improved; the best verse of Collins, Gray, Johnson, and even Goldsmith satisfies some of our fastidious demands better than that of Donne or Marvell or King. But while the language became more refined, the feeling became more crude. The feeling, the sensibility, expressed in the *Country Churchyard* (to say nothing of Tennyson and Browning) is cruder than that in the *Coy Mistress.*

The second effect of the influence of Milton and Dryden followed from the first, and was therefore slow in manifestation. The sentimental age began early in the eighteenth century, and continued. The poets revolted against the ratiocinative, the descriptive; they thought and felt by fits, unbalanced; they reflected. In one or two passages of Shelley's *Triumph of Life,* in the second *Hyperion,* there are traces of a struggle toward unification of sensibility. But Keats and Shelley died, and Tennyson and Browning ruminated.

After this brief exposition of a theory—too brief, perhaps, to carry conviction—we may ask, what would have been the fate of the "metaphysical" had the current of poetry descended in a direct line from them, as it descended in a direct line to them? They would not, certainly, be classified as metaphysical. The possible interests of a poet are unlimited; the more intelligent he is the better; the more intelligent he is the more likely that he will have interests: our only condition is that he turn them into poetry, and not merely meditate on them poetically. A philosophical theory which has entered into poetry is established, for its truth or falsity in one sense ceases to matter, and its truth in another sense is proved. The poets in question have, like other poets, various faults. But they were, at best, engaged in the task of trying to find the verbal equivalent for states of mind and feeling. And this means both that they are more mature, and that they wear better, than later poets of certainly not less literary ability.

It is not a permanent necessity that poets should be interested in philosophy, or in any other subject. We can only say that it appears likely that poets in our civilization, as it exists at present, must be *difficult.* Our civilization comprehends great variety and complexity, and this variety and complexity, playing upon a refined sensibility, must produce various and complex results. The poet must become more and more comprehensive, more allusive, more indirect, in order to force, to dislocate if necessary, language into his meaning. (A brilliant and extreme statement of this view, with which it is not requisite to associate oneself, is that of M. Jean Epstein, *La Poésie d'aujourd-hui.*) Hence we get something which looks very much like the conceit—we get, in fact, a method curiously similar to that of the "metaphysical poets," similar also in its use of obscure words and of simple phrasing.

> O géraniums diaphanes, guerroyeurs sortilèges,
> Sacrilèges monomanes!
> Emballages, dévergondages, douches! O pressoirs
> Des vendanges des grands soirs!
> Layettes aux abois,
> Thyrses au fond des bois!
> Transfusions, représailles,
> Relevailles, compresses et l'éternal potion,

Angélus! n'en pouvoir plus
De débâcles nuptiales! de débâcles nuptiales!*

The same poet could write also simply:

Elle est bien loin, elle pleure,
Le grand vent se lamente aussi . . .†

Jules Laforgue, and Tristan Corbière in many of his poems, are nearer
to the "school of Donne" than any modern English poet. But poets
more classical than they have the same essential quality of transmuting
ideas into sensations, of transforming an observation into a state of mind.

Pour l'enfant, amoureux de cartes et d'estampes,
L'univers est égal à son vaste appétit.
Ah, que le monde est grand à la clarté des lampes!
Aux yeux du souvenir que le monde est petit! ‡

In French literature the great master of the seventeenth century—
Racine—and the great master of the nineteenth—Baudelaire—are in
some ways more like each other than they are like any one else. The
greatest two masters of diction are also the greatest two psychologists,
the most curious explorers of the soul. It is interesting to speculate
whether it is not a misfortune that two of the greatest masters of diction
in our language, Milton and Dryden, triumph with a dazzling disregard
of the soul. If we continued to produce Miltons and Drydens it might
not so much matter, but as things are it is a pity that English poetry
has remained so incomplete. Those who object to the "artificiality" of
Milton or Dryden sometimes tell us to "look into our hearts and write."
But that is not looking deep enough; Racine or Donne looked into a
good deal more than the heart. One must look into the cerebral cortex,
the nervous system, and the digestive tracts.

    May we not conclude, then, that Donne, Crashaw, Vaughan, Herbert
and Lord Herbert, Marvell, King, Cowley at his best, are in the direct
current of English poetry, and that their faults should be reprimanded
by this standard rather than coddled by antiquarian affection? They

---

    * ["Oh diaphanous geraniums, knight-errant sorcery,
      Monomaniac sacrileges!
      Bursts of enthusiasm, licentiousness, cold showers! Oh wine-presses
    For the harvests of the revolution!
    Layettes at bay,
    Thyrsus deep in the woods,
    Transfusions, reprisals,
    Churching, compresses and the eternal potion,
    Angelus! Fed up with
    Nuptial disasters! with nuptial disasters!"—Ed.]
        † ["She is far away, she weeps,
            The high wind moans too . . ."—Ed.]
        ‡ ["For the child, fond of cards and prints,
            The world is as large as his vast appetite.
            Ah, how big the world is in the lamp light!
            In the eyes of memory, how small it is!"—Ed.]

have been enough praised in terms which are implicit limitations because they are "metaphysical" or "witty," "quaint" or "obscure," though at their best they have not these attributes more than other serious poets. On the other hand, we must not reject the criticism of Johnson (a dangerous person to disagree with) without having mastered it, without having assimilated the Johnsonian canons of taste. In reading the celebrated passage in his essay on Cowley we must remember that by wit he clearly means something more serious than we usually mean today; in his criticism of their versification we must remember in what a narrow discipline he was trained, but also how well trained; we must remember that Johnson tortures chiefly the chief offenders, Cowley and Cleveland. It would be a fruitful work, and one requiring a substantial book, to break up the classification of Johnson (for there has been none since) and exhibit these poets in all their difference of kind and of degree, from the massive music of Donne to the faint, pleasing tinkle of Aurelian Townshend—whose *Dialogue between a Pilgrim and Time* is one of the few regrettable omissions from the excellent anthology of Professor Grierson.

T. S. ELIOT
Tradition and the Individual Talent

T. S. Eliot's *Selected Essays*, certainly the most celebrated work of criticism of our time, opens with an exposition of the tradition in relation to the individual talent. Eliot defines as an aesthetic principle the obligation of the present to the past in art, and the metamorphosis of the past in works of our contemporaries. In the process of developing his consciousness of the past, the poet undergoes a continual self-sacrifice, "a continual extinction of personality."

This theory of the depersonalization of art is one of the well-known doctrines of modern poetics which Eliot made famous. His remarks about the exclusion of "actual emotions" from poetry in favor of *significant* emotion recall the criticism of Poe. "Tradition and the Individual Talent" has gone far in molding the poetic sensibility of a generation of modern Classicists.

I

*I*n English writing we seldom speak of tradition, though we occasionally apply its name in deploring its absence. We cannot refer

to "the tradition" or to "a tradition"; at most, we employ the adjective
in saying that the poetry of So-and-so is "traditional" or even "too
traditional." Seldom, perhaps, does the word appear except in a phrase
of censure. If otherwise, it is vaguely approbative, with the implication,
as to the work approved, of some pleasing archaeological reconstruction.
You can hardly make the word agreeable to English ears without this
comfortable reference to the reassuring science of archaeology.

Certainly the word is not likely to appear in our appreciations of
living or dead writers. Every nation, every race, has not only its own
creative, but its own critical turn of mind; and is even more oblivious of
the shortcomings and limitations of its critical habits than of those of its
creative genius. We know, or think we know, from the enormous mass
of critical writing that has appeared in the French language the critical
method or habit of the French; we only conclude (we are such unconscious people) that the French are "more critical" than we, and sometimes even plume ourselves a little with the fact, as if the French were
the less spontaneous. Perhaps they are; but we might remind ourselves
that criticism is as inevitable as breathing, and that we should be none
the worse for articulating what passes in our minds when we read a
book and feel an emotion about it, for criticizing our own minds in
their work of criticism. One of the facts that might come to light in this
process is our tendency to insist, when we praise a poet, upon those
aspects of his work in which he least resembles any one else. In these
aspects or parts of his work we pretend to find what is individual, what
is the peculiar essence of the man. We dwell with satisfaction upon the
poet's difference from his predecessors, especially his immediate predecessors; we endeavour to find something that can be isolated in order
to be enjoyed. Whereas if we approach a poet without this prejudice we
shall often find that not only the best, but the most individual parts of
his work may be those in which the dead poets, his ancestors, assert their
immortality most vigorously. And I do not mean the impressionable
period of adolescence, but the period of full maturity.

Yet if the only form of tradition, of handing down, consisted in following the ways of the immediate generation before us in a blind or timid
adherence to its successes, "tradition" should positively be discouraged.
We have seen many such simple currents soon lost in the sand; and
novelty is better than repetition. Tradition is a matter of much wider
significance. It cannot be inherited, and if you want it you must obtain
it by great labour. It involves, in the first place, the historical sense,
which we may call nearly indispensable to any one who would continue
to be a poet beyond his twenty-fifth year; and the historical sense
involves a perception, not only of the pastness of the past, but of its
presence; the historical sense compels a man to write not merely with
his own generation in his bones, but with a feeling that the whole of
the literature of Europe from Homer and within it the whole of the
literature of his own country has a simultaneous existence and composes
a simultaneous order. This historical sense, which is a sense of the

timeless as well as of the temporal and of the timeless and of the
temporal together, is what makes a writer traditional. And it is at the
same time what makes a writer most acutely conscious of his place in
time, of his own contemporaneity.

No poet, no artist of any art, has his complete meaning alone. His
significance, his appreciation is the appreciation of his relation to the
dead poets and artists. You cannot value him alone; you must set him,
for contrast and comparison, among the dead. I mean this as a principle
of aesthetic, not merely historical, criticism. The necessity that he shall
conform, that he shall cohere, is not onesided; what happens when a
new work of art is created is something that happens simultaneously to
all the works of art which preceded it. The existing monuments form
an ideal order among themselves, which is modified by the introduction
of the new (the really new) work of art among them. The existing order
is complete before the new work arrives; for order to persist after the
supervention of novelty, the *whole* existing order must be, if ever so
slightly, altered; and so the relations, proportions, values of each work
of art toward the whole are readjusted; and this is conformity between
the old and the new. Whoever has approved this idea of order, of the
form of European, of English literature will not find it preposterous that
the past should be altered by the present as much as the present is
directed by the past. And the poet who is aware of this will be aware of
great difficulties and responsibilities.

In a peculiar sense he will be aware also that he must inevitably be
judged by the standards of the past. I say judged, not amputated, by
them; not judged to be as good as, or worse or better than, the dead;
and certainly not judged by the canons of dead critics. It is a judgment,
a comparison, in which two things are measured by each other. To
conform merely would be for the new work not really to conform at
all; it would not be new, and would therefore not be a work of art. And
we do not quite say that the new is more valuable because it fits in; but
its fitting in is a test of its value—a test, it is true, which can only be
slowly and cautiously applied, for we are none of us infallible judges
of conformity. We say: it appears to conform, and is perhaps individual,
or it appears individual, and many conform; but we are hardly likely
to find that it is one and not the other.

To proceed to a more intelligible exposition of the relation of the
poet to the past: he can neither take the past as a lump, an indiscriminate
bolus, nor can he form himself wholly on one or two private admirations,
nor can he form himself wholly upon one preferred period. The first
course is inadmissible, the second is an important experience of youth,
and the third is a pleasant and highly desirable supplement. The poet
must be very conscious of the main current, which does not at all flow
invariably through the most distinguished reputations. He must be quite
aware of the obvious fact that art never improves, but that the material
of art is never quite the same. He must be aware that the mind of
Europe—the mind of his own country—a mind which he learns in time

to be much more important than his own private mind—is a mind which changes, and that this change is a development which abandons nothing *en route*, which does not superannuate either Shakespeare, or Homer, or the rock drawing of the Magdalenian draughtsmen. That this development, refinement perhaps, complication certainly, is not, from the point of view of the artist, any improvement. Perhaps not even an improvement from the point of view of the psychologist or not to the extent which we imagine; perhaps only in the end based upon a complication in economics and machinery. But the difference between the present and the past is that the conscious present is an awareness of the past in a way and to an extent which the past's awareness of itself cannot show.

Some one said: "The dead writers are remote from us because we *know* so much more than they did." Precisely, and they are that which we know.

I am alive to a usual objection to what is clearly part of my programme for the *métier* of poetry. The objection is that the doctrine requires a ridiculous amount of erudition (pedantry), a claim which can be rejected by appeal to the lives of poets in any pantheon. It will even be affirmed that much learning deadens or perverts poetic sensibility. While, however, we persist in believing that a poet ought to know as much as will not encroach upon his necessary receptivity and necessary laziness, it is not desirable to confine knowledge to whatever can be put into a useful shape for examinations, drawing-rooms, or the still more pretentious modes of publicity. Some can absorb knowledge, the more tardy must sweat for it. Shakespeare acquired more essential history from Plutarch than most men could from the whole British Museum. What is to be insisted upon is that the poet must develop or procure the consciousness of the past and that he should continue to develop this consciousness throughout his career.

What happens is a continual surrender of himself as he is at the moment to something which is more valuable. The progress of an artist is a continual self-sacrifice, a continual extinction of personality.

There remains to define this process of depersonalization and its relation to the sense of tradition. It is in this depersonalization that art may be said to approach the condition of science. I, therefore, invite you to consider, as a suggestive analogy, the action which takes place when a bit of finely filiated platinum is introduced into a chamber containing oxygen and sulphur dioxide.

II

Honest criticism and sensitive appreciation are directed not upon the poet but upon the poetry. If we attend to the confused cries of the newspaper critics and the *susurrus* of popular repetition that follows, we shall hear the names of poets in great numbers; if we seek not Blue-book knowledge but the enjoyment of poetry, and ask for a poem, we shall seldom find it. I have tried to point out the importance of the relation of the poem to other poems by other authors, and suggested the conception of poetry as a living whole of all the poetry that has ever been written. The other aspect of this Impersonal theory of poetry is the relation of the poem to its author. And I hinted, by an analogy, that the mind of the mature poet differs from that of the immature one not precisely in any valuation of "personality," not being necessarily more interesting, or having "more to say," but rather by being a more finely perfected medium in which special, or very varied, feelings are at liberty to enter into new combinations.

The analogy was that of the catalyst. When the two gases previously mentioned are mixed in the presence of a filament of platinum, they form sulphurous acid. This combination takes place only if the platinum is present; nevertheless the newly formed acid contains no trace of platinum, and the platinum itself is apparently unaffected; has remained inert, neutral, and unchanged. The mind of the poet is the shred of platinum. It may partly or exclusively operate upon the experience of the man himself; but, the more perfect the artist, the more completely separate in him will be the man who suffers and the mind which creates; the more perfectly will the mind digest and transmute the passions which are its material.

The experience, you will notice, the elements which enter the presence of the transforming catalyst, are of two kinds: emotions and feelings. The effect of a work of art upon the person who enjoys it is an experience different in kind from any experience not of art. It may be formed out of one emotion, or may be a combination of several; and various feelings, inhering for the writer in particular words or phrases or images, may be added to compose the final result. Or great poetry may be made without the direct use of any emotion whatever: composed out of feelings solely. Canto XV of the *Inferno* (Brunetto Latini) is a working up of the emotion evident in the situation; but the effect, though single as that of any work of art, is obtained by considerable complexity of detail. The last quatrain gives an image, a feeling attaching to an image, which "came," which did not develop simply out of what precedes, but which was probably in suspension in the poet's mind until the proper combination arrived for it to add itself to. The poet's mind is in fact a receptacle for seizing and storing up numberless feelings, phrases, images, which remain there until all the particles which can unite to form a new compound are present together.

If you compare several representative passages of the greatest poetry you see how great is the variety of types of combination, and also how completely any semi-ethical criterion of "sublimity" misses the mark. For it is not the "greatness," the intensity, of the emotions, the components, but the intensity of the artistic process, the pressure, so to speak, under which the fusion takes place, that counts. The episode of Paolo and Francesca employs a definite emotion, but the intensity of the poetry is something quite different from whatever intensity in the

supposed experience it may give the impression of. It is no more
intense, furthermore, than Canto XXVI, the voyage of Ulysses, which
has not the direct dependence upon an emotion. Great variety is possible
in the process of transmutation of emotion: the murder of Agamemnon,
or the agony of Othello, gives an artistic effect apparently closer to a
possible original than the scenes from Dante. In the *Agamemnon,* the
artistic emotion approximates to the emotion of an actual spectator; in
Othello to the emotion of the protagonist himself. But the difference
between art and the event is always absolute; the combination which is
the murder of Agamemnon is probably as complex as that which is the
voyage of Ulysses. In either case there has been a fusion of elements. The
ode of Keats contains a number of feelings which have nothing particular
to do with the nightingale, but which the nightingale, partly, perhaps,
because of its attractive name, and partly because of its reputation,
served to bring together.

The point of view which I am struggling to attack is perhaps related
to the metaphysical theory of the substantial unity of the soul: for my
meaning is, that the poet has, not a "personality" to express, but a
particular medium, which is only a medium and not a personality, in
which impressions and experiences combine in peculiar and unexpected
ways. Impressions and experiences which are important for the man
may take no place in the poetry, and those which become important in
the poetry may play quite a negligible part in the man, the personality.

I will quote a passage which is unfamiliar enough to be regarded with
fresh attention in the light—or darkness—of these observations:

> And now methinks I could e'en chide myself
> For doating on her beauty, though her death
> Shall be revenged after no common action.
> Does the silkworm expend her yellow labours
> For thee? For thee does she undo herself?
> Are lordships sold to maintain ladyships
> For the poor benefit of a bewildering minute?
> Why does yon fellow falsify highways,
> And put his life between the judge's lips,
> To refine such a thing—keeps horse and men
> To beat their valours for her? . . .

In this passage (as is evident if it is taken in its context) there is a
combination of positive and negative emotions: an intensely strong
attraction toward beauty and an equally intense fascination by the
ugliness which is contrasted with it and which destroys it. This balance
of contrasted emotion is in the dramatic situation to which the speech
is pertinent, but that situation alone is inadequate to it. This is, so to
speak, the structural emotion, provided by the drama. But the whole
effect, the dominant tone, is due to the fact that a number of floating
feelings, having an affinity to this emotion by no means superficially
evident, have combined with it to give us a new art emotion.

It is not in his personal emotions, the emotions provoked by particular events in his life, that the poet is in any way remarkable or interesting. His particular emotions may be simple, or crude, or flat. The emotion in his poetry will be a very complex thing, but not with the complexity of the emotions of people who have very complex or unusual emotions in life. One error, in fact, of eccentricity in poetry is to seek for new human emotions to express; and in this search for novelty in the wrong place it discovers the perverse. The business of the poet is not to find new emotions, but to use the ordinary ones and, in working them up into poetry, to express feelings which are not in actual emotions at all. And emotions which he has never experienced will serve his turn as well as those familiar to him. Consequently, we must believe that "emotion recollected in tranquillity" is an inexact formula. For it is neither emotion, nor recollection, nor, without distortion of meaning, tranquillity. It is a concentration, and a new thing resulting from the concentration, of a very great number of experiences which to the practical and active person would not seem to be experiences at all; it is a concentration which does not happen consciously or of deliberation. These experiences are not "recollected," and they finally unite in an atmosphere which is "tranquil" only in that it is a passive attending upon the event. Of course this is not quite the whole story. There is a great deal, in the writing of poetry, which must be conscious and deliberate. In fact, the bad poet is usually unconscious where he ought to be conscious, and conscious where he ought to be unconscious. Both errors tend to make him "personal." Poetry is not a turning loose of emotion, but an escape from emotion; it is not the expression of personality, but an escape from personality. But, of course, only those who have personality and emotions know what it means to want to escape from these things.

III

ὁ δὲ νοῦς ἴσως θειότερόν τι καὶ ἀπαθές ἐστιν.*

This essay proposes to halt at the frontier of metaphysics or mysticism, and confine itself to such practical conclusions as can be applied by the responsible person interested in poetry. To divert interest from the poet to the poetry is a laudable aim: for it would conduce to a juster estimation of actual poetry, good and bad. There are many people who appreciate the expression of sincere emotion in verse, and there is a smaller number of people who can appreciate technical excellence. But very few know when there is an expression of *significant* emotion, emotion which has its life in the poem and not in the history of the poet. The emotion of art is impersonal. And the poet cannot reach this impersonality without surrendering himself wholly to the work to be done. And he is not likely to know what is to be done unless he lives in what is not merely the present, but the present moment of the past, unless he is conscious, not of what is dead, but of what is already living.

* ["Perhaps the mind is too divine, and is therefore unaffected."—Ed.]

SIR JAMES FRAZER

from

THE GOLDEN BOUGH

One of the chief characteristics of modern Classicist poetry is its reliance on the studies of anthropology and comparative mythology. Sir James Frazer's *The Golden Bough* is an exhaustive study of a particular myth which led him to an examination of related myths and customs throughout the world and in all ages. The influence of his research on modern poetic sensibility is incalculable. Suffice it to say that without Frazer we would probably not have such works as *The Waste Land*, the *Cantos*, or even Joyce's *Ulysses*.

Our inclusion of the introduction to *The Golden Bough* serves only to familiarize the reader of modern poetry with the vast mythologic scope of modern anthropology and modern poetry. Frazer's study of magic alone has helped revolutionize poetry in our time.

Who does not know Turner's picture of the Golden Bough? The scene, suffused with the golden glow of imagination in which the divine mind of Turner steeped and transfigured even the fairest natural landscape, is a dream-like vision of the little woodland lake of Nemi, "Diana's Mirror," as it was called by the ancients. No one who has seen that calm water, lapped in a green hollow of the Alban Hills, can ever forget it. The two characteristic Italian villages which slumber on its banks, and the equally Italian palace whose terraced gardens descend steeply to the lake, hardly break the stillness, and even the solitariness, of the scene. Dian herself might still linger by this lonely shore, still haunt these woodlands wild.

In antiquity this sylvan landscape was the scene of a strange and recurring tragedy. On the northern shore of the lake, right under the precipitous cliffs on which the modern village of Nemi is perched, stood the sacred grove and sanctuary of Diana Nemorensis, or Diana of the Wood. The lake and the grove were sometimes known as the lake and grove of Aricia. But the town of Aricia (the modern La Riccia) was situated about three miles off, at the foot of the Alban Mount, and separated by a steep descent from the lake, which lies in a small crater-like hollow on the mountain side. In this sacred grove there grew a certain tree round which at any time of the day, and probably far into the night, a grim figure might be seen to prowl. In his hand he carried a drawn sword, and he kept peering warily about him as if every instant he expected to be set upon by an enemy. He was a priest and a murderer; and the man for whom he looked was sooner or later to murder him and hold the priesthood in his stead. Such was the rule of the sanctuary. A candidate for the priesthood could only succeed to office by slaying the priest, and having slain him, he retained office till he was himself slain by a stronger or a craftier.

The post which he held by this precarious tenure carried with it the title of king; but surely no crowned head ever lay uneasier, or was visited by more evil dreams, than his. For year in year out, in summer and winter, in fair weather and in foul, he had to keep his lonely watch, and whenever he snatched a troubled slumber it was at the peril of his life. The least relaxation of his vigilance, the smallest abatement of his strength of limb or skill of fence, put him in jeopardy; gray hairs might seal his death-warrant. To gentle and pious pilgrims at the shrine the sight of him may well have appeared to darken the fair landscape, as when a cloud suddenly blots the sun on a bright day. The dreamy blue of Italian skies, the dappled shade of summer woods, and the sparkle of waves in the sun can have accorded but ill with that stern and sinister figure. Rather we picture to ourselves the scene as it may have been witnessed by a belated wayfarer on one of those wild autumn nights when the dead leaves are falling thick, and the winds seem to sing the dirge of the dying year. It is a sombre picture, set to melancholy music—the background of forest showing black and jagged against a lowering and stormy sky, the sighing of the wind in the branches, the rustle of the withered leaves under foot, the lapping of the cold water on the shore, and in the foreground, pacing to and fro, now in twilight and now in gloom, a dark figure with a glitter as of steel at the shoulder whenever the pale moon, riding clear of the cloud-rack, peers down at him through the matted boughs.

The strange rule of his priesthood has no parallel in classical antiquity, and cannot be explained from it. To find an explanation we must go farther afield. No one will probably deny that such a custom savours of a barbarous age, and, surviving into imperial times, stands out in striking isolation from the polished Italian society of the day, like a primeval rock rising from a smooth-shaven lawn. It is the very rudeness and barbarity of the custom which allow us a hope of explaining it. For recent researches into the early history of man have revealed the essential similarity with which, under many superficial differences, the human mind has elaborated its first crude philosophy of life. Accordingly, if we can show that a barbarous custom, like that of the priesthood of Nemi, has existed elsewhere; if we can detect the motives which led to its institution; if we can prove that these motives have operated widely, perhaps universally, in human society, producing in varied circumstances a variety of institutions specifically different but generically alike; if we can show, lastly, that these very motives, with some of their derivative institutions, were actually at work in classical antiquity; then we may fairly infer that at a remoter age the same motives gave birth to the priesthood of Nemi. Such an inference, in default of direct evidence as to how the priesthood did actually arise, can never amount to demonstration.

But it will be more or less probable according to the degree of completeness with which it fulfils the conditions indicated above. The object of this book is, by meeting these conditions, to offer a fairly probable explanation of the priesthood of Nemi.

I begin by setting forth the few facts and legends which have come down to us on the subject. According to one story the worship of Diana at Nemi was instituted by Orestes, who, after killing Thoas, King of Tauric Chersonese (the Crimea), fled with his sister to Italy, bringing with him the image of the Tauric Diana. The bloody ritual which legend ascribed to that goddess is familiar to classical readers; it is said that every stranger who landed on the shore was sacrificed on her altar. But transported to Italy, the rite assumed a milder form. Within the sanctuary at Nemi grew a certain tree of which no branch might be broken. Only a runaway slave was allowed to break off, if he could, one of its boughs. Success in the attempt entitled him to fight the priest in single combat, and if he slew him he reigned in his stead with the title of King of the Wood (*Rex Nemorensis*). Tradition averred that the fateful branch was that Golden Bough which, at the Sibyl's bidding, Aeneas plucked before he essayed the perilous journey to the world of the dead. The flight of the slave represented, it was said, the flight of Orestes; his combat with the priest was a reminiscence of the human sacrifices once offered to the Tauric Diana. This rule of succession by the sword was observed down to imperial times; for amongst his other freaks Caligula, thinking that the priest of Nemi had held office too long, hired a more stalwart ruffian to slay him; and a Greek traveller, who visited Italy in the age of the Antonines, remarks that down to his time the priesthood was still the prize of victory in a single combat.

Of the worship of Diana at Nemi two leading features can still be made out. First, from the votive offerings found in modern times on the site, it appears that she was especially worshipped by women desirous of children or of an easy delivery. Second, fire seems to have played a foremost part in her ritual. For during her annual festival, celebrated at the hottest time of the year, her grove shone with a multitude of torches, whose ruddy glare was reflected by the waters of the lake; and throughout the length and breadth of Italy the day was kept with holy rites at every domestic hearth. Moreover, women whose prayers had been heard by the goddess brought lighted torches to the grove in fulfilment of their vows. Lastly, the title of Vesta borne by the Arician Diana points almost certainly to the maintenance of a perpetual holy fire in her sanctuary.

At her annual festival all young people went through a purificatory ceremony in her honour; dogs were crowned; and the feast consisted of a young kid, wine, and cakes, served up piping hot on platters of leaves.

But Diana did not reign alone in her grove at Nemi. Two lesser divinities shared her forest sanctuary. One was Egeria, the nymph of the clear water which, bubbling from the basaltic rocks, used to fall in graceful cascades into the lake at the place called Le Mole. According to one story the grove was first consecrated to Diana by a Manius Egerius, who was the ancestor of a long and distinguished line. Hence the proverb "There are many Manii at Ariciae." Others explained the proverb very differently. They said it meant that there were a great many ugly and deformed people, and they referred to the word *Mania,* which meant a bogey or bugbear to frighten children.

The other of these minor deities was Virbius. Legend had it that Virbius was the youthful Greek hero Hippolytus, who had been killed by his horses on the sea-shore of the Saronic Gulf. Him, to please Diana, the leech Aesculapius brought to life again by his simples. But Jupiter, indignant that a mortal man should return from the gates of death, thrust down the meddling leech himself to Hades; and Diana, for the love she bore Hippolytus, carried him away to Italy and hid him from the angry god in the dells of Nemi, where he reigned a forest king under the name of Virbius. Horses were excluded from the grove and sanctuary, because horses had killed Hippolytus. Some thought that Virbius was the sun. It was unlawful to touch his image. His worship was cared for by a special priest, the Flamen Virbialis.

Such, then, are the facts and theories bequeathed to us by antiquity on the subject of the priesthood of Nemi. From materials so slight and scanty it is impossible to extract a solution of the problem. It remains to try whether the survey of a wider field may not yield us the clue we seek. The questions to be answered are two: first, why had the priest to slay his predecessor? and second, why, before he slew him, had he to pluck the Golden Bough? The rest of this book will be an attempt to answer these questions.

JESSIE L. WESTON

from FROM RITUAL TO ROMANCE

The Fisher King

Central to the doctrine and technique of modern Classicism is mythopoeia (myth-making). When *From Ritual to Romance* was published in 1920, it provided for mythic poets like T. S. Eliot not only a vast corpus of symbolic material for poetry but a technique of relationship as well. Eliot acknowledges his greatest debt to Miss Weston for her study of the Grail legends; her book, Eliot says, will do more to clear up the difficulties of *The Waste Land*

than any other source, even *The Golden Bough*. Miss Weston's
chapter on "The Fisher King," while a highly scholarly study,
indicates the tremendous range of a particular myth.

*T*he gradual process of our investigation has led us to the conclusion that the elements forming the existing Grail legend—the setting
of the story, the nature of the task which awaits the hero, the symbols
and their significance—one and all, while finding their counterpart in
prehistoric record, present remarkable parallels to the extant practice and
belief of countries so widely separate as the British Isles, Russia, and
Central Africa.

The explanation of so curious a fact, for it is a fact, and not a mere
hypothesis, may, it was suggested, most probably be found in the theory
that in this fascinating literature we have the, sometimes partially understood, sometimes wholly misinterpreted, record of a ritual, originally
presumed to exercise a life-giving potency, which, at one time of universal
observance, has, even in its decay, shown itself possessed of elements of
the most persistent vitality.

That if the ritual, which according to our theory lies at the root of
the Grail story, be indeed the ritual of a Life Cult, it should, *in* and
per se, possess precisely these characteristics, will, I think, be admitted
by any fair-minded critic; the point of course is, can we definitely
prove our theory, *i.e.*, not merely point to striking parallels, but select,
from the figures and incidents composing our story, some one element,
which, by showing itself capable of explanation on this theory, and on
this theory alone, may be held to afford decisive proof of the soundness
of our hypothesis?

It seems to me that there is one such element in the bewildering complex, by which the theory can be thus definitely tested, that is the
personality of the central figure and the title by which he is known. If
we can prove that the Fisher King, *qua* Fisher King, is an integral part
of the ritual, and can be satisfactorily explained alike by its intention,
and inherent symbolism, we shall, I think, have taken the final step
which will establish our theory upon a sure basis. On the other hand, if
the Fisher King, *qua* Fisher King, does not fit into our framework we
shall be forced to conclude that, while the *provenance* of certain elements of the Grail literature is practically assured, the *ensemble* has been
complicated by the introduction of a terminology, which, whether the
outcome of serious intention, or of mere literary caprice, was foreign to
the original source, and so far, defies explanation. In this latter case
our theory would not necessarily be *manqué*, but would certainly be
seriously incomplete.

We have already seen that the personality of the King, the nature of
the disability under which he is suffering, and the reflex effect exercised upon his folk and his land, correspond, in a most striking manner,
to the intimate relation at one time held to exist between the ruler and

his land; a relation mainly dependent upon the identification of the King with the Divine principle of Life and Fertility.

This relation, as we have seen above, exists to-day among certain African tribes.

If we examine more closely into the existing variants of our romances, we shall find that those very variants are not only thoroughly *dans le cadre* of our proposed solution, but also afford a valuable, and hitherto unsuspected, indication of the relative priority of the versions.

In Chapter 1, I discussed the task of the hero in general, here I propose to focus attention upon his host, and while in a measure traversing the same ground, to do so with a view to determining the true character of this enigmatic personage.

In the *Bleheris* version,[1] the lord of the castle is suffering under no disability whatever; he is described as "tall, and strong of limb, of no great age, but somewhat bald." Besides the King there is a Dead Knight upon a bier, over whose body Vespers for the Dead are solemnly sung. The wasting of the land, partially restored by Gawain's question concerning the Lance, has been caused by the 'Dolorous Stroke,' *i.e.*, the stroke which brought about the death of the Knight, whose identity is here never revealed. Certain versions which interpolate the account of Joseph of Arimathea and the Grail, allude to 'Le riche Pescheur' and his heirs as Joseph's descendants, and, presumably, for it is not directly stated, guardians of the Grail,[2] but the King himself is here never called by that title. From his connection with the Waste Land it seems more probable that it was the Dead Knight who filled that *rôle*.

In the second version of which Gawain is the hero, that of *Diû Crône*[3] the Host is an old and infirm man. After Gawain has asked the question we learn that he is really dead, and only compelled to retain the semblance of life till the task of the Quester be achieved. Here, again, he is not called the Fisher King.

In the *Perceval* versions, on the contrary, we find the name invariably associated with him, but he is not always directly connected with the misfortunes which have fallen upon his land. Thus, while the Wauchier texts are incomplete, breaking off at the critical moment of asking the question, Manessier who continues, and ostensibly completes, Wauchier, introduces the Dead Knight, here Goondesert, or Gondefer (which I suspect is the more correct form), brother of the King, whose death by treachery has plunged the land in misery, and been the direct cause of the self-wounding of the King.[4] The healing of the King and the restoration of the land depend upon Perceval's slaying the murderer Partinal. These two versions show a combination of Perceval and

[1] Cf. my *Sir Gawain at the Grail Castle*, pp. 3–30. The best text is that of MS. B.N., fonds Franç. 12576, ff. 87*vo*–91. The above remarks apply also to the *Elucidation*, which is using a version of the *Bleheris* form.
[2] B.N. 12577, fo. 136*vo*.
[3] Cf. *Sir Gawain at the Grail Castle*, pp. 33–46.
[4] Cf. B.N. 12576, ff. 220–222*vo* and fo. 258.

Gawain themes, such as their respective dates might lead us to expect.

Robert de Borron is the only writer who gives a clear, and tolerably reasonable, account of why the guardian of the Grail bears the title of Fisher King; in other cases, such as the poems of Chrétien and Wolfram, the name is connected with his partiality for fishing, an obviously *post hoc* addition.

The story in question is found in Borron's *Joseph of Arimathea*.[5] Here we are told how, during the wanderings of that holy man and his companions in the wilderness, certain of the company fell into sin. By the command of God, Brons, Joseph's brother-in-law, caught a Fish, which, with the Grail, provided a mystic meal of which the unworthy cannot partake; thus the sinners were separated from the righteous. Henceforward Brons was known as 'The Rich Fisher.' It is noteworthy, however, that in the Perceval romance, ascribed to Borron, the title is as a rule, *Roi* Pescheur, not *Riche* Pescheur.[6]

In this romance the King is not suffering from any special malady, but is the victim of extreme old age; not surprising, as he is Brons himself, who has survived from the dawn of Christianity to the days of King Arthur. We are told that the effect of asking the question will be to restore him to youth;[7] as a matter of fact it appears to bring about his death, as he only lives three days after his restoration.[8]

When we come to Chrétien's poem we find ourselves confronted with a striking alteration in the presentment. There are, not one, but two, disabled kings; one suffering from the effects of a wound, the other in extreme old age. Chrétien's poem being incomplete we do not know what he intended to be the result of the achieved Quest, but we may I think reasonably conclude that the wounded King at least was healed.[9]

The *Parzival* of von Eschenbach follows the same tradition, but is happily complete. Here we find the wounded King was healed, but what becomes of the aged man (here the grandfather, not as in Chrétien the father, of the Fisher King) we are not told.[10]

The *Perlesvaus* is, as I have noted above,[11] very unsatisfactory. The illness of the King is badly motived, and he dies before the achievement of the Quest. This romance, while retaining certain interesting, and undoubtedly primitive features, is, as a whole, too late, and *remaniée* a redaction to be of much use in determining the question of origins.

---

[5] Hucher, *Le Saint Graal*, Vol. I. pp. 251 *et seq.*, 315 *et seq.*

[6] Cf. Modena MS. pp. 11, 12, 21, etc.; Dr Nitze, *The Fisher-King in the Grail Romances*, p. 373, says Borron uses the term *Rice* Pescheur, as opposed to the *Roi* Pescheur of Chrétien. This remark is only correct as applied to the *Joseph*.

[7] Modena MS. p. 61 and note.

[8] *Ibid.* p. 63.

[9] The evidence of the *Parzival* and the parallel Grail sections of *Sone de Nansai*, which appear to repose ultimately on a source common to all three authors, makes this practically certain.

[10] This is surely a curious omission, if the second King were as essential a part of the scheme as Dr Nitze supposes.

[11] Cf. Chapter 2, p. 15.

The same may be said of the *Grand Saint Graal* and *Queste* versions, both of which are too closely connected with the prose *Lancelot,* and too obviously intended to develop and complete the *données* of that romance to be relied upon as evidence for the original form of the Grail legend.[12] The version of the *Queste* is very confused: there are two kings at the Grail castle, Pelles, and his father; sometimes the one, sometimes the other, bears the title of Roi Pescheur.[13] There is besides, an extremely old, and desperately wounded, king, Mordrains, a contemporary of Joseph, who practically belongs, not to the Grail tradition, but to a Conversion legend embodied in the *Grand Saint Graal.*[14] Finally, in the latest cyclic texts, we have three Kings, all of whom are wounded.[15]

The above will show that the presentment of this central figure is much confused; generally termed Le Roi Pescheur, he is sometimes described as in middle life, and in full possession of his bodily powers. Sometimes while still comparatively young he is incapacitated by the effects of a wound, and is known also by the title of Roi Mehaigné, or Maimed King. Sometimes he is in extreme old age, and in certain closely connected versions the two ideas are combined, and we have a wounded Fisher King, and an aged father, or grandfather. But I would draw attention to the significant fact that in no case is the Fisher King a youthful character; that distinction is reserved for his Healer, and successor.

Now is it possible to arrive at any conclusion as to the relative value and probable order of these conflicting variants? I think that if we admit that they do, in all probability, represent a more or less coherent survival of the Nature ritual previously discussed, we may, by help of what we know as to the varying forms of that ritual, be enabled to bring some order out of this confusion.

If we turn back to Chapters 4, 5, and 7, and consult the evidence there given as to the Adonis cults, the Spring Festivals of European Folk, the Mumming Plays of the British Isles, the main fact that emerges is that in the great majority of these cases the representative of the Spirit of Vegetation is considered as dead, and the object of these ceremonies is to restore him to life. This I hold to be the primary form.

This section had already been written when I came across the important article by Dr Jevons, referred to in a previous chapter.[16]

---

[12] I cannot agree with Dr Nitze's remark (*op. cit.* p. 374) that "in most versions the Fisher King has a mysterious double." I hold the feature to be a peculiarity of the Chrétien-Wolfram group. It is not found in the Gawain versions, in Wauchier, nor in Manessier. Gerbert is using the *Queste* in the passage relative to Mordrains, and for the reason stated above I hold that neither *Queste* nor *Grand Saint Graal* should be cited when we are dealing as Dr Nitze is here dealing, with questions of ultimate origin.

[13] Cf. my *Legend of Sir Lancelot,* pp. 167 and 168.

[14] Cf. Heinzel, *Ueber die Alt-Franz. Gral-Romanen,* pp. 136 and 137.

[15] Cf. *Legend of Sir Perceval,* Vol. II. p. 343, note. These three kings are found in the curious *Merlin* MS. B.N., f. Franç. 337, fo. 249 *et seq.*

[16] *Vide supra,* pp. 91, 92.

Certain of his remarks are here so much to the point that I cannot refrain from quoting them. Speaking of the Mumming Plays, the writer says: "The one point in which there is no variation is that—the character is killed and brought to life again. The play is a ceremonial performance, or rather it is the development in dramatic form of what was originally a religious or magical rite, representing or realizing the revivification of the character slain. This revivification is the one essential and invariable feature of all the Mummer's plays in England." [17]

In certain cases, e.g., the famous Roman Spring festival of Mamurius Veturius and the Swabian ceremony referred to above,[18] the central figure is an old man. In no case do I find that the representative of Vegetation is merely wounded, although the nature of the ritual would obviously admit of such a variant.

Thus, taking the extant and recognized forms of the ritual into consideration, we might expect to find that in the earliest, and least contaminated, version of the Grail story the central figure would be dead, and the task of the Quester that of restoring him to life. Viewed from this standpoint the *Gawain* versions (the priority of which is maintainable upon strictly literary grounds, Gawain being the original Arthurian romantic hero) are of extraordinary interest. In the one form we find a Dead Knight, whose fate is distinctly stated to have involved his land in desolation, in the other, an aged man who, while preserving the semblance of life, is in reality dead.

This last version appears to me, in view of our present knowledge, to be of extreme critical value. There can, I think, be little doubt that in the primary form underlying our extant versions the King was dead, and restored to life; at first, I strongly suspect, by the agency of some mysterious herb, or herbs, a feature retained in certain forms of the Mumming play.

In the next stage, that represented by Borron, he is suffering from extreme old age, and the task of the Quester is to restore him to youth. This version is again supported by extant parallels. In each of these cases it seems most probable that the original ritual (I should wish it to be clearly understood that I hold the Grail story to have been primarily dramatic, and actually performed) involved an act of substitution. The Dead King in the first case being probably represented by a mere effigy, in the second being an old man, his place was, at a given moment of the ritual, taken by the youth who played the *rôle* of the Quester. It is noteworthy that, while both Perceval and Galahad are represented as mere lads, Gawain, whatever his age at the moment of the Grail quest, was, as we learn from *Diû Crône,* dowered by his fairy Mistress with the gift of eternal youth.[19]

---

[17] *Op. cit.* p. 184.
[18] Cf. Chapter 5, p. 52, Chap. 7, p. 88.
[19] *Diû Crône,* ll. 17329 *et seq.*

The versions of Chrétien and Wolfram, which present us with a wounded Fisher King, and a father, or grandfather,[20] in extreme old age, are due in my opinion to a literary device, intended to combine two existing variants. That the subject matter was well understood by the original redactor of the common source is proved by the nature of the injury,[21] but I hold that in these versions we have passed from the domain of ritual to that of literature. Still, we have a curious indication that the Wounding variant may have had its place in the former. The suggestion made above as to the probable existence in the primitive ritual of a substitution ceremony, seems to me to provide a possible explanation of the feature found alike in Wolfram, and in the closely allied Grail section of *Sone de Nansai; i.e.,* that the wound of the King was a punishment for sin, he had conceived a passion for a Pagan princess.[22] Now there would be no incongruity in representing the Dead King as reborn in youthful form, the aged King as *revenu dans sa juvence,* but when the central figure was a man in the prime of life some reason had to be found, his strength and vitality being restored, for his supersession by the appointed Healer. This supersession was adequately motived by the supposed transgression of a fundamental Christian law, entailing as consequence the forfeiture of his crown.

I would thus separate the *doubling* theme, as found in Chrétien and Wolfram, from the *wounded* theme, equally common to these poets. This latter might possibly be accounted for on the ground of a ritual variant; the first is purely literary, explicable neither on the exoteric, nor the esoteric, aspect of the ceremony. From the exoteric point of view there are not, and there cannot be, two Kings suffering from parallel disability; the ritual knows one Principle of Life, and one alone. Equally from the esoteric standpoint Fisher King, and Maimed King, representing two different aspects of the same personality, may, and probably were, represented as two individuals, but one alone is disabled. Further, as the two are, in very truth, one, they should be equals in age, not of different generations. Thus the *Bleheris* version which gives us a Dead Knight, presumably, from his having been slain in battle, still in vigorous manhood, and a hale King is, ritually, the more correct. The original of Manessier's version must have been similar, but the fact that by the time it was compiled the Fisher King was generally accepted as being also the Maimed King led to the introduction of the very awkward, and poorly motived, self-wounding incident. It will be noted that in this case the King is not healed either at the moment of the slaying of his brother's murderer (which would be the logical result of the *données* of

---

[20] In the *Parzival* Titurel is grandfather to Anfortas, Frimutel intervening; critics of the poem are apt to overlook this difference between the German and French versions.

[21] Cf. Chapter 2, p. 20.

[22] Cf. here my notes on *Sone de Nansai* (*Romania*, Vol. XLIII. p. 412).

the tale), nor at the moment of contact with the successful Quester, but at the mere announcement of his approach.[23]

Thus, if we consider the King, apart from his title, we find that alike from his position in the story, his close connection with the fortunes of his land and people, and the varying forms of the disability of which he is the victim, he corresponds with remarkable exactitude to the central figure of a well-recognized Nature ritual, and may therefore justly be claimed to belong *ab origine* to such a hypothetical source.

But what about his title, why should he be called the *Fisher* King?

Here we strike what I hold to be the main *crux* of the problem, a feature upon which scholars have expended much thought and ingenuity, a feature which the authors of the romances themselves either did not always understand, or were at pains to obscure by the introduction of the obviously *post hoc* "motif" above referred to, *i.e.*, that he was called the Fisher King because of his devotion to the pastime of fishing: *à-propos* of which Heinzel sensibly remarks, that the story of the Fisher King "presupposes a legend of this personage only vaguely known and remembered by Chrétien." [24]

Practically the interpretations already attempted fall into two main groups, which we may designate as the Christian-Legendary, and the Celtic-Folk-lore interpretations. For those who hold that the Grail story is essentially, and fundamentally, Christian, finding its root in Eucharistic symbolism, the title is naturally connected with the use of the Fish symbol in early Christianity: the *Icthys* anagram, as applied to Christ, the title 'Fishers of Men,' bestowed upon the Apostles, the Papal ring of the Fisherman—though it must be noted that no manipulation of the Christian symbolism avails satisfactorily to account for the lamentable condition into which the bearer of the title has fallen.[25]

The advocates of the Folk-lore theory, on the other hand, practically evade this main difficulty, by basing their interpretation upon Borron's story of the catching of the Fish by Brons, equating this character with the Bran of Welsh tradition, and pointing to the existence, in Irish and Welsh legend, of a Salmon of Wisdom, the tasting of whose flesh confers

---

[23] In connection with my previous remarks on the subject [p. 79] I would point out that the *Queste* and *Grand Saint Graal* versions repeat the Maimed King *motif* in the most unintelligent manner. The element of old age, inherent in the Evalach-Mordrains incident, is complicated and practically obscured, by an absurdly exaggerated wounding element, here devoid of its original significance.

[24] Heinzel, *op. cit.* p. 13.

[25] For an instance of the extravagances to which a strictly Christian interpretation can lead, cf. Dr Sebastian Evans's theories set forth in his translation of the *Perlesvaus* (*The High History of the Holy Grail*) and in his *The Quest of the Holy Grail*. The author places the origin of the cycle in the first quarter of the thirteenth century, and treats it as an allegory of the position in England during the Interdict pronounced against King John, and the consequent withholding of the Sacraments. His identification of the characters with historical originals is most ingenious, an extraordinary example of misapplied learning.

all knowledge. Hertz acutely remarks that the incident, as related by Borron, is not of such importance as to justify the stress laid upon the name, Rich Fisher, by later writers.[26] We may also note in this connection that the Grail romances never employ the form 'Wise Fisher,' which, if the origin of the name were that proposed above, we might reasonably expect to find. It is obvious that a satisfactory solution of the problem must be sought elsewhere.

In my opinion the key to the puzzle is to be found in the rightful understanding of the *Fish-Fisher* symbolism. Students of the Grail literature have been too prone to treat the question on the Christian basis alone, oblivious of the fact that Christianity did no more than take over, and adapt to its own use, a symbolism already endowed with a deeply rooted prestige and importance.

So far the subject cannot be said to have received adequate treatment; certain of its aspects have been more or less fully discussed in monographs and isolated articles, but we still await a comprehensive study on this most important question.[27]

So far as the present state of our knowledge goes we can affirm with certainty that the Fish is a Life symbol of immemorial antiquity, and that the title of Fisher has, from the earliest ages, been associated with Deities who were held to be specially connected with the origin and preservation of Life.

In Indian cosmogony Manu finds a little fish in the water in which he would wash his hands; it asks, and receives, his protection, asserting that when grown to full size it will save Manu from the universal deluge. This is Jhasa, the greatest of all fish.[28]

The first Avatar of Vishnu the Creator is a Fish. At the great feast in honour of this god, held on the twelfth day of the first month of the Indian year, Vishnu is represented under the form of a golden Fish, and addressed in the following terms: "Wie Du, O Gott, in Gestalt eines Fisches die in der Unterwelt befindlichen Veden gerettet hast, so rette auch mich." [29] The Fish Avatar was afterwards transferred to Buddha.

In Buddhist religion the symbols of the Fish and Fisher are freely employed. Thus in Buddhist monasteries we find drums and gongs in the shape of a fish, but the true meaning of the symbol, while still regarded

---

[26] For a general discussion of the conflicting views cf. Dr Nitze's study, referred to above. The writer devotes special attention to the works of the late Prof. Heinzel and Mr Alfred Nutt as leading representatives of their respective schools.

[27] R. Pischel's *Ueber die Ursprung des Christlichen Fisch-Symbols* is specially devoted to the possible derivation from Indian sources. Scheftelowitz, *Das Fischsymbolik in Judentum und Christentum* (*Archiv fur Religionswissenschaft*, Vol. XIV.), contains a great deal of valuable material. R. Eisler, *Orpheus the Fisher* (*The Quest*, Vols. I. and II.), *John, Jonas, Oannes* (ibid. Vol. III.), *The Messianic Fish-meal of the Primitive Church* (ibid. Vol. IV.), are isolated studies, forming part of a comprehensive work on the subject, the publication of which has unfortunately been prevented by the War.

[28] *Mahâbhârata*, Bk. III.

[29] Cf. Scheftelowitz, *op. cit.* p. 51.

as sacred, has been lost, and the explanations, like the explanations of the Grail romances, are often fantastic afterthoughts.

In the Māhāyana scriptures Buddha is referred to as the Fisherman who draws fish from the ocean of Samsara to the light of Salvation. There are figures and pictures which represent Buddha in the act of fishing, an attitude which, unless interpreted in a symbolic sense, would be utterly at variance with the tenets of the Buddhist religion.[30]

This also holds good for Chinese Buddhism. The goddess Kwanyin (= Avalokiteśvara), the female Deity of Mercy and Salvation, is depicted either on, or holding, a Fish. In the Han palace of Kun-Ming-Ch'ih there was a Fish carved in jade to which in time of drought sacrifices were offered, the prayers being always answered.

Both in India and China the Fish is employed in funeral rites. In India a crystal bowl with Fish handles was found in a reputed tomb of Buddha. In China the symbol is found on stone slabs enclosing the coffin, on bronze urns, vases, etc. Even as the Babylonians had the Fish, or Fisher, god, Oannes who revealed to them the arts of Writing, Agriculture, etc., and was, as Eisler puts it, 'teacher and lord of all wisdom,' so the Chinese Fu-Hi, who is pictured with the mystic tablets containing the mysteries of Heaven and Earth, is, with his consort and retinue, represented as having a fish's tail.[31]

The writer of the article in *The Open Court* asserts that "the Fish was sacred to those deities who were supposed to lead men back from the shadows of death to life." [32] If this be really the case we can understand the connection of the symbol first with Orpheus, later with Christ, as Eisler remarks: "Orpheus is connected with nearly all the mystery, and a great many of the ordinary chthonic, cults in Greece and Italy. Christianity took its first tentative steps into the reluctant world of Graeco-Roman Paganism under the benevolent patronage of Orpheus." [33]

There is thus little reason to doubt that, if we regard the Fish as a Divine Life symbol, of immemorial antiquity, we shall not go very far astray.

We may note here there was a fish known to the Semites by the name of Adonis, although as the title signifies 'Lord,' and is generic rather than specific, too much stress cannot be laid upon it. It is more interesting to know that in Babylonian cosmology Adapa the Wise, the son of Ea, is represented as a Fisher.[34] In the ancient Sumerian laments for Tammuz, previously referred to, that god is frequently addressed as *Divine Lamgar, Lord of the Net*, the nearest equivalent I have so far

[30] Cf. *The Open Court*, June and July, 1911, where reproductions of these figures will be found.
[31] *Op. cit.* p. 403. Cf. here an illustration in Miss Harrison's *Themis* (p. 262), which shows Cecrops, who played the same rôle with regard to the Greeks, with a serpent's tail.
[32] *Ibid.* p. 168. In this connection note the prayer to Vishnu, quoted above.
[33] Cf. Eisler, *Orpheus the Fisher* (*The Quest*, Vol I. p. 126).
[34] Cf. W. Staerk, *Ueber den Ursprung der Gral-Legende*, pp. 55, 56.

found to our 'Fisher King.' [35] Whether the phrase is here used in an actual or a symbolic sense the connection of idea is sufficiently striking.

In the opinion of the most recent writers on the subject the Christian Fish symbolism derives directly from the Jewish, the Jews, on their side having borrowed freely from Syrian belief and practice.[36]

What may be regarded as the central point of Jewish Fish symbolism is the tradition that, at the end of the world, Messias will catch the great Fish Leviathan, and divide its flesh as food among the faithful. As a foreshadowing of this Messianic Feast the Jews were in the habit of eating fish upon the Sabbath. During the Captivity, under the influence of the worship of the goddess Atargatis, they transferred the ceremony to the Friday, the eve of the Sabbath, a position which it has retained to the present day. Eisler remarks that "in Galicia one can see Israelite families in spite of their being reduced to the extremest misery, procuring on Fridays a single gudgeon, to eat, divided into fragments, at night-fall. In the 16th century Rabbi Solomon Luria protested strongly against this practice. Fish, he declared, should be eaten on the Sabbath itself, not on the Eve." [37]

This Jewish custom appears to have been adopted by the primitive Church, and early Christians, on their side, celebrated a Sacramental Fish-meal. The Catacombs supply us with numerous illustrations, fully described by the two writers referred to. The elements of this mystic meal were Fish, Bread, and Wine, the last being represented in the Messianic tradition: "At the end of the meal God will give to the most worthy, *i.e.*, to King David, the Cup of Blessing—one of fabulous dimensions." [38]

Fish play an important part in Mystery Cults, as being the 'holy' food. Upon a tablet dedicated to the Phrygian *Mater Magna* we find Fish and Cup; and Dolger, speaking of a votive tablet discovered in the Balkans, says, "Hier ist der Fisch immer und immer wieder allzu deutlich als die heilige Speise eines Mysterien-Kultes hervorgehoben." [39]

Now I would submit that here, and not in Celtic Folk-lore, is to be found the source of Borron's Fish-meal. Let us consider the circumstances. Joseph and his followers, in the course of their wanderings, find themselves in danger of famine. The position is somewhat curious, as apparently the leaders have no idea of the condition of their followers till the latter appeal to Brons.[40]

---

[35] Cf. S. Langdon, *Sumerian and Babylonian Psalms*, pp. 301, 305, 307, 313.

[36] Cf. Eisler, *The Messianic Fish-meal of the Primitive Church* (*The Quest*, Vol. IV.), where the various frescoes are described; also the article by Scheftelowitz, already referred to. While mainly devoted to Jewish beliefs and practices, this study contains much material derived from other sources. So far it is the fullest and most thoroughly *documenté* treatment of the subject I have met with.

[37] Cf. Eisler, *op. cit.* and Scheftelowitz, pp. 19, 20.

[38] Cf. Eisler, *op. cit.* p. 508.

[39] Cf. Scheftelowitz, *op. cit.* pp. 337, 338 and note 4.

[40] Hucher, *Le Saint Graal*, Vol. I. pp. 251 *et seq.*, 315 *et seq.*

Brons informs Joseph, who prays for aid and counsel from the Grail.
A Voice from Heaven bids him send his brother-in-law, Brons, to catch
a fish. Meanwhile he, Joseph, is to prepare a table, set the Grail, covered
with a cloth, in the centre opposite his own seat, and the fish which
Brons shall catch, on the other side. He does this, and the seats are
filled—"Si s'i asieent une grant partie et plus i ot de cels qui n'i sistrent
mie, que de cels qui sistrent." Those who are seated at the table are
conscious of a great "douceur," and "l'accomplissement de lor cuers,"
the rest feel nothing.

Now compare this with the Irish story of the Salmon of Wisdom.[41]

Finn Mac Cumhail enters the service of his namesake, Finn Eger, who
for seven years had remained by the Boyne watching the Salmon of Lynn
Feic, which it had been foretold Finn should catch. The younger lad,
who conceals his name, catches the fish. He is set to watch it while it
roasts but is warned not to eat it. Touching it with his thumb he is
burned, and puts his thumb in his mouth to cool it. Immediately he
becomes possessed of all knowledge, and thereafter has only to chew
his thumb to obtain wisdom. Mr Nutt remarks: "The incident in Borron's poem has been recast in the mould of mediaeval Christian Symbolism, but I think the older myth can still be clearly discerned, and is
wholly responsible for the incident as found in the *Conte du Graal.*"

But when these words were written we were in ignorance of the
Sacramental Fish-meal, common alike to Jewish, Christian, and Mystery
Cults, a meal which offers a far closer parallel to Borron's romance than
does the Finn story, in which, beyond the catching of a fish, there is
absolutely no point of contact with our romance, neither Joseph nor
Brons derives wisdom from the eating thereof; it is not they who detect
the sinners, the severance between the good and the evil is brought
about automatically. The Finn story has no common meal, and no idea
of spiritual blessings such as are connected therewith.

In the case of the Messianic Fish-meal, on the other hand, the parallel
is striking; in both cases it is a communal meal, in both cases the
privilege of sharing it is the reward of the faithful, in both cases it is a
foretaste of the bliss of Paradise.

Furthermore, as remarked above, the practice was at one time of
very widespread prevalence.

Now whence did Borron derive his knowledge, from Jewish, Christian
or Mystery sources?

This is a question not very easy to decide. In view of the pronounced
Christian tone of Borron's romance I should feel inclined to exclude
the first, also the Jewish Fish-meal seems to have been of a more open,
general and less symbolic character than the Christian; it was frankly an
anticipation of a promised future bliss, obtainable by all.

Orthodox Christianity, on the other hand, knows nothing of a Sacred
Fish-meal, so far as I am aware it forms no part of any Apocalyptic

---

[41] Cf. A. Nutt, *Studies in the Legend of the Holy Grail,* p. 209.

expectation, and where this special symbolism does occur it is often under conditions which place its interpretation outside the recognized category of Christian belief.

A noted instance in point is the famous epitaph of Bishop Aberkios, over the correct interpretation of which scholars have spent much time and ingenuity.[42] In this curious text Aberkios, after mentioning his journeys, says:

> "Paul I had as my guide,
> Faith however always went ahead and set before me as food
> a *Fish* from a *Fountain*, a huge one, a clean one,
> Which a *Holy Virgin* has *caught*.
> This she gave to the friends ever to eat as food,
> Having good *Wine*, and offering it watered together with *Bread*.
> Aberkios had this engraved when 72 years of age in truth.
> *Whoever can understand this* let him pray for Aberkios."

Eisler (I am here quoting from the *Quest* article) remarks, "As the last line of our quotation gives us quite plainly to understand, a number of words which we have italicized are obviously used in an unusual, metaphorical, sense, that is to say as terms of the Christian Mystery language." While Harnack, admitting that the Christian character of the text is indisputable, adds significantly: *"aber das Christentum der Grosskirche ist es nicht."*

Thus it is possible that, to the various points of doubtful orthodoxy which scholars have noted as characteristic of the Grail romances, Borron's Fish-meal should also be added.

Should it be objected that the dependence of a medieval romance upon a Jewish tradition of such antiquity is scarcely probable, I would draw attention to the *Voyage of Saint Brandan,* where the monks, during their prolonged wanderings, annually 'kept their Resurrection,' *i.e.,* celebrate their Easter Mass, on the back of a great Fish.[43] On their first meeting with this monster Saint Brandan tells them it is the greatest of all fishes, and is named Jastoni, a name which bears a curious resemblance to the Jhasa of the Indian tradition cited above.[44] In this last instance the connection of the Fish with life, renewed and sustained, is undeniable.

The original source of such a symbol is most probably to be found in the belief, referred to in a previous chapter,[45] that all life comes from the water, but that a more sensual and less abstract idea was also operative appears from the close connection of the Fish with the goddess Astarte or Atargatis, a connection here shared by the Dove. Cumont, in his *Les Religions Orientales dans le Paganisme Romain,* says: "Two

---

[42] Cf. Eisler, *The Mystic Epitaph of Bishop Aberkios* (*The Quest,* Vol. V. pp. 302–312); Scheftelowitz, *op. cit.* p. 8.

[43] Cf. *The Voyage of Saint Brandan,* ll. 372 *et seq.,* 660 *et seq.*

[44] *Op. cit.* ll. 170 *et seq.,* and *supra,* p. 119.

[45] *Vide supra,* p. 70.

animals were held in general reverence, namely, Dove and Fish. Count-
less flocks of Doves greeted the traveller when he stepped on shore at
Askalon, and in the outer courts of all the temples of Astarte one
might see the flutter of their white wings. The Fish were preserved in
ponds near to the Temple, and superstitious dread forbade their capture,
for the goddess punished such sacrilege, smiting the offender with
ulcers and tumours." [46]

But at certain mystic banquets priests and initiates partook of this
otherwise forbidden food, in the belief that they thus partook of the
flesh of the goddess. Eisler and other scholars are of opinion that it was
the familiarity with this ritual gained by the Jews during the Captivity
that led to the adoption of the Friday Fish-meal, already referred to,
Friday being the day dedicated to the goddess and, later, to her equivalent, Venus. From the Jews the custom spread to the Christian Church,
where it still flourishes, its true origin, it is needless to say, being
wholly unsuspected. [47]

Dove and Fish also appear together in ancient iconography. In Comte
Goblet d'Alviella's work *The Migration of Symbols* there is an illustration of a coin of Cyzicus, on which is represented an Omphalus,
flanked by two Doves, with a Fish beneath; [48] and a whole section is
devoted to the discussion of the representations of two Doves on either
side of a Temple entrance, or of an Omphalus. In the author's opinion
the origin of the symbol may be found in the sacred dove-cotes of
Phoenicia, referred to by Cumont.

Scheftelowitz instances the combination of Fish-meal and Dove,
found on a Jewish tomb of the first century at Syracuse, and remarks
that the two are frequently found in combination on Christian tomb-
stones. [49]

Students of the Grail romances will not need to be reminded that
the Dove makes its appearance in certain of our texts. In the *Parzival*
it plays a somewhat important rôle; every Good Friday a Dove brings
from Heaven a Host, which it lays upon the Grail; and the Dove is the
badge of the Grail Knights. [50] In the prose *Lancelot* the coming of the
Grail procession is heralded by the entrance through the window of a
Dove, bearing a censer in its beak. [51] Is it not possible that it was the
already existing connection in Nature ritual of these two, Dove and
Fish, which led to the introduction of the former into our romances,
where its rôle is never really adequately motived? It is further to be
noted that besides Dove and Fish the Syrians reverenced Stones, more

[46] *Op. cit.* p. 168.
[47] Cf. *The Messianic Fish-meal.*
[48] *Op. cit.* p. 92, fig. 42a.
[49] *Op. cit.* p. 23, and note, p. 29.
[50] *Parzival,* Bk. IX. ll. 1109 *et seq.,* Bk. XVI. ll. 175 *et seq.*
[51] Cf. *Sir Gawain at the Grail Castle,* p. 55. Certain of the *Lancelot* MSS.,
e.g., B.N., f. Fr. 123, give two doves.

especially meteoric Stones, which they held to be endowed with life potency, another point of contact with our romances.[52]

That the Fish was considered a potent factor in ensuring fruitfulness is proved by certain prehistoric tablets described by Scheftelowitz, where Fish, Horse, and Swastika, or in another instance Fish and Reindeer, are found in a combination which unmistakeably denotes that the object of the votive tablet was to ensure the fruitfulness of flocks and herds.[53]

With this intention its influence was also invoked in marriage ceremonies. The same writer points out that the Jews in Poland were accustomed to hold a Fish feast immediately on the conclusion of the marriage ceremony and that a similar practice can be proved for the ancient Greeks.[54] At the present day the Jews of Tunis exhibit a Fish's tail on a cushion at their weddings.[55] In some parts of India the newly-wedded pair waded knee-deep into the water, and caught fish in a new garment. During the ceremony a Brahmin student, from the shore, asked solemnly, "What seest thou?" to which the answer was returned, "Sons and Cattle." [56] In all these cases there can be no doubt that it was the prolific nature of the Fish, a feature which it shares in common with the Dove, which inspired practice and intention.

Surely the effect of this cumulative body of evidence is to justify us in the belief that Fish and Fisher, being, as they undoubtedly are, Life symbols of immemorial antiquity, are, by virtue of their origin, entirely in their place in a sequence of incidents which there is solid ground for believing derive ultimately from a Cult of this nature. That Borron's Fish-meal, that the title of Fisher King, are not accidents of literary invention but genuine and integral parts of the common body of tradition which has furnished the incidents and *mise-en-scène* of the Grail drama. Can it be denied that, while from the standpoint of a Christian interpretation the character of the Fisher King is simply incomprehensible, from the standpoint of Folk-tale inadequately explained, from that of a Ritual survival it assumes a profound meaning and significance? He is not merely a deeply symbolic figure, but the essential centre of the whole cult, a being semi-divine, semi-human, standing between his people and land, and the unseen forces which control their destiny. If the Grail story be based upon a Life ritual the character of the Fisher King is of the very essence of the tale, and his title, so far from being meaningless, expresses, for those who are at pains to seek,

---

[52] Cf. Scheftelowitz, p. 338. Hagen, *Der Gral,* has argued that Wolfram's stone is such a meteoric stone, a Boetylus. I am not prepared to take up any position as to the exact nature of the stone itself, whether precious stone or meteor; the real point of importance being its Life-giving potency.

[53] *Op. cit.* p. 381.

[54] *Ibid.* p. 376 *et seq.*

[55] *Ibid.* p. 20.

[56] *Ibid.* p. 377.

the intention and object of the perplexing whole. The Fisher King is, as I suggested above, the very heart and centre of the whole mystery, and I contend that with an adequate interpretation of this enigmatic character the soundness of the theory providing such an interpretation may be held to be definitely proved.

SYSTEMS AND TECHNIQUES

T. E. HULME

Romanticism and Classicism

Regardless of its intrinsic importance, or lack of it, this essay is probably the most important single twentieth-century prose document in the formation of modern poetry. Both T. S. Eliot and Ezra Pound draw upon it heavily for the sanction of a new Classical philosophy in literature. In this essay Hulme predicts the death of Romanticism and offers the ancient doctrine of Original Sin as a starting point for a more restricted, "finite" view of man and of civilization. According to Hulme's attitude, the control of man (since he cannot control himself) rests upon precedent, written tradition, and established methods of policing humanity. Hulme was a paradoxical thinker—a disciple of the French philosopher Bergson (an anti-intellectualist) and an advocate of absolute order in society and the arts. The fact that he caught the imagination of the leading expatriate American poets is a major clue to modern poetry.

I want to maintain that after a hundred years of romanticism, we are in for a classical revival, and that the particular weapon of this new classical spirit, when it works in verse, will be fancy. And in this I imply the superiority of fancy—not superior generally or absolutely, for that would be obvious nonsense, but superior in the sense that we use the word good in empirical ethics—good for something, superior for something. I shall have to prove then two things, first that a classical revival is coming, and, secondly, for its particular purposes, fancy will be superior to imagination.

So banal have the terms Imagination and Fancy become that we imagine they must have always been in the language. Their history as two differing terms in the vocabulary of criticism is comparatively short. Originally, of course, they both mean the same thing; they first began to be differentiated by the German writers on æsthetics in the eighteenth century.

I know that in using the words "classic" and "romantic" I am doing a dangerous thing. They represent five or six different kinds of antitheses, and while I may be using them in one sense you may be interpreting them in another. In this present connection I am using them in a perfectly precise and limited sense. I ought really to have coined a couple of new words, but I prefer to use the ones I have used, as I then conform to the practice of the group of polemical writers who make most use of them at the present day, and have almost succeeded in making them political catchwords. I mean Maurras, Lasserre and all the group connected with L'Action Française.

At the present time this is the particular group with which the distinction is most vital. Because it has become a party symbol. If you asked a man of a certain set whether he preferred the classics or the romantics, you could deduce from that what his politics were.

The best way of gliding into a proper definition of my terms would be to start with a set of people who are prepared to fight about it—for in them you will have no vagueness. (Other people take the infamous attitude of the person with catholic tastes who says he likes both.)

About a year ago, a man whose name I think was Fauchois gave a lecture at the Odéon on Racine, in the course of which he made some disparaging remarks about his dullness, lack of invention and the rest of it. This caused an immediate riot: fights took place all over the house; several people were arrested and imprisoned, and the rest of the series of lectures took place with hundreds of gendarmes and detectives scattered all over the place. These people interrupted because the classical ideal is a living thing to them and Racine is the great classic. That is what I call a real vital interest in literature. They regard romanticism as an awful disease from which France had just recovered.

The thing is complicated in their case by the fact that it was romanticism that made the revolution. They hate the revolution, so they hate romanticism.

I make no apology for dragging in politics here; romanticism both in England and France is associated with certain political views, and it is in taking a concrete example of the working out of a principle in action that you can get its best definition.

What was the positive principle behind all the other principles of '89? I am talking here of the revolution in as far as it was an idea; I leave out material causes—they only produce the forces. The barriers which could easily have resisted or guided these forces had been previously rotted away by ideas. This always seems to be the case in successful changes; the privileged class is beaten only when it has lost faith in itself, when it has itself been penetrated with the ideas which are working against it.

It was not the rights of man—that was a good solid practical war-cry. The thing which created enthusiasm, which made the revolution practically a new religion, was something more positive than that. People of all classes, people who stood to lose by it, were in a positive ferment about the idea of liberty. There must have been some idea which enabled them to think that something positive could come out of so essentially negative a thing. There was, and here I get my definition of romanticism. They had been taught by Rousseau that man was by nature good, that it was only bad laws and customs that had suppressed him. Remove all these and the infinite possibilities of man would have a chance. This is what made them think that something positive could come out of disorder, this is what created the religious enthusiasm. Here is the root of all romanticism: that man, the individual, is an infinite reservoir of possibilities; and if you can so rearrange society by the destruction of oppressive order then these possibilities will have a chance and you will get Progress.

One can define the classical quite clearly as the exact opposite to this. Man is an extraordinarily fixed and limited animal whose nature is absolutely constant. It is only by tradition and organisation that anything decent can be got out of him.

This view was a little shaken at the time of Darwin. You remember his particular hypothesis, that new species came into existence by the cumulative effect of small variations—this seems to admit the possibility of future progress. But at the present day the contrary hypothesis makes headway in the shape of De Vries's mutation theory, that each new species comes into existence, not gradually by the accumulation of small steps, but suddenly in a jump, a kind of sport, and that once in existence it remains absolutely fixed. This enables me to keep the classical view with an appearance of scientific backing.

Put shortly, these are the two views, then. One, that man is intrinsically good, spoilt by circumstance; and the other that he is intrinsically limited, but disciplined by order and tradition to something fairly decent. To the one party man's nature is like a well, to the other like a bucket. The view which regards man as a well, a reservoir full of possibilities, I call the romantic; the one which regards him as a very finite and fixed creature, I call the classical.

One may note here that the Church has always taken the classical view since the defeat of the Pelagian heresy and the adoption of the sane classical dogma of original sin.

It would be a mistake to identify the classical view with that of materialism. On the contrary it is absolutely identical with the normal religious attitude. I should put it in this way: That part of the fixed nature of man is the belief in the Deity. This should be as fixed and true for every man as belief in the existence of matter and in the objective world. It is parallel to appetite, the instinct of sex, and all the other fixed qualities. Now at certain times, by the use of either force or rhetoric, these instincts have been suppressed—in Florence, under Savonarola, in Geneva under Calvin, and here under the Roundheads. The inevitable result of such a process is that the repressed instinct bursts out in some abnormal direction. So with religion. By the perverted rhetoric of Rationalism, your natural instincts are suppressed and you are converted into an agnostic. Just as in the case of the other instincts, Nature has her revenge. The instincts that find their right and proper outlet in religion must come out in some other way. You don't believe in a God, so you begin to believe that man is a god. You don't believe in Heaven, so you begin to believe in a heaven on earth. In other words, you get romanticism. The concepts that are right and proper in their own sphere are spread over, and so mess up, falsify and blur the clear outlines of human experience. It is like pouring a pot of treacle over the dinner table. Romanticism then, and this is the best definition I can give of it, is spilt religion.

I must now shirk the difficulty of saying exactly what I mean by romantic and classical in verse. I can only say that it means the result of these two attitudes towards the cosmos, towards man, in so far as it gets reflected in verse. The romantic, because he thinks man infinite, must always be talking about the infinite; and as there is always the bitter contrast between what you think you ought to be able to do and what man actually can, it always tends, in its later stages at any rate, to be gloomy. I really can't go any further than to say it is the reflection of these two temperaments, and point out examples of the different spirits. On the one hand I would take such diverse people as Horace, most of the Elizabethans and the writers of the Augustan age, and on the other side Lamartine, Hugo, parts of Keats, Coleridge, Byron, Shelley and Swinburne.

I know quite well that when people think of classical and romantic in verse, the contrast at once comes into their mind between, say, Racine and Shakespeare. I don't mean this; the dividing line that I intend is here misplaced a little from the true middle. That Racine is on the extreme classical side I agree, but if you call Shakespeare romantic, you are using a different definition to the one I give. You are thinking of the difference between classic and romantic as being merely one between restraint and exuberance. I should say with Nietzsche that there are two kinds of classicism, the static and the dynamic. Shakespeare is the classic of motion.

What I mean by classical in verse, then, is this. That even in the most imaginative flights there is always a holding back, a reservation. The classical poet never forgets this finiteness, this limit of man. He remembers always that he is mixed up with earth. He may jump, but he always returns back; he never flies away into the circumambient gas.

You might say if you wished that the whole of the romantic attitude seems to crystallise in verse round metaphors of flight. Hugo is always flying, flying over abysses, flying up into the eternal gases. The word infinité in every other line.

In the classical attitude you never seem to swing right along to the infinite nothing. If you say an extravagant thing which does exceed the limits inside which you know man to be fastened, yet there is always conveyed in some way at the end an impression of yourself standing outside it, and not quite believing it, or consciously putting it forward as a flourish. You never go blindly into an atmosphere more than the truth, an atmosphere too rarefied for man to breathe for long. You are always faithful to the conception of a limit. It is a question of pitch; in romantic verse you move at a certain pitch of rhetoric which you know, man being what he is, to be a little high-falutin. The kind of thing you get in Hugo or Swinburne. In the coming classical reaction that will feel just wrong. For an example of the opposite thing, a verse written in the proper classical spirit, I can take the song from Cymbeline beginning with "Fear no more the heat of the sun." I am just using this as a parable. I don't quite mean what I say here. Take the last two lines:

> "Golden lads and girls all must,
> Like chimney sweepers come to dust."

Now, no romantic would have ever written that. Indeed, so ingrained is romanticism, so objectionable is this to it, that people have asserted that these were not part of the original song.

Apart from the pun, the thing that I think quite classical is the word lad. Your modern romantic could never write that. He would have to write golden youth, and take up the thing at least a couple of notes in pitch.

I want now to give the reasons which make me think that we are nearing the end of the romantic movement.

The first lies in the nature of any convention or tradition in art. A particular convention or attitude in art has a strict analogy to the phenomena of organic life. It grows old and decays. It has a definite period of life and must die. All the possible tunes get played on it and then it is exhausted; moreover its best period is its youngest. Take the case of the extraordinary efflorescence of verse in the Elizabethan period. All kinds of reasons have been given for this—the discovery of the new world and all the rest of it. There is a much simpler one. A new medium had been given them to play with—namely, blank verse. It was new and so it was easy to play new tunes on it.

The same law holds in other arts. All the masters of painting are born into the world at a time when the particular tradition from which they start is imperfect. The Florentine tradition was just short of full ripeness when Raphael came to Florence, the Bellinesque was still young when Titian was born in Venice. Landscape was still a toy or an appanage of figure-painting when Turner and Constable arose to reveal its independent power. When Turner and Constable had done with landscape they left little or nothing for their successors to do on the same lines. Each field of artistic activity is exhausted by the first great artist who gathers a full harvest from it.

This period of exhaustion seems to me to have been reached in romanticism. We shall not get any new efflorescence of verse until we get a new technique, a new convention, to turn ourselves loose in.

Objection might be taken to this. It might be said that a century as an organic unity doesn't exist, that I am being deluded by a wrong metaphor, that I am treating a collection of literary people as if they were an organism or state department. Whatever we may be in other things, an objector might urge, in literature in as far as we are anything at all—in as far as we are worth considering—we are individuals, we are persons, and as distinct persons we cannot be subordinated to any general treatment. At any period at any time, an individual poet may be a classic or a romantic just as he feels like it. You at any particular moment may think that you can stand outside a movement. You may think that as an individual you observe both the classic and the romantic spirit and decide from a purely detached point of view that one is superior to the other.

The answer to this is that no one, in a matter of judgment of beauty, can take a detached standpoint in this way. Just as physically you are not born that abstract entity, man, but the child of particular parents, so you are in matters of literary judgment. Your opinion is almost entirely of the literary history that came just before you, and you are governed by that whatever you may think. Take Spinoza's example of a stone falling to the ground. If it had a conscious mind it would, he said, think it was going to the ground because it wanted to. So you with your pretended free judgment about what is and what is not beautiful. The amount of freedom in man is much exaggerated. That we are free on certain rare occasions, both my religion and the views I get from metaphysics convince me. But many acts which we habitually label free are in reality automatic. It is quite possible for a man to write a book almost automatically. I have read several such products. Some observations were recorded more than twenty years ago by Robertson on reflex speech, and he found that in certain cases of dementia, where the people were quite unconscious so far as the exercise of reasoning went, that very intelligent answers were given to a succession of questions on politics and such matters. The meaning of these questions could not possibly have been understood. Language here acted after the manner of a reflex. So that certain extremely complex mechanisms, subtle enough to imitate beauty, can work by themselves—I certainly think that this is the case with judgments about beauty.

I can put the same thing in slightly different form. Here is a question of a conflict of two attitudes, as it might be of two techniques. The critic, while he has to admit that changes from one to the other occur, persists in regarding them as mere variations to a certain fixed normal, just as a pendulum might swing. I admit the analogy of the pendulum as far as movement, but I deny the further consequence of the analogy, the existence of the point of rest, the normal point.

When I say that I dislike the romantics, I dissociate two things: the part of them in which they resemble all the great poets, and the part in which they differ and which gives them their character as romantics. It is this minor element which constitutes the particular note of a century, and which, while it excites contemporaries, annoys the next generation. It was precisely that quality in Pope which pleased his friends, which we detest. Now, anyone just before the romantics who felt that, could have predicted that a change was coming. It seems to me that we stand just in the same position now. I think that there is an increasing proportion of people who simply can't stand Swinburne.

When I say that there will be another classical revival I don't necessarily anticipate a return to Pope. I say merely that now is the time for such a revival. Given people of the necessary capacity, it may be a vital thing; without them we may get a formalism something like Pope. When it does come we may not even recognise it as classical. Although it will be classical it will be different because it has passed through a romantic period. To take a parallel example: I remember being very surprised, after seeing the Post Impressionists, to find in Maurice Denis's account of the matter that they consider themselves classical in the sense that they were trying to impose the same order on the mere flux of new material provided by the impressionist movement, that existed in the more limited materials of the painting before.

There is something now to be cleared away before I get on with my argument, which is that while romanticism is dead in reality, yet the critical attitude appropriate to it still continues to exist. To make this a little clearer: For every kind of verse, there is a corresponding receptive attitude. In a romantic period we demand from verse certain qualities. In a classical period we demand others. At the present time I should say that this receptive attitude has outlasted the thing from which it was formed. But while the romantic tradition has run dry, yet the critical attitude of mind, which demands romantic qualities from verse, still survives. So that if good classical verse were to be written to-morrow very few people would be able to stand it.

I object even to the best of the romantics. I object still more to the receptive attitude. I object to the sloppiness which doesn't consider that a poem is a poem unless it is moaning or whining about something or other. I always think in this connection of the last line of a poem of John Webster's which ends with a request I cordially endorse:

"End your moan and come away."

The thing has got so bad now that a poem which is all dry and hard, a properly classical poem, would not be considered poetry at all. How many people now can lay their hands on their hearts and say they like either Horace or Pope? They feel a kind of chill when they read them.

The dry hardness which you get in the classics is absolutely repugnant to them. Poetry that isn't damp isn't poetry at all. They cannot see that accurate description is a legitimate object of verse. Verse to them always means a bringing in of some of the emotions that are grouped round the word infinite.

The essence of poetry to most people is that it must lead them to a beyond of some kind. Verse strictly confined to the earthly and the definite (Keats is full of it) might seem to them to be excellent writing, excellent craftsmanship, but not poetry. So much has romanticism debauched us, that, without some form of vagueness, we deny the highest.

In the classic it is always the light of ordinary day, never the light that never was on land or sea. It is always perfectly human and never exaggerated: man is always man and never a god.

But the awful result of romanticism is that, accustomed to this strange light, you can never live without it. Its effect on you is that of a drug.

There is a general tendency to think that verse means little else than the expression of unsatisfied emotion. People say: "But how can you have verse without sentiment?" You see what it is: the prospect alarms them. A classical revival to them would mean the prospect of an arid desert and the death of poetry as they understand it, and could only come to fill the gap caused by that death. Exactly why this dry classical spirit should have a positive and legitimate necessity to express itself in poetry is utterly inconceivable to them. What this positive need is, I shall show later. It follows from the fact that there is another quality, not the emotion produced, which is at the root of excellence in verse. Before I get to this I am concerned with a negative thing, a theoretical point, a prejudice that stands in the way and is really at the bottom of this reluctance to understand classical verse.

It is an objection which ultimately I believe comes from a bad metaphysic of art. You are unable to admit the existence of beauty without the infinite being in some way or another dragged in.

I may quote for purposes of argument, as a typical example of this kind of attitude made vocal, the famous chapters in Ruskin's *Modern Painters*, Vol. II, on the imagination. I must say here, parenthetically, that I use this word without prejudice to the other discussion with which I shall end the paper. I only use the word here because it is Ruskin's word. All that I am concerned with just now is the attitude behind it, which I take to be the romantic.

"Imagination cannot but be serious; she sees too far, too darkly, too solemnly, too earnestly, ever to smile. There is something in the heart of everything, if we can reach it, that we shall not be inclined to laugh at. . . . Those who have so pierced and seen the melancholy deeps of things, are filled with intense passion and gentleness of sympathy." (Part III, Chap. III, § 9.)

"There is in every word set down by the imaginative mind an awful undercurrent of meaning, and evidence and shadow upon it of the deep places out of which it has come. It is often obscure, often half-told; for he who wrote it, in his clear seeing of the things beneath, may have been impatient of detailed interpretation; for if we choose to dwell upon it and trace it, it will lead us always securely back to that metropolis of the soul's dominion from which we may follow out all the ways and tracks to its farthest coasts." (Part III, Chap. III, § 5.)

Really in all these matters the act of judgment is an instinct, an absolutely unstateable thing akin to the art of the tea taster. But you must talk, and the only language you can use in this matter is that of analogy. I have no material clay to mould to the given shape; the only thing which one has for the purpose, and which acts as a substitute for it, a kind of mental clay, are certain metaphors modified into theories of æsthetic and rhetoric. A combination of these, while it cannot state the essentially unstateable intuition, can yet give you a sufficient analogy to enable you to see what it was and to recognise it on condition that you yourself have been in a similar state. Now these phrases of Ruskin's convey quite clearly to me his taste in the matter.

I see quite clearly that he thinks the best verse must be serious. That is a natural attitude for a man in the romantic period. But he is not content with saying that he prefers this kind of verse. He wants to deduce his opinion like his master, Coleridge, from some fixed principle which can be found by metaphysic.

Here is the last refuge of this romantic attitude. It proves itself to be not an attitude but a deduction from a fixed principle of the cosmos.

One of the main reasons for the existence of philosophy is not that it enables you to find truth (it can never do that) but that it does provide you a refuge for definitions. The usual idea of the thing is that it provides you with a fixed basis from which you can deduce the things you want in æsthetics. The process is the exact contrary. You start in the confusion of the fighting line, you retire from that just a little to the rear to recover, to get your weapons right. Quite plainly, without metaphor this—it provides you with an elaborate and precise language in which you really can explain definitely what you mean, but what you want to say is decided by other things. The ultimate reality is the hurly-burly, the struggle; the metaphysic is an adjunct to clear-headedness in it.

To get back to Ruskin and his objection to all that is not serious. It seems to me that involved in this is a bad metaphysical æsthetic. You have the metaphysic which in defining beauty or the nature of art always drags in the infinite. Particularly in Germany, the land where theories of æsthetics were first created, the romantic æsthetes collated all beauty to an impression of the infinite involved in the identification of our being in absolute spirit. In the least element of beauty we have a total intuition of the whole world. Every artist is a kind of pantheist.

Now it is quite obvious to anyone who holds this kind of theory that any poetry which confines itself to the finite can never be of the highest kind. It seems a contradiction in terms to them. And as in

metaphysics you get the last refuge of a prejudice, so it is now necessary for me to refute this.

Here follows a tedious piece of dialectic, but it is necessary for my
purpose. I must avoid two pitfalls in discussing the idea of beauty. On
the one hand there is the old classical view which is supposed to define
it as lying in conformity to certain standard fixed forms; and on the
other hand there is the romantic view which drags in the infinite. I
have got to find a metaphysic between these two which will enable me
to hold consistently that a neo-classic verse of the type I have indicated
involves no contradiction in terms. It is essential to prove that beauty
may be in small, dry things.

The great aim is accurate, precise and definite description. The first
thing is to recognise how extraordinarily difficult this is. It is no mere
matter of carefulness; you have to use language, and language is by its
very nature a communal thing; that is, it expresses never the exact
thing but a compromise—that which is common to you, me and everybody. But each man sees a little differently, and to get out clearly and
exactly what he does see, he must have a terrific struggle with
language, whether it be with words or the technique of other arts.
Language has its own special nature, its own conventions and communal ideas. It is only by a concentrated effort of the mind that you
can hold it fixed to your own purpose. I always think that the fundamental process at the back of all the arts might be represented by the
following metaphor. You know what I call architect's curves—flat
pieces of wood with all different kinds of curvature. By a suitable
selection from these you can draw approximately any curve you like.
The artist I take to be the man who simply can't bear the idea of that
'approximately.' He will get the exact curve of what he sees whether it
be an object or an idea in the mind. I shall here have to change my
metaphor a little to get the process in his mind. Suppose that instead
of your curved pieces of wood you have a springy piece of steel of the
same types of curvature as the wood. Now the state of tension or concentration of mind, if he is doing anything really good in this struggle
against the ingrained habit of the technique, may be represented by
a man employing all his fingers to bend the steel out of its own curve
and into the exact curve which you want. Something different to what
it would assume naturally.

There are then two things to distinguish, first the particular faculty
of mind to see things as they really are, and apart from the conventional
ways in which you have been trained to see them. This is itself rare
enough in all consciousness. Second, the concentrated state of mind,
the grip over oneself which is necessary in the actual expression of what
one sees. To prevent one falling into the conventional curves of ingrained technique, to hold on through infinite detail and trouble to the
exact curve you want. Wherever you get this sincerity, you get the
fundamental quality of good art without dragging in infinite or serious.

I can now get at that positive fundamental quality of verse which constitutes excellence, which has nothing to do with infinity, with mystery or with emotions.

This is the point I aim at, then, in my argument. I prophesy that a period of dry, hard, classical verse is coming. I have met the preliminary objection founded on the bad romantic æsthetic that in such verse, from which the infinite is excluded, you cannot have the essence of poetry at all.

After attempting to sketch out what this positive quality is, I can get on to the end of my paper in this way: That where you get this quality exhibited in the realm of the emotions you get imagination, and that where you get this quality exhibited in the contemplation of finite things you get fancy.

In prose as in algebra concrete things are embodied in signs or counters which are moved about according to rules, without being visualised at all in the process. There are in prose certain type situations and arrangements of words, which move as automatically into certain other arrangements as do functions in algebra. One only changes the X's and the Y's back into physical things at the end of the process. Poetry, in one aspect at any rate, may be considered as an effort to avoid this characteristic of prose. It is not a counter language, but a visual concrete one. It is a compromise for a language of intuition which would hand over sensations bodily. It always endeavours to arrest you, and to make you continuously see a physical thing, to prevent you gliding through an abstract process. It chooses fresh epithets and fresh metaphors, not so much because they are new, and we are tired of the old, but because the old cease to convey a physical thing and become abstract counters. A poet says a ship 'coursed the seas' to get a physical image, instead of the counter word 'sailed.' Visual meanings can only be transferred by the new bowl of metaphor; prose is an old pot that lets them leak out. Images in verse are not mere decoration, but the very essence of an intuitive language. Verse is a pedestrian taking you over the ground, prose—a train which delivers you at a destination.

I can now get on to a discussion of two words often used in this connection, "fresh" and "unexpected." You praise a thing for being "fresh." I understand what you mean, but the word besides conveying the truth conveys a secondary something which is certainly false. When you say a poem or drawing is fresh, and so good, the impression is somehow conveyed that the essential element of goodness is freshness, that it is good because it is fresh. Now this is certainly wrong, there is nothing particularly desirable about freshness *per se*. Works of art aren't eggs. Rather the contrary. It is simply an unfortunate necessity due to the nature of language and technique that the only way the element which does constitute goodness, the only way in which its presence can be detected externally, is by freshness. Freshness convinces you, you feel at once that the artist was in an actual physical state. You feel that for a minute.

Real communication is so very rare, for plain speech is unconvincing. It is in this rare fact of communication that you get the root of æsthetic pleasure.

I shall maintain that wherever you get an extraordinary interest in a thing, a great zest in its contemplation which carries on the contemplator to accurate description in the sense of the word accurate I have just analysed, there you have sufficient justification for poetry. It must be an intense zest which heightens a thing out of the level of prose. I am using contemplation here just in the same way that Plato used it, only applied to a different subject; it is a detached interest. "The object of æsthetic contemplation is something framed apart by itself and regarded without memory or expectation, simply as being itself, as end not means, as individual not universal."

To take a concrete example. I am taking an extreme case. If you are walking behind a woman in the street, you notice the curious way in which the skirt rebounds from her heels. If that peculiar kind of motion becomes of such interest to you that you will search about until you can get the exact epithet which hits it off, there you have a properly æsthetic emotion. But it is the zest with which you look at the thing which decides you to make the effort. In this sense the feeling that was in Herrick's mind when he wrote "the tempestuous petticoat" was exactly the same as that which in bigger and vaguer matters makes the best romantic verse. It doesn't matter an atom that the emotion produced is not of dignified vagueness, but on the contrary amusing; the point is that exactly the same activity is at work as in the highest verse. That is the avoidance of conventional language in order to get the exact curve of the thing.

I have still to show that in the verse which is to come, fancy will be the necessary weapon of the classical school. The positive quality I have talked about can be manifested in ballad verse by extreme directness and simplicity, such as you get in "On Fair Kirkconnel Lea." But the particular verse we are going to get will be cheerful, dry and sophisticated, and here the necessary weapon of the positive quality must be fancy.

Subject doesn't matter; the quality in it is the same as you get in the more romantic people.

It isn't the scale or kind of emotion produced that decides, but this one fact: Is there any real zest in it? Did the poet have an actually realised visual object before him in which he delighted? It doesn't matter if it were a lady's shoe or the starry heavens.

Fancy is not mere decoration added on to plain speech. Plain speech is essentially inaccurate. It is only by new metaphors, that is, by fancy, that it can be made precise.

When the analogy has not enough connection with the thing described to be quite parallel with it, where it overlays the thing it described and there is a certain excess, there you have the play of fancy—that I grant is inferior to imagination.

But where the analogy is every bit of it necessary for accurate description in the sense of the word accurate I have previously described, and your only objection to this kind of fancy is that it is not serious in the effect it produces, then I think the objection to be entirely invalid. If it is sincere in the accurate sense, when the whole of the analogy is necessary to get out the exact curve of the feeling or thing you want to express—there you seem to me to have the highest verse, even though the subject be trivial and the emotions of the infinite far away.

It is very difficult to use any terminology at all for this kind of thing. For whatever word you use is at once sentimentalised. Take Coleridge's word "vital." It is used loosely by all kinds of people who talk about art, to mean something vaguely and mysteriously significant. In fact, vital and mechanical is to them exactly the same antithesis as between good and bad.

Nothing of the kind; Coleridge uses it in a perfectly definite and what I call dry sense. It is just this: A mechanical complexity is the sum of its parts. Put them side by side and you get the whole. Now vital or organic is merely a convenient metaphor for a complexity of a different kind, that in which the parts cannot be said to be elements as each one is modified by the other's presence, and each one to a certain extent is the whole. The leg of a chair by itself is still a leg. My leg by itself wouldn't be.

Now the characteristic of the intellect is that it can only represent complexities of the mechanical kind. It can only make diagrams, and diagrams are essentially things whose parts are separate one from another. The intellect always analyses—when there is a synthesis it is baffled. That is why the artist's work seems mysterious. The intellect can't represent it. This is a necessary consequence of the particular nature of the intellect and the purposes for which it is formed. It doesn't mean that your synthesis is ineffable, simply that it can't be definitely stated.

Now this is all worked out in Bergson, the central feature of his whole philosophy. It is all based on the clear conception of these vital complexities which he calls "intensive" as opposed to the other kind which he calls "extensive," and the recognition of the fact that the intellect can only deal with the extensive multiplicity. To deal with the intensive you must use intuition.

Now, as I said before, Ruskin was perfectly aware of all this, but he had no such metaphysical background which would enable him to state definitely what he meant. The result is that he has to flounder about in a series of metaphors. A powerfully imaginative mind seizes and combines at the same instant all the important ideas of its poem or picture, and while it works with one of them, it is at the same instant working with and modifying all in their relation to it and never losing sight of their bearings on each other—as the motion of a snake's body goes through all parts at once and its volition acts at the same instant in coils which go contrary ways.

A romantic movement must have an end of the very nature of the thing. It may be deplored, but it can't be helped—wonder must cease to be wonder.

I guard myself here from all the consequences of the analogy, but it expresses at any rate the inevitableness of the process. A literature of wonder must have an end as inevitably as a strange land loses its strangeness when one lives in it. Think of the lost ecstasy of the Elizabethans. "Oh my America, my new found land," think of what it meant to them and of what it means to us. Wonder can only be the attitude of a man passing from one stage to another, it can never be a permanently fixed thing.

EZRA POUND

from

A Retrospect[1]

The prose of Ezra Pound is personal and eccentric, violent and scrappy, yet it has the wholehearted sanction of T. S. Eliot. Eliot considers Pound a great critic.

The following two essays are a good illustration of Pound's criticism. They present, among other things, the famous "Imagist manifesto"; advice for right poetic diction and versification; and definitions of the three main categories of poetry, which Pound calls Melopoeia, Phanopoeia, and Logopoeia. The second essay ends with a provocative list of indispensable books, from Homer and Ovid to the moderns—one of the representative book lists which Pound and Eliot have advocated throughout their lifetime literary relationship. To Pound the book list stands for the "key" to a new civilization.

𝒯here has been so much scribbling about a new fashion in poetry, that I may perhaps be pardoned this brief recapitulation and retrospect.

In the spring or early summer of 1912, 'H. D.', Richard Aldington and myself decided that we were agreed upon the three principles following:

1. Direct treatment of the 'thing' whether subjective or objective.

---

[1] A group of early essays and notes which appeared under this title in *Pavannes and Divisions* (1918). 'A Few Don'ts' was first printed is *Poetry*, I, 6 (March, 1913).

2. To use absolutely no word that does not contribute to the presentation.

3. As regarding rhythm: to compose in the sequence of the musical phrase, not in sequence of a metronome.

Upon many points of taste and predilection we differed, but agreeing upon these three positions we thought we had as much right to a group name, at least as much right, as a number of French 'schools' proclaimed by Mr Flint in the August number of Harold Monro's magazine for 1911.

This school has since been 'joined' or 'followed' by numerous people who, whatever their merits, do not show any signs of agreeing with the second specification. Indeed *vers libre* has become as prolix and as verbose as any of the flaccid varieties that preceded it. It has brought faults of its own. The actual language and phrasing is often as bad as that of our elders without even the excuse that the words are shovelled in to fill a metric pattern or to complete the noise of a rhyme-sound. Whether or no the phrases followed by the followers are musical must be left to the reader's decision. At times I can find a marked metre in 'vers libres', as stale and hackneyed as any pseudo-Swinburnian, at times the writers seem to follow no musical structure whatever. But it is, on the whole, good that the field should be ploughed. Perhaps a few good poems have come from the new method, and if so it is justified.

Criticism is not a circumscription or a set of prohibitions. It provides fixed points of departure. It may startle a dull reader into alertness. That little of it which is good is mostly in stray phrases; or if it be an older artist helping a younger it is in great measure but rules of thumb, cautions gained by experience.

I set together a few phrases on practical working about the time the first remarks on imagisme were published. The first use of the word 'Imagiste' was in my note to T. E. Hulme's five poems, printed at the end of my 'Ripostes' in the autumn of 1912. I reprint my cautions from *Poetry* for March, 1913.

A Few Don'ts

An 'Image' is that which presents an intellectual and emotional complex in an instant of time. I use the term 'complex' rather in the technical sense employed by the newer psychologists, such as Hart, though we might not agree absolutely in our application.

It is the presentation of such a 'complex' instantaneously which gives that sense of sudden liberation; that sense of freedom from time limits and space limits; that sense of sudden growth, which we experience in the presence of the greatest works of art.

It is better to present one Image in a lifetime than to produce voluminous works.

All this, however, some may consider open to debate. The immediate

necessity is to tabulate A LIST OF DON'TS for those beginning to write
verses. I can not put all of them into Mosaic negative.

To begin with, consider the three propositions (demanding direct
treatment, economy of words, and the sequence of the musical phrase),
not as dogma—never consider anything as dogma—but as the result of
long contemplation, which, even if it is some one else's contemplation,
may be worth consideration.

Pay no attention to the criticism of men who have never themselves
written a notable work. Consider the discrepancies between the actual
writing of the Greek poets and dramatists, and the theories of the Graeco-
Roman grammarians, concocted to explain their metres.

Language

Use no superfluous word, no adjective which does not reveal something.

Don't use such an expression as 'dim lands *of peace*'. It dulls the
image. It mixes an abstraction with the concrete. It comes from the
writer's not realizing that the natural object is always the *adequate*
symbol.

Go in fear of abstractions. Do not retell in mediocre verse what has
already been done in good prose. Don't think any intelligent person is
going to be deceived when you try to shirk all the difficulties of the
unspeakably difficult art of good prose by chopping your composition
into line lengths.

What the expert is tired of today the public will be tired of tomorrow.

Don't imagine that the art of poetry is any simpler than the art of
music, or that you can please the expert before you have spent at least
as much effort on the art of verse as the average piano teacher spends on
the art of music.

Be influenced by as many great artists as you can, but have the
decency either to acknowledge the debt outright, or to try to conceal it.

Don't allow 'influence' to mean merely that you mop up the particular
decorative vocabulary of some one or two poets whom you happen to
admire. A Turkish war correspondent was recently caught red-handed
babbling in his despatches of 'dove-grey' hills, or else it was 'pearl-pale',
I can not remember.

Use either no ornament or good ornament.

Rhythm and Rhyme

Let the candidate fill his mind with the finest cadences he can
discover, preferably in a foreign language,[2] so that the meaning of the
words may be less likely to divert his attention from the movement;
e.g. Saxon charms, Hebridean Folk Songs, the verse of Dante, and the

[2] This is for rhythm, his vocabulary must of course be found in his native
tongue.

lyrics of Shakespeare—if he can dissociate the vocabulary from the cadence. Let him dissect the lyrics of Goethe coldly into their component sound values, syllables long and short, stressed and unstressed, into vowels and consonants.

It is not necessary that a poem should rely on its music, but if it does rely on its music that music must be such as will delight the expert.

Let the neophyte know assonance and alliteration, rhyme immediate and delayed, simple and polyphonic, as a musician would expect to know harmony and counterpoint and all the minutiae of his craft. No time is too great to give to these matters or to any one of them, even if the artist seldom have need of them.

Don't imagine that a thing will 'go' in verse just because it's too dull to go in prose.

Don't be 'viewy'—leave that to the writers of pretty little philosophic essays. Don't be descriptive; remember that the painter can describe a landscape much better than you can, and that he has to know a deal more about it.

When Shakespeare talks of the 'Dawn in russet mantle clad' he presents something which the painter does not present. There is in this line of his nothing that one can call description; he presents.

Consider the way of the scientists rather than the way of an advertising agent for a new soap.

The scientist does not expect to be acclaimed as a great scientist until he has *discovered* something. He begins by learning what has been discovered already. He goes from that point onward. He does not bank on being a charming fellow personally. He does not expect his friends to applaud the results of his freshman class work. Freshmen in poetry are unfortunately not confined to a definite and recognizable class room. They are 'all over the shop'. Is it any wonder 'the public is indifferent to poetry?'

Don't chop your stuff into separate *iambs*. Don't make each line stop dead at the end, and then begin every next line with a heave. Let the beginning of the next line catch the rise of the rhythm wave, unless you want a definite longish pause.

In short, behave as a musician, a good musician, when dealing with that phase of your art which has exact parallels in music. The same laws govern, and you are bound by no others.

Naturally, your rhythmic structure should not destroy the shape of your words, or their natural sound, or their meaning. It is improbable that, at the start, you will be able to get a rhythm-structure strong enough to affect them very much, though you may fall a victim to all sorts of false stopping due to line ends and cæsurae.

The Musician can rely on pitch and the volume of the orchestra. You can not. The term harmony is misapplied in poetry; it refers to simultaneous sounds of different pitch. There is, however, in the best verse a sort of residue of sound which remains in the ear of the hearer and acts more or less as an organ-base.

A rhyme must have in it some slight element of surprise if it is to give pleasure; it need not be bizarre or curious, but it must be well used if used at all.

Vide further Vildrac and Duhamel's notes on rhyme in *'Technique Poétique'*.

That part of your poetry which strikes upon the imaginative *eye* of the reader will lose nothing by translation into a foreign tongue; that which appeals to the ear can reach only those who take it in the original.

Consider the definiteness of Dante's presentation, as compared with Milton's rhetoric. Read as much of Wordsworth as does not seem too unutterably dull.

If you want the gist of the matter go to Sappho, Catullus, Villon, Heine when he is the vein, Gautier when he is not too frigid; or, if you have not the tongues, seek out the leisurely Chaucer. Good prose will do you no harm, and there is good discipline to be had by trying to write it.

Translation is likewise good training, if you find that your original matter 'wobbles' when you try to rewrite it. The meaning of the poem to be translated can not 'wobble'.

If you are using a symmetrical form, don't put in what you want to say and then fill up the remaining vacuums with slush.

Don't mess up the perception of one sense by trying to define it in terms of another. This is usually only the result of being too lazy to find the exact word. To this clause there are possibly exceptions.

The first three simple prescriptions will throw out nine-tenths of all the bad poetry now accepted as standard and classic; and will prevent you from many a crime of production.

'. . . *Mais d'abord il faut être un poète'*, as MM. Duhamel and Vildrac have said at the end of their little book, *'Notes sur la Technique Poétique.'*

Since March 1913, Ford Madox Hueffer has pointed out that Wordsworth was so intent on the ordinary or plain word that he never thought of hunting for *le mot juste*.

John Butler Yeats has handled or man-handled Wordsworth and the Victorians, and his criticism, contained in letters to his son, is now printed and available.

I do not like writing *about* art, my first, at least I think it was my first essay on the subject, was a protest against it.

.   .   .   .   .

Credo

Rhythm.—I believe in an 'absolute rhythm', a rhythm, that is, in poetry which corresponds exactly to the emotion or shade of emotion to be expressed. A man's rhythm must be interpretative, it will be, therefore, in the end, his own, uncounterfeiting, uncounterfeitable.

Symbols.—I believe that the proper and perfect symbol is the natural object, that if a man use 'symbols' he must so use them that their symbolic function does not obtrude; so that *a* sense, and the poetic quality of the passage, is not lost to those who do not understand the symbol as such, to whom, for instance, a hawk is a hawk.

Technique.—I believe in technique as the test of a man's sincerity; in law when it is ascertainable; in the trampling down of every convention that impedes or obscures the determination of the law, or the precise rendering of the impulse.

Form.—I think there is a 'fluid' as well as a 'solid' content, that some poems may have form as a tree has form, some as water poured into a vase. That most symmetrical forms have certain uses. That a vast number of subjects cannot be precisely, and therefore not properly rendered in symmetrical forms.

'Thinking that alone worthy wherein the whole art is employed'.[3] I think the artist should master all known forms and systems of metric, and I have with some persistence set about doing this, searching particularly into those periods wherein the systems came to birth or attained their maturity. It has been complained, with some justice, that I dump my note-books on the public. I think that only after a long struggle will poetry attain such a degree of development, or, if you will, modernity, that it will vitally concern people who are accustomed, in prose, to Henry James and Anatole France, in music to Debussy. I am constantly contending that it took two centuries of Provence and one of Tuscany to develop the media of Dante's masterwork, that it took the latinists of the Renaissance, and the Pleiade, and his own age of painted speech to prepare Shakespeare his tools. It is tremendously important that great poetry be written, it makes no jot of difference who writes it. The experimental demonstrations of one man may save the time of many —hence my furore over Arnaut Daniel—if a man's experiments try out one new rime, or dispense conclusively with one iota of currently accepted nonsense, he is merely playing fair with his colleagues when he chalks up his result.

No man ever writes very much poetry that 'matters'. In bulk, that is, no one produces much that is final, and when a man is not doing this highest thing, this saying the thing once for all and perfectly; when he is not matching Ποικιλόθρον᾽, ἀθάνατ᾽ Ἀφρόδιτα, or 'Hist—said Kate the Queen', he had much better be making the sorts of experiment which may be of use to him in his later work, or to his successors.

'The lyf so short, the craft so long to lerne.' It is a foolish thing for a man to begin his work on a too narrow foundation, it is a disgraceful thing for a man's work not to show steady growth and increasing fineness from first to last.

---

[3] Dante, *De Volgari Eloquio.*

As for 'adaptations'; one finds that all the old masters of painting recommend to their pupils that they begin by copying masterwork, and proceed to their own composition.

As for 'Every man his own poet', the more every man knows about poetry the better. I believe in every one writing poetry who wants to; most do. I believe in every man knowing enough of music to play 'God bless our home' on the harmonium, but I do not believe in every man giving concerts and printing his sin.

The mastery of any art is the work of a lifetime. I should not discriminate between the 'amateur' and the 'professional'. Or rather I should discriminate quite often in favour of the amateur, but I should discriminate between the amateur and the expert. It is certain that the present chaos will endure until the Art of poetry has been preached down the amateur gullet, until there is such a general understanding of the fact that poetry is an art and not a pastime; such a knowledge of technique; of technique of surface and technique of content, that the amateurs will cease to try to drown out the masters.

If a certain thing was said once for all in Atlantis or Arcadia, in 450 Before Christ or in 1290 after, it is not for us moderns to go saying it over, or to go obscuring the memory of the dead by saying the same thing with less skill and less conviction.

My pawing over the ancients and semi-ancients has been one struggle to find out what has been done, once for all, better than it can ever be done again, and to find out what remains for us to do, and plenty does remain, for if we still feel the same emotions as those which launched the thousand ships, it is quite certain that we come on these feelings differently, through different nuances, by different intellectual gradations. Each age has its own abounding gifts yet only some ages transmute them into matter of duration. No good poetry is ever written in a manner twenty years old, for to write in such a manner shows conclusively that the writer thinks from books, convention and *cliché,* and not from life, yet a man feeling the divorce of life and his art may naturally try to resurrect a forgotten mode if he finds in that mode some leaven, or if he thinks he sees in it some element lacking in contemporary art which might unite that art again to its sustenance, life.

In the art of Daniel and Cavalcanti, I have seen that precision which I miss in the Victorians, that explicit rendering, be it of external nature, or of emotion. Their testimony is of the eyewitness, their symptoms are first hand.

As for the nineteenth century, with all respect to its achievements, I think we shall look back upon it as a rather blurry, messy sort of a period, a rather sentimentalistic, mannerish sort of a period. I say this without any self-righteousness, with no self-satisfaction.

As for there being a 'movement' or my being of it, the conception of poetry as a 'pure art' in the sense in which I use the term, revived with Swinburne. From the puritanical revolt to Swinburne, poetry had been merely the vehicle—yes, definitely, Arthur Symon's scruples and feelings

about the word not withholding—the ox-cart and post-chaise for trans-
mitting thoughts poetic or otherwise. And perhaps the 'great Victorians',
though it is doubtful, and assuredly the 'nineties' continued the development of the art, confining their improvements, however, chiefly to
sound and to refinements of manner.

Mr Yeats has once and for all stripped English poetry of its perdam-
nable rhetoric. He has boiled away all that is not poetic—and a good
deal that is. He has become a classic in his own lifetime and *nel mezzo
del cammin*. He has made our poetic idiom a thing pliable, a speech
without inversions.

Robert Bridges, Maurice Hewlett and Frederic Manning are[4] in their
different ways seriously concerned with overhauling the metric, in testing the language and its adaptability to certain modes. Ford Hueffer
is making some sort of experiments in modernity. The Provost of Oriel
continues his translation of the *Divina Commedia*.

As to Twentieth century poetry, and the poetry which I expect to
see written during the next decade or so, it will, I think, move against
poppy-cock, it will be harder and saner, it will be what Mr Hewlett
calls 'nearer the bone'. It will be as much like granite as it can be, its
force will lie in its truth, its interpretative power (of course, poetic
force does always rest there); I mean it will not try to seem forcible by
rhetorical din, and luxurious riot. We will have fewer painted adjectives
impeding the shock and stroke of it. At least for myself, I want it so,
austere, direct, free from emotional slither.

What is there now, in 1917, to be added?

Re Vers Libre

I think the desire for vers libre is due to the sense of quantity re-
asserting itself after years of starvation. But I doubt if we can take over,
for English, the rules of quantity laid down for Greek and Latin, mostly
by Latin grammarians.

I think one should write vers libre only when one 'must', that is
to say, only when the 'thing' builds up a rhythm more beautiful than
that of set metres, or more real, more a part of the emotion of the
'thing', more germane, intimate, interpretative than the measure of
regular accentual verse; a rhythm which discontents one with set iambic
or set anapaestic.

Eliot has said the thing very well when he said, 'No *vers* is *libre* for
the man who wants to do a good job.'

As a matter of detail, there is vers libre with accent heavily marked
as a drum-beat (as par example my 'Dance Figure'), and on the other
hand I think I have gone as far as can profitably be gone in the other
direction (and perhaps too far). I mean I do not think one can use to

---

[4] (Dec. 1911).

any advantage rhythms much more tenuous and imperceptible than some I have used. I think progress lies rather in an attempt to approximate classical quantitative metres (NOT to copy them) than in a carelessness regarding such things.[5]

I agree with John Yeats on the relation of beauty to certitude. I prefer satire, which is due to emotion, to any sham of emotion.

I have had to write, or at least I have written a good deal about art, sculpture, painting and poetry. I have seen what seemed to me the best of contemporary work reviled and obstructed. Can any one write prose of permanent or durable interest when he is merely saying for one year what nearly every one will say at the end of three or four years? I have been battistrada for a sculptor, a painter, a novelist, several poets. I wrote also of certain French writers in *The New Age* in nineteen twelve or eleven.

I would much rather that people would look at Brzeska's sculpture and Lewis's drawings, and that they would read Joyce, Jules Romains, Eliot, than that they should read what I have said of these men, or that I should be asked to republish argumentative essays and reviews.

All that the critic can do for the reader or audience or spectator is to focus his gaze or audition. Rightly or wrongly I think my blasts and essays have done their work, and that more people are now likely to go to the sources than are likely to read this book.

Jammes's 'Existences' in *'La Triomphe de la Vie'* is available. So are his early poems. I think we need a convenient anthology rather than descriptive criticism. Carl Sandburg wrote me from Chicago, 'It's hell when poets can't afford to buy each other's books.' Half the people who care, only borrow. In America so few people know each other that the difficulty lies more than half in distribution. Perhaps one should make an anthology: Romains's 'Un Etre en Marche' and 'Prières', Vildrac's 'Visite'. Retrospectively the fine wrought work of Laforgue, the flashes of Rimbaud, the hard-bit lines of Tristan Corbière, Tailhade's sketches in 'Poèmes Aristophanesques', the 'Litanies' of De Gourmont.

It is difficult at all times to write of the fine arts, it is almost impossible unless one can accompany one's prose with many reproductions. Still I would seize this chance or any chance to reaffirm my belief in Wyndham Lewis's genius, both in his drawings and his writings. And I would name an out of the way prose book, the *'Scenes and Portraits'* of Frederic Manning, as well as James Joyce's short stories and novel, 'Dubliners' and the now well known 'Portrait of the Artist' as well as Lewis's 'Tarr', if, that is, I may treat my strange reader as if he were a new friend come into the room, intent on ransacking my bookshelf.

---

[5] Let me date this statement 20 Aug. 1917.

EZRA POUND

from

How to Read

Part II: Or What May Be an Introduction to Method

*I*t is as important for the purpose of thought to keep language efficient as it is in surgery to keep tetanus bacilli out of one's bandages.

In introducing a person to literature one would do well to have him examine works where language is efficiently used; to devise a system for getting directly and expeditiously at such works, despite the smoke-screens erected by half-knowing and half-thinking critics. To get at them, despite the mass of dead matter that these people have heaped up and conserved round about them in the proportion: one barrel of sawdust to each half-bunch of grapes.

Great literature is simply language charged with meaning to the utmost possible degree.

When we set about examining it we find that this charging has been done by several clearly definable sorts of people, and by a periphery of less determinate sorts.

(*a*) *The inventors*, discoverers of a particular process or of more than one mode and process. Sometimes these people are known, or discoverable; for example, we know, with reasonable certitude, that Arnaut Daniel introduced certain methods of rhyming, and we know that certain finenesses of perception appeared first in such a troubadour or in G. Cavalcanti. We do not know, and are not likely to know, anything definite about the precursors of Homer.

(*b*) *The masters*. This is a very small class, and there are very few real ones. The term is properly applied to inventors who, apart from their own inventions, are able to assimilate and co-ordinate a large number of preceding inventions. I mean to say they either start with a core of their own and accumulate adjuncts, or they digest a vast mass of subject-matter, apply a number of known modes of expression, and succeed in pervading the whole with some special quality or some special character of their own, and bring the whole to a state of homogeneous fullness.

(*c*) *The diluters*, these who follow either the inventors or the 'great writers', and who produce something of lower intensity, some flabbier variant, some diffuseness or tumidity in the wake of the valid.

(*d*) (And this class produces the great bulk of all writing.) The men who do more or less good work in the more or less good style of a period. Of these the delightful anthologies, the song books, are full, and choice among them is the matter of taste, for you prefer Wyatt to Donne, Donne to Herrick, Drummond of Hawthornden to Browne, in response to some purely personal sympathy, these people add but some slight personal flavour, some minor variant of a mode, without affecting the main course of the story.

At their faintest 'Ils n'existent pas, leur ambiance leur confert une existence.' They do not exist: their ambience confers existence upon them. When they are most prolific they produce dubious cases like Virgil and Petrarch, who probably pass, among the less exigeant, for colossi.

(e) Belles Lettres. Longus, Prévost, Benjamin Constant, who are not exactly 'great masters', who can hardly be said to have originated a form, but who have nevertheless brought some mode to a very high development.

(f) And there is a supplementary or sixth class of writers, the starters of crazes, the Ossianic McPhersons, the Gongoras[1] whose wave of fashion flows over writing for a few centuries or a few decades, and then subsides, leaving things as they were.

It will be seen that the first two classes are the more sharply defined: that the difficulty of classification for particular lesser authors increases as one descends the list, save for the last class, which is again fairly clear.

The point is, that if a man knows the facts about the first two categories, he can evaluate almost any unfamiliar book at first sight. I mean he can form a just estimate of its worth, and see how and where it belongs in this schema.

As to crazes, the number of possible diseases in literature is perhaps not very great, the same afflictions crop up in widely separated countries without any previous communication. The good physician will recognize a known malady, even if the manifestation be superficially different.

The fact that six different critics will each have a different view concerning what author belongs in which of the categories here given, does not in the least invalidate the categories. When a man knows the facts about the first two categories, the reading of work in the other categories will not greatly change his opinion about those in the first two.

Language

Obviously this knowledge cannot be acquired without knowledge of various tongues. The same discoveries have served a number of races. If a man has not time to learn different languages he can at least, and with very little delay, be told what the discoveries were. If he wish to be a good critic he will have to look for himself.

---

[1] One should perhaps apologize, or express a doubt as to the origin of Gongorism, or redefine it or start blaming it on some other spaniard.

Bad critics have prolonged the use of demoded terminology, usually a terminology originally invented to describe what had been done before 300 B.C., and to describe it in a rather exterior fashion. Writers of second order have often tried to produce works to fit some category or term not yet occupied in their own local literature. If we chuck out the classifications which apply to the outer shape of the work, or to its occasion, and if we look at what actually happens, in, let us say, poetry, we will find that the language is charged or energized in various manners.

That is to say, there are three 'kinds of poetry':

MELOPŒIA, wherein the words are charged, over and above their plain meaning, with some musical property, which directs the bearing or trend of that meaning.

PHANOPŒIA, which is a casting of images upon the visual imagination.

LOGOPŒIA, 'the dance of the intellect among words', that is to say, it employs words not only for their direct meaning, but it takes count in a special way of habits of usage, of the context we *expect* to find with the word, its usual concomitants, of its known acceptances, and of ironical play. It holds the aesthetic content which is peculiarly the domain of verbal manifestation, and cannot possibly be contained in plastic or in music. It is the latest come, and perhaps most tricky and undependable mode.

The *melopœia* can be appreciated by a foreigner with a sensitive ear, even though he be ignorant of the language in which the poem is written. It is practically impossible to transfer or translate it from one language to another, save perhaps by divine accident, and for half a line at a time.

Phanopœia can, on the other hand, be translated almost, or wholly, intact. When it is good enough, it is practically impossible for the translator to destroy it save by very crass bungling, and the neglect of perfectly well-known and formulative rules.

Logopœia does not translate; though the attitude of mind it expresses may pass through a paraphrase. Or one might say, you can *not* translate it 'locally', but having determined the original author's state of mind, you may or may not be able to find a derivative or an equivalent.

Prose

The language of prose is much less highly charged, that is perhaps the only availing distinction between prose and poesy. Prose permits greater factual presentation, explicitness, but a much greater amount of language is needed. During the last century or century and a half, prose has, perhaps for the first time, perhaps for the second or third time, arisen to challenge the poetic pre-eminence. That is to say, *Cœur Simple*, by Flaubert, is probably more important than Théophile Gautier's *Carmen*, etc.

The total charge in certain nineteenth-century prose works possibly surpasses the total charge found in individual poems of that period; but that merely indicates that the author has been able to get his effect cumulatively, by a greater heaping up of factual data; imagined fact, if you will, but nevertheless expressed in factual manner.

By using several hundred pages of prose, Flaubert, by force of architectonics, manages to attain an intensity comparable to that in Villon's *Heaulmière*, or his prayer for his mother. This does not invalidate my dissociation of the two terms: poetry, prose.

In *Phanopœia* we find the greatest drive toward utter precision of word; this art exists almost exclusively by it.

In *melopœia* we find a contrary current, a force tending often to lull, or to distract the reader from the exact sense of the language. It is poetry on the borders of music and music is perhaps the bridge between consciousness and the unthinking sentient or even insentient universe.

All writing is built up of these three elements, plus 'architectonics' or 'the form of the whole', and to know anything about the relative efficiency of various works one must have some knowledge of the maximum already attained by various authors, irrespective of where and when.[2]

It is not enough to know that the Greeks attained to the greatest skill in melopœia, or even that the Provençaux added certain diverse developments and that some quite minor, nineteenth-century Frenchmen achieved certain elaborations.

It is not quite enough to have the general idea that the Chinese (more particularly Rihaku and Omakitsu) attained the known maximum of *phanopœia*, due perhaps to the nature of their written ideograph, or to wonder whether Rimbaud is, at rare moments, their equal. One wants one's knowledge in more definite terms.

It is an error to think that vast reading will automatically produce any such knowledge or understanding. Neither Chaucer with his forty books, nor Shakespeare with perhaps half a dozen, in folio, can be considered illiterate. A man can learn more music by working on a Bach fugue until he can take it apart and put it together, than by playing through ten dozen heterogeneous albums.

You may say that for twenty-seven years I have thought consciously about this particular matter, and read or read at a great many books, and that with the subject never really out of my mind, I don't yet know half there is to know about *melopœia*.

There are, on the other hand, a few books that I still keep on my desk, and a great number that I shall never open again. But the books that a man needs to know in order to 'get his bearings', in order to have a sound judgment of any bit of writing that may come before him, are very few. The list is so short, indeed, that one wonders that people, professional writers in particular, are willing to leave them ignored and to continue dangling in mid-chaos emitting the most imbecile estimates, and often vitiating their whole lifetime's production.

[2] Lacuna at this point to be corrected in criticism of Hindemith's 'Schwandreher'. E.P. Sept. 1938.

Limiting ourselves to the authors who actually invented something, or who are the 'first known examples' of the process in working order, we find:

OF THE GREEKS: Homer, Sappho. (The 'great dramatists' decline from Homer, and depend immensely on him for their effects; their 'charge', at its highest potential, depends so often, and so greatly on their being able to count on their audience's knowledge of the *Iliad*. Even Æschylus is rhetorical.)[3]

OF THE ROMANS: As we have lost Philetas, and most of Callimachus, we may suppose that the Romans added a certain sophistication; at any rate, Catullus, Ovid, Propertius, all give us something we cannot find now in Greek authors.

A specialist may read Horace if he is interested in learning the precise demarcation between what can be learned about writing, and what cannot. I mean that Horace is the perfect example of a man who acquired all that is acquirable, without having the root. I beg the reader to observe that I am being exceedingly iconoclastic, that I am omitting thirty established names for every two I include. I am chucking out Pindar, and Virgil, without the slightest compunction. I do not suggest a 'course' in Greek or Latin literature, I name a few isolated writers; five or six pages of Sappho. One can throw out at least one-third of Ovid. That is to say, I am omitting the authors who can teach us no new or no more effective method of 'charging' words.

OF THE MIDDLE AGES: The Anglo-Saxon *Seafarer,* and some more cursory notice of some medieval narrative, it does not so greatly matter what narrative, possibly the *Beowulf,* the *Poema del Cid,* and the sages of *Grettir* and *Burnt Nial.* And then, in contrast, troubadours, perhaps thirty poems in Provençal, and for comparison with them a few songs by Von Morungen, or Wolfram von Essenbach, and von der Vogelweide; and then Bion's *Death of Adonis.*

From which mixture, taken in this order, the reader will get his bearings on the art of poetry made to be sung; for there are three kinds of *melopœia:* (1) that made to be sung to a tune; (2) that made to be intoned or sung to a sort of chant; and (3) that made to be spoken; and the art of joining words in each of these kinds is different, and cannot be clearly understood until the reader knows that there are three different objectives.

OF THE ITALIANS: Guido Cavalcanti and Dante; perhaps a dozen and a half poems of Guido's, and a dozen poems by his contemporaries, and the *Divina Commedia.*

In Italy, around the year 1300, there were new values established, things said that had not been said in Greece, or in Rome or elsewhere.

VILLON: After Villon and for several centuries, poetry can be considered as *fioritura,* as an efflorescence, almost an effervescence, and without any new roots. Chaucer is an enrichment, one might say a

---

[3] E.P.'s later and unpublished notes, revise all this in so far as they demand much greater recognition of Sophokles.

more creamy version of the 'matter of France', and he in some measure preceded the verbal richness of the classic revival, but beginning with the Italians after Dante, coming through the Latin writers of the Renaissance, French, Spanish, English, Tasso, Ariosto, etc., the Italians always a little in the lead, the whole is elaboration, medieval basis, and wash after wash of Roman or Hellenic influence. I mean one need not read any particular part of it for purpose of learning one's comparative values.

If one were studying history and not poetry, one might discover the medieval mind more directly in the opening of Mussato's *Ecerinus* than even in Dante. The culture of Chaucer is the same as that which went contemporaneously into Ferrara, with the tongue called *'francoveneto'*.

One must emphasize one's contrasts in the quattrocento. One can take Villon as pivot for understanding them. After Villon, and having begun before his time, we find this *fioritura*, and for centuries we find little else. Even in Marlowe and Shakespeare there is this embroidery of language, this talk about the matter, rather than presentation. I doubt if anyone ever acquired discrimination in studying 'The Elizabethans'. You have grace, richness of language, abundance, but you have probably nothing that isn't replaceable by something else, no ornament that wouldn't have done just as well in some other connection, or for which some other figure of rhetoric couldn't have served, or which couldn't have been distilled from literary antecedents.

The 'language' had not been heard on the London stage, but it had been heard in the Italian law courts, etc.; there were local attempts, all over Europe, to teach the public (in Spain, Italy, England) Latin diction. 'Poetry' was considered to be (as it still is considered by a great number of drivelling imbeciles) synonymous with 'lofty and flowery language'.

One Elizabethan specialist has suggested that Shakespeare, disgusted with his efforts, or at least despairing of success, as a poet, took to the stage. The drama is a mixed art; it does not rely on the charge that can be put into the word, but calls on gesture and mimicry and 'impersonation' for assistance. The actor must do a good half of the work. One does no favour to drama by muddling the two sets of problems.

Apologists for the drama are continually telling us in one way or another that drama either cannot use at all, or can make but a very limited use of words charged to their highest potential. This is perfectly true. Let us try to keep our minds on the problem we started with, i.e., the art of writing, the art of 'charging' language with meaning.

After 1450 we have the age of *fioritura*; after Marlowe and Shakespeare came what was called a 'classic' movement, a movement that restrained without inventing. Anything that happens to mind in England has usually happened somewhere else first. Someone invents something, then someone develops, or some dozens develop a frothy or at any rate creamy enthusiasm or over-abundance, then someone tries to tidy things up. For example, the estimable Pleiad emasculating the French tongue, and the French classicists, and the English classicists, etc., all of which things should be relegated to the subsidiary zone: period interest, historical interest, bric-à-brac for museums.

At this point someone says: 'O, but the ballads'. All right, I will allow the voracious peruser a half-hour for ballads (English and Spanish, or Scottish, Border, and Spanish). There is nothing easier than to be distracted from one's point, or from the main drive of one's subject by a desire for utterly flawless equity and omniscience.

Let us say, but directly in parenthesis, that there was a very limited sort of *logopœia* in seventeenth- and eighteenth-century satire. And that Rochester and Dorset may have introduced a new note, or more probably re-introduced an old one, that reappears later in Heine.

Let us also cut loose from minor details and minor exceptions: the main fact is that we 'have come' or that 'humanity came' to a point where verse-writing can or could no longer be clearly understood without the study of prose-writing.

Say, for the sake of argument, that after the slump of the Middle Ages, prose 'came to' again in Machiavelli; admit that various sorts of prose had existed, in fact nearly all sorts had existed. Herodotus wrote history that is literature. Thucydides was a journalist. (It is a modern folly to suppose that vulgarity and cheapness have the merit of novelty; they have always existed, and are of no interest in themselves.)

There have been bombast, oratory, legal speech, balanced sentences, Ciceronian impressiveness; Petronius had written a satiric novel, Longus had written a delicate nouvelle. The prose of the Renaissance leaves us Rabelais, Brantôme, Montaigne. A determined specialist can dig interesting passages, or sumptuous passages, or even subtle passages out of Pico, the medieval mystics, scholastics, platonists, none of which will be the least use to a man trying to learn the art of 'changing language'.

I mean to say that from the beginning of literature up to A.D. 1750 poetry was the superior art, and was so considered to be, and if we read books written before that date we find the number of interesting books in verse at least equal to the number of prose books still readable; and the poetry contains the quintessence. When we want to know what people were like before 1750, when we want to know that they had blood and bones like ourselves, we go to the poetry of the period.

But, as I have said, the '*fioritura* business' set in. And one morning Monsieur Stendhal, not thinking of Homer, or Villon, or Catullus, but having a very keen sense of actuality, noticed that 'poetry', *la poésie*, as the term was then understood, the stuff written by his French contemporaries, or sonorously rolled at him from the French stage, was a damn nuisance. And he remarked that poetry, with its bagwigs and its bobwigs, and its padded calves and its periwigs, its 'fustian à la Louis XIV', was greatly inferior to prose for conveying a clear idea of the diverse states of our consciousness ('les mouvements du coeur').

And at that moment the serious art of writing 'went over to prose', and for some time the important developments of language as means of expression were the developments of prose. And a man cannot clearly understand or justly judge the value of verse, modern verse, any verse, unless he has grasped this.

CONFUCIUS

from

THE ANALECTS

A few sentences from Book XIII of *The Analects* provide Ezra Pound with the central doctrine of his epic poem, the *Cantos*. The doctrine asserts the primacy of correct or precise language as the key to the regulation of civilized government and the arts. Imprecise language, according to these sayings, leads to the degeneration and collapse of civilization. The poet thus has the high responsibility to guard the precision of language and, therefore, the State itself.

The term "the precise definition" is used throughout the *Cantos* both in English and in Chinese ideograms. The passage that follows is translated and paraphrased in the poem frequently.

𝒯zu-lu said, If the prince of Wei were waiting for you to come and administer his country for him, what would be your first measure? The Master said, It would certainly be to correct language. Tzu-lu said, Can I have heard you aright? Surely what you say has nothing to do with the matter. Why should language be corrected? The Master said, Yu! How boorish you are! A gentleman, when things he does not understand are mentioned, should maintain an attitude of reserve. If language is incorrect, then what is said does not concord with what was meant; and if what is said does not concord with what was meant, what is to be done cannot be effected. If what is to be done cannot be effected, then rites and music will not flourish. If rites and music do not flourish, then mutilations and lesser punishments will go astray. And if mutilations and lesser punishments go astray, then the people have nowhere to put hand or foot.

Therefore the gentleman uses only such language as is proper for speech, and only speaks of what it would be proper to carry into effect. The gentleman, in what he says, leaves nothing to mere chance.

WILLIAM BUTLER YEATS

from A VISION

The Great Wheel

A Vision is a literary curiosity by one of the most renowned poets of our century. Purportedly dictated to Yeats's wife by spirits and set down in a species of automatic writing, it is actually an occult system of ideas which gave the poet a philosophical framework for many of his poems. Yeats's celestial geometry has many parallels in medieval cabalism, astrology, and ancient gnosticism; by means of the Wheel diagram he could classify the great figures and events of the past and prophesy for the future. *A Vision* is by no means a frivolous book but a serious attempt to understand and cope with the cultural history of the West. The chapter given below details the mechanics and the symbolism of the Wheel.

Part I: The Principal Smybol

I

When Discord," writes Empedocles, "has fallen into the lowest depths of the vortex"—the extreme bound, not the centre, Burnet points out—"Concord has reached the centre, into it do all things come together so as to be only one, not all at once but gradually from different quarters, and as they come Discord retires to the extreme boundary . . . in proportion as it runs out Concord in a soft immortal boundless stream runs in." And again: "Never will boundless time be emptied of that pair; and they prevail in turn as that circle comes round, and pass away before one another and increase in their appointed turn." It was this Discord or War that Heraclitus called "God of all and Father of all, some it has made gods and some men, some bond and some free," and I recall that Love and War came from the eggs of Leda.

II

According to Simplicius,[1] a late commentator upon Aristotle, the Concord of Empedocles fabricates all things into "an homogeneous sphere," and then Discord separates the elements and so makes the world we inhabit, but even the sphere formed by Concord is not the changeless eternity, for Concord or Love but offers us the image of that which is changeless.

If we think of the vortex attributed to Discord as formed by circles diminishing until they are nothing, and of the opposing sphere attributed to Concord as forming from itself an opposing vortex, the apex of each vortex in the middle of the other's base, we have the fundamental symbol of my instructors.

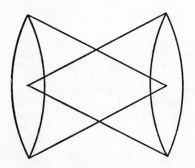 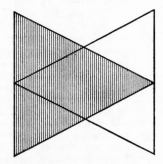

If I call the unshaded cone "Discord" and the other "Concord" and think of each as the bound of a gyre, I see that the gyre of "Concord" diminishes as that of "Discord" increases, and can imagine after that the gyre of "Concord" increasing while that of "Discord" diminishes, and so on, one gyre within the other always. Here the thought of Heraclitus dominates all: "Dying each other's life, living each other's death."

The first gyres clearly described by philosophy are those described in the *Timaeus* which are made by the circuits of "the Other" (creators of all particular things), of the planets as they ascend or descend above or below the equator. They are opposite in nature to that circle of the fixed stars which constitutes "the Same" and confers upon us the knowledge of Universals. Alcemon, a pupil of Pythagoras, thought that men die because they cannot join their beginning and their end. Their serpent has not its tail in its mouth. But my friend the poet and scholar Dr. Sturm sends me an account of gyres in St. Thomas Aquinas: the circular movement of the angels which, though it imitates the circle of "the Same," seems as little connected with the visible heavens as figures drawn by my instructors, his straight line of the human intellect and his gyre, the combination of both movements, made by the ascent and

---

[1] Quoted by Pierre Duhem in *Le Système du monde*, vol. i, page 75.

descent[2] of angels between God and man. He has also found me passages in Dr. Dee, in Macrobius, in an unknown mediaeval writer, which describe souls changing from gyre to sphere and from sphere to gyre. Presently I shall have much to say of the sphere as the final place of rest.

Gyres are occasionally alluded to, but left unexplored, in Swedenborg's mystical writings. In the *Principia*, a vast scientific work written before his mystical life, he describes the double cone. All physical reality, the universe as a whole, every solar system, every atom, is a double cone; where there are "two poles one opposite to the other, these two poles have the form of cones." [3] I am not concerned with his explanation of how these cones have evolved from the point and the sphere, nor with his arguments to prove that they govern all the movements of the planets, for I think, as did Swedenborg in his mystical writings, that the forms of geometry can have but a symbolic relation to spaceless reality, *Mundus Intelligibilis*. Flaubert is the only writer known to me who has so used the double cone. He talked much of writing a story called "La Spirale." He died before he began it, but something of his talk about it has been collected and published. It would have described a man whose dreams during sleep grew in magnificence as his life grew more and more unlucky, the wreck of some love affair coinciding with his marriage to a dream princess.

III

The double cone or vortex, as used by my instructors, is more complicated than that of Flaubert. A line is a movement without extension, and so symbolical of time—subjectivity—Berkeley's stream of ideas—in Plotinus[4] it is apparently "sensation"—and a plane cutting it at right angles is symbolical of space or objectivity. Line and plane are combined in a gyre which must expand or contract according to whether mind grows in objectivity or subjectivity.

The identification of time[5] with subjectivity is probably as old as

[2] In an essay called "The Friends of the People of Faery" in my *Celtic Twilight* I describe such an ascent and descent. I found the same movement in some story I picked up at Kiltartan, and suspected a mediaeval symbolism unknown to me at the time.

[3] Vol. ii, p. 555 of the Swedenborg Society's translation.

[4] *Ennead*, vi. i. 8 (MacKenna's translation).

[5] Giovanni Gentile summarises Kant on time and space as follows: "Kant said that space is a form of external sense, time a form of internal sense. He meant that we represent nature, that is what we call the external world and think of as having been in existence before our knowledge and spiritual life began, in space, then we represent the multiplicity of the objects of our internal experience, or what we distinguish as diverse and manifold in the development of our spiritual life, not in space but in time" (*Theory of Mind as Pure Art*, chap. ix, H. Wildon Carr's translation). He thinks these definitions which seem to separate time and space from one another require restatement. It will be seen, however, when I come to what I have called the *Four Principles*, that my symbols imply his description of time as a spatialising act.

philosophy; all that we can touch or handle, and for the moment I mean no other objectivity, has shape or magnitude, whereas our thoughts and emotions have duration and quality, a thought recurs or is habitual, a lecture or a musical composition is measured upon the clock. At the

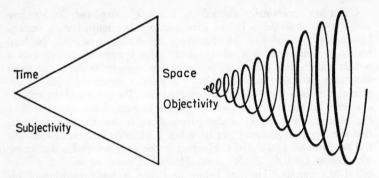

same time pure time and pure space, pure subjectivity and pure objectivity —the plane at the bottom of the cone and the point at its apex—are abstractions or figments of the mind.

IV

My instructors used this single cone or vortex once or twice but soon changed it for a double cone or vortex, preferring to consider subjectivity and objectivity as intersecting states struggling one against the other. If the musical composition seek to suggest the howling of dogs or of the sea waves it is not altogether in time, it suggests bulk and weight. In what I call the cone of the *Four Faculties* which are what man has made in a past or present life—I shall speak later of what makes man —the subjective cone is called that of the *antithetical tincture* because it is achieved and defended by continual conflict with its opposite; the objective cone is called that of the *primary tincture* because whereas subjectivity—in Empedocles "Discord" as I think—tends to separate

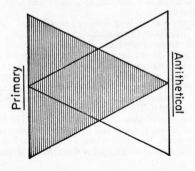

man from man, objectivity brings us back to the mass where we begin. I had suggested the word *tincture,* a common word in Boehme, and my instructors took the word *antithetical* from *Per Amica Silentia Lunae.*

I had never read Hegel, but my mind had been full of Blake from boyhood up and I saw the world as a conflict—Spectre and Emanation —and could distinguish between a contrary and a negation. "Contraries are positive," wrote Blake, "a negation is not a contrary," "How great the gulph between simplicity and insipidity," and again, "There is a place at the bottom of the graves where contraries are equally true."

I had never put the conflict in logical form,[6] never thought with Hegel that the two ends of the see-saw are one another's negation, nor that the spring vegetables were refuted when over.

The cones of the *tinctures* mirror reality but are in themselves pursuit and illusion. As will be presently seen, the sphere is reality. By the *antithetical* cone, which is left unshaded in my diagram, we express more and more, as it broadens, our inner world of desire and imagination, whereas by the *primary,* the shaded cone, we express more and more, as it broadens, that objectivity of mind which, in the words of Murray's Dictionary, lays "stress upon that which is external to the mind" or treats "of outward things and events rather than of inward thought" or seeks "to exhibit the actual facts, not coloured by the opinions or feelings." The *antithetical tincture* is emotional and aesthetic whereas the *primary tincture* is reasonable and moral. Within these cones move what are called the *Four Faculties: Will* and *Mask, Creative Mind* and *Body of Fate.*

It will be enough until I have explained the geometrical diagrams in detail to describe *Will* and *Mask* as the will and its object, or the Is and the Ought (or that which should be), *Creative Mind* and *Body of Fate* as thought and its object, or the Knower and the Known, and to say that the first two are lunar or *antithetical* or natural, the second two solar or *primary* or reasonable. A particular man is classified according to the place of *Will,* or choice, in the diagram. At first sight there are only two *Faculties,* because only two of the four, *Will* and *Creative Mind,* are active, but it will be presently seen that the *Faculties* can be represented by two opposing cones so drawn that the *Will* of the one is the *Mask* of the other, the *Creative Mind* of the one the *Body of Fate* of the other. Everything that wills can be desired, resisted or accepted, every creative act can be seen as fact, every *Faculty* is alternately shield and sword.

V

These pairs of opposites whirl in contrary directions, *Will* and *Mask* from right to left, *Creative Mind* and *Body of Fate* like the hands of a

---

[6] Though reality is not logical it becomes so in our minds if we discover logical refutations of the writer or movement that is going out of fashion. There is always error, which has nothing to do with "the conflict" which creates all life. Croce in his study of Hegel identifies error with negation.

clock, from left to right. I will confine myself for the moment to *Will*
and *Creative Mind*, will and thought. As *Will* approaches the utmost
expansion of its *antithetical* cone it drags *Creative Mind* with it—

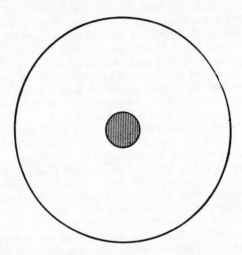

thought is more and more dominated by will—but *Creative Mind* remains at the same distance from its cone's narrow end that *Will* is from
the broad end of the *antithetical* cone. Then, as though satiated by
the extreme expansion of its cone, *Will* lets *Creative Mind* dominate,
and is dragged by it until *Creative Mind* weakens once more. As
Creative Mind, let us say, is dragged by *Will* towards the utmost
expansion of its *antithetical* cone it is more and more contaminated by
Will, while *Will* frees itself from contamination. We can, however,
represent the two *Faculties* as they approach the full expansion of the
antithetical cone by the same cross-sections of the cone.

The shaded, or *primary* part, is a contamination of *Will*; the unshaded, or *antithetical* part, a contamination of *Creative Mind* We can
substitute positions in the cones for either symbol: we can represent
Creative Mind as approaching the extreme expansion of the *antithetical*
cone and then as changing into the narrow end of the *primary* cone and
expanding once more; the *Will* as approaching the narrow end of the
primary cone and then, at the same instant when the *Creative Mind*
changes cones, passing into the broad end of the *antithetical* cone, and
contracting once more. The diagram is sometimes so used by my
instructors and gives them a phrase which constantly occurs, "the interchange of the *tinctures*," but it is inconvenient. For this reason they
generally represent the *Faculties* as moving always along the outside
of the diagram. Just before complete *antithetical* expression they are
placed thus:

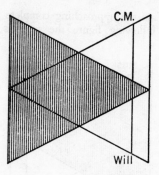

Just after it, thus:

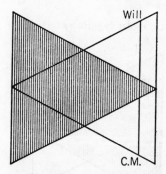

I think of the gyre of *Will* as approaching complete *antithetical* expansion—unshaded cone—along the lower side of the diagram or moving from right to left, and the gyre of *Creative Mind* as approaching it along the upper side, left to right, and then of their passing one another at complete expansion, then of their receding from it, *Will* upon the upper side, *Creative Mind* upon the lower, and always on the outside of the diagram until they pass one another at complete *primary* expansion. These movements are but a convenient pictorial summary of what is more properly a double movement of two gyres. These gyres move not only forward to the *primary* and *antithetical* expansion, but have their own circular movement, the gyre of *Will* from right to left, that of *Creative Mind* from left to right. I shall consider presently the significance of these circlings.

VI

The *Mask* and *Body of Fate* occupy those positions which are most opposite in character to the positions of *Will* and *Creative Mind*. If *Will* and *Creative Mind* are approaching complete *antithetical* expansion,

Mask and *Body of Fate* are approaching complete *primary* expansion, and so on. In the following figure the man is almost completely *antithetical* in nature.

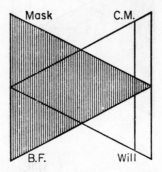

In the following almost completely *primary*.

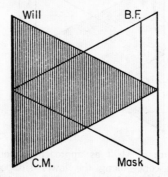

In the following he is completely *primary*, a state which is like the completely *antithetical* state, as I must show presently, only a supernatural or ideal existence.

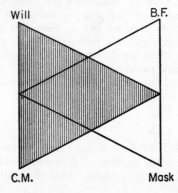

In the following he is midway between *primary* and *antithetical* and moving towards *antithetical* expansion. All four gyres are superimposed.

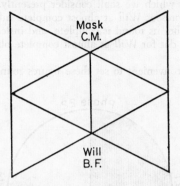

I have only to set a row of numbers upon the sides to possess a classification, as I will show presently, of every possible movement of thought and of life, and I have been told to make these numbers correspond to the phases of the moon, including among them full moon and the moonless night when the moon is nearest to the sun. The moonless night is called Phase 1, and the full moon is Phase 15. Phase 8 begins the *antithetical* phases, those where the bright part of the moon is greater than the dark, and Phase 22 begins the *primary* phases, where the dark part is greater than the bright. At Phases 15 and 1 respectively, the *antithetical* and *primary tinctures* come to a climax. A man of, say, Phase 13 is a man whose *Will* is at that phase, and the diagram which shows the position of the *Faculties* for a *Will* so placed, describes his character and

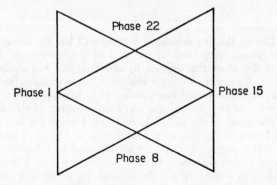

destiny. The last phase is Phase 28, and the twenty-eight phases constitute a month of which each day and night constitute an incarnation and the discarnate period which follows. I am for the moment only concerned with the incarnation, symbolised by the moon at night.

Phase 1 and Phase 28 are not human incarnations because human life is impossible without strife between the *tinctures*. They belong to an order of existence which we shall consider presently. The figure which I have used to represent *Will* at almost complete subjectivity represents the moon just before its round is complete, and instead of using a black disc with a white dot for *Will* at almost complete objectivity I think of the last crescent.

But it is more convenient to set these figures round a circle thus:

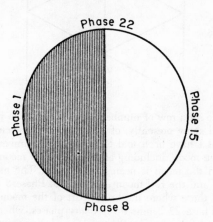

Part II: Examination of the Wheel

I

During the first months of instruction I had the Great Wheel of the lunar phases as printed at the end of this paragraph, but knew nothing of the cones that explain it, and though I had abundant definitions and descriptions of the *Faculties* at their different stations, did not know why they passed one another at certain points, nor why two moved from left to right like the sun's daily course, two from right to left like the moon in the zodiac. Even when I wrote the first edition of this book I thought the geometrical symbolism so difficult, I understood it so little, that I put it off to a later section; and as I had at that time, for a reason I have explained, to use a romantic setting, I described the Great Wheel as danced on the desert sands by mysterious dancers who left the traces of their feet to puzzle the Caliph of Bagdad and his learned men. I tried to interest my readers in an unexplained rule of thumb that somehow explained the world.

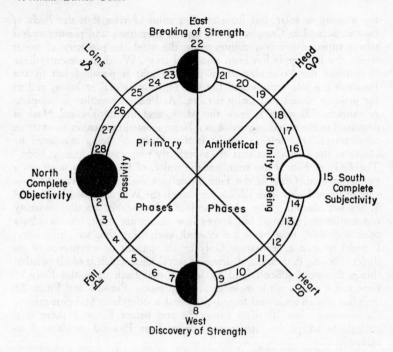

II

This wheel is every completed movement of thought or life, twenty-eight incarnations, a single incarnation, a single judgment or act of thought. Man seeks his opposite or the opposite of his condition, attains his object so far as it is attainable, at Phase 15 and returns[7] to Phase 1 again.

Phase 15 is called Sun in Moon because the solar or *primary tincture* is consumed by the lunar, but from another point of view it is *Mask* consumed in *Will*; all is beauty. The *Mask* as it were wills itself as beauty, but because, as Plotinus says, things that are of one kind are unconscious, it is an ideal or supernatural incarnation. Phase 1 is called Moon in Sun because the lunar or *antithetical tincture* is consumed in

[7] A similar circular movement fundamental in the works of Giovanni Gentile is, I read somewhere, the half-conscious foundation of the political thought of modern Italy. Individuals and classes complete their personality and then sink back to enrich the mass. Government must, it is held, because all good things have been created by class war, recognise that class war though it may be regulated must never end. It is the old saying of Heraclitus, "War is God of all, and Father of all, some it has made Gods and some men, some bond and some free," and the converse of Marxian Socialism.

the *primary* or solar, but from another point of view it is the *Body of Fate* consumed in *Creative Mind;* man is submissive and plastic: unless where supersensual power intervenes, the steel-like plasticity of water where the last ripple has been smoothed away. We shall presently have to consider the *Principles* where pure thought is possible, but in the *Faculties* the sole activity and the sole unity is natural or lunar, and in the *primary* phases that unity is moral. At Phase 1 morality is complete submission. All unity is from the *Mask,* and the *antithetical Mask* is described in the automatic script as a "form created by passion to unite us to ourselves," the self so sought is that Unity of Being compared by Dante in the *Convito* to that of "a perfectly proportioned human body." The *Body of Fate* is the sum, not the unity, of fact, fact as it affects a particular man. Only in the Four *Principles* shall we discover the concord of Empedocles. The *Will* is very much the Will described by Croce.[8] When not affected by the other *Faculties* it has neither emotion, morality nor intellectual interest, but knows how things are done, how windows open and shut, how roads are crossed, everything that we call utility. It seeks its own continuance. Only by the pursuit or acceptance of its direct opposite, that object of desire or moral ideal which is of all possible things the most difficult, and by forcing that form upon the *Body of Fate,* can it attain self-knowledge and expression. Phase 8 and Phase 22 are phases of struggle and tragedy, the first a struggle to find personality, the second to lose it. After Phase 22 and before Phase 1 there is a struggle to accept the fate-imposed unity, from Phase 1 to Phase 8 to escape it.

All such abstract statements are, however, misleading, for we are dealing always with a particular man, the man of Phase 13 or Phase 17 let us say. The *Four Faculties* are not the abstract categories of philosophy, being the result of the four memories of the *Daimon* or ultimate self of that man. His *Body of Fate,* the series of events forced upon him from without, is shaped out of the *Daimon's* memory of the events of his past incarnations; his *Mask* or object of desire or idea of the good, out of its memory of the moments of exaltation in his past lives; his *Will* or normal ego out of its memory of all the events of his present life, whether consciously remembered or not; his *Creative Mind* from its memory of ideas—or universals—displayed by actual men in past lives, or their spirits between lives.

III

When I wish for some general idea which will describe the Great Wheel as an individual life I go to the *Commedia dell' Arte* or improvised drama of Italy. The stage-manager, or *Daimon,* offers his actor an inherited scenario, the *Body of Fate,* and a *Mask* or rôle as unlike as

---

[8] The *Four Faculties* somewhat resemble the four moments to which Croce has dedicated four books; that the resemblance is not closer is because Croce makes little use of antithesis and antinomy.

possible to his natural ego or *Will*, and leaves him to improvise through his *Creative Mind* the dialogue and details of the plot. He must discover or reveal a being which only exists with extreme effort, when his muscles are as it were all taut and all his energies active. But this is *antithetical* man. For *primary* man I go to the *Commedia dell' Arte* in its decline. The *Will* is weak and cannot create a rôle, and so, if it transform itself, does so after an accepted pattern, some traditional clown or pantaloon. It has perhaps no object but to move the crowd, and if it "gags" it is that there may be plenty of topical allusions. In the *primary* phases man must cease to desire *Mask* and Image by ceasing from self-expression, and substitute a motive of service for that of self-expression. Instead of the created *Mask* he has an imitative *Mask*; and when he recognises this, his *Mask* may become the historical norm, or an image of mankind. The author of the *Imitation of Christ* was certainly a man of a late *primary* phase. The *antithetical Mask* and *Will* are *free*, and the *primary Mask* and *Will* *enforced*; and the *free Mask* and *Will* are personality, while the *enforced Mask* and *Will* are code, those limitations which give strength precisely because they are *enforced*. Personality, no matter how habitual, is a constantly renewed choice, varying from an individual charm, in the more *antithetical* phases, to a hard objective dramatisation; but when the *primary* phases begin man is moulded more and more from without.

Antithetical men are, like Landor, violent in themselves because they hate all that impedes their personality, but are in their intellect (*Creative Mind*) gentle, whereas *primary* men whose hatreds are impersonal are violent in their intellect but gentle in themselves, as doubtless Robespierre was gentle.

The *Mask* before Phase 15 is described as a "revelation" because through it the being obtains knowledge of itself, sees itself in personality; while after Phase 15 it is a "concealment," for the being grows incoherent, vague and broken, as its intellect (*Creative Mind*) is more and more concerned with objects that have no relation to its unity but a relation to the unity of society or of material things known through the *Body of Fate*. It adopts a personality which it more and more casts outward, more and more dramatises. It is now a dissolving violent phantom which would grip itself and hold itself together. The being of *antithetical* man is described as full of rage before Phase 12, against all in the world that hinders its expression, after Phase 12, but before Phase 15, the rage is a knife turned against itself. After Phase 15, but before Phase 19, the being is full of phantasy, a continual escape from and yet acknowledgment of all that allures in the world, a continual playing with all that must engulf it. The *primary* is that which serves, the *antithetical* is that which creates.

At Phase 8 is the "Discovery of Strength," its embodiment in sensuality. The imitation that held it to the enforced *Mask*, the norm of the race now a hated convention, has ceased and its own norm has not begun. *Primary* and *antithetical* are equal and fight for mastery; and when this fight is ended through the conviction of weakness and the preparation for rage, the *Mask* becomes once more voluntary. At Phase 22 is the "Breaking of Strength," for here the being makes its last attempt to impose its personality upon the world before the *Mask* becomes enforced once more, character substituted for personality. To these two phases, perhaps to all phases, the being may return up to four times, my instructors say, before it can pass on. It is claimed, however, that four times is the utmost possible. By being is understood that which divides into *Four Faculties,* by individuality the *Will* analysed in relation to itself, by personality the *Will* analysed in relation to the free *Mask,* by character *Will* analysed in relation to the enforced *Mask.* Personality is strongest near Phase 15, individuality near Phase 22 and Phase 8.

In the last phases, Phases 26, 27 and 28, the *Faculties* wear away, grow transparent, and man may see himself as it were arrayed against the supersensual; but of this I shall speak when I consider the *Principles.*

IV

The *Will* looks into a painted picture, the *Creative Mind* looks into a photograph, but both look into something that is the opposite of themselves. The *Creative Mind* contains all the universals in so far as its memory permits their employment, whereas the photograph is heterogeneous. The picture is chosen, the photograph is fated, because by Fate and Necessity—for I need both words—is understood that which comes from without, whereas the *Mask* is predestined, Destiny being that which comes to us from within. We can best explain the heterogeneity of the photograph when we call it the photograph of a crowded street, which the *Creative Mind* when not under the influence of the *Mask* contemplates coldly; while the picture contains but few objects and the contemplating *Will* is impassioned and solitary. When the *Will* predominates the *Mask* or Image is "sensuous"; when *Creative Mind* predominates it is "abstract," when *Mask* predominates it is "idealised," when *Body of Fate* predominates it is "concrete." The automatic script defines "sensuous" in an unexpected way. An object is sensuous if I relate it to myself, "my fire, my chair, my sensation," whereas "a fire, a chair, a sensation," are all concrete or appertain to the *Body of Fate;* while "the fire, the chair, the sensation," because they are looked upon as representative of their kind, are "abstract." To a miser his own money would be "sensuous," another's money "concrete," the money he lacked "idealised," the money economists speak of "abstract."

V

In the Table in section XII the characters of the *Faculties* at all the different phases are described, and the phasal characteristics of a man at any particular phase can be discovered by their means. The descriptions should not be considered as exhaustive but as suggestions to call into imagination the *Four Faculties* at any particular phase.

They were written in the automatic script sometimes two or three, sometimes eight or nine at a time. Even now after years of use I could not re-create them if the Table were lost. I should say they proved a use more prolonged than my own did I not remember that the creators of the script claim a rapidity of thought impossible to our minds. I think of the elaborate pictures one sees between sleeping and waking and often showing powers of design and invention that would have taken hours of an artist's time.

At Phases 11 and 12 occurs what is called the *opening of the tinc- tures,* at Phase 11 the *antithetical* opens, at Phase 12 the *primary.* A cone is for the moment substituted for the wheel, a gyre encircles the cone, ascending or descending, which completes its journey round the cone, while the larger movement completes a phase. The opening means the reflection inward of the *Four Faculties:* all are as it were mirrored in personality, Unity of Being becomes possible. Hitherto we have been part of something else, but now discover everything within our own nature. Sexual love becomes the most important event in life, for the opposite sex is nature chosen and fated. Personality seeks personality. Every emotion begins to be related to every other as musical notes are related. It is as though we touched a musical string that set other strings vibrating. The *antithetical tincture* (*Will* and *Mask*) opens first because the phases signified by odd numbers are *antithetical,* the *primary tincture* at Phase 12 because those signified by even numbers are *primary.* Though all phases from Phase 8 to Phase 22 are *antithetical,* taken as a whole, and all phases from Phase 22 to Phase 8 *primary;* seen by different analysis the individual phases are alternately *antithetical* and *primary.* At Phase 18 the *primary tincture* closes once more, and at Phase 19 the *antithetical.* At Phases 25 and 26 there is a new opening, and at Phases 4 and 5 a new closing, but this time the *tinctures* open not into personality but into its negation. The whole objectively perceived. One may regard the subjective phases as forming a separate wheel, its Phase 8 between Phases 11 and 12 of larger wheel, its Phase 22 be- tween Phases 19 and 20; the objective phases as another separate wheel, its Phase 8 between Phases 25 and 26, its Phase 22 between Phases 4 and 5. This wheel between its Phases 8 and 22 is not sub- jective, from the point of man, but a sharing of or submission to divine personality experienced as spiritual objectivity, whereas its three first and three last phases are physical objectivity. During this spiritual ob- jectivity, or spiritual *primary,* the *Faculties* "wear thin," the *Principles,* which are, when evoked from the point of view of the Faculties, a sphere, shine through. At Phase 15 and Phase 1 occurs what is called the *interchange of the tinctures,* those thoughts, emotions, energies, which were *primary* before Phase 15 or Phase 1 are *antithetical* after, those that were *antithetical* are *primary.* I was told, for instance, that before the historical Phase 15 the *antithetical tincture* of the average

European was dominated by reason and desire, the *primary* by race and emotion, and that after Phase 15 this was reversed, his subjective nature had been passionate and logical but was now enthusiastic and sentimental. I have made little use of this interchange in my account of the twenty-eight incarnations because when I wrote it I did not understand the relation between the change and Unity of Being. Every phase is in itself a wheel; the individual soul is awakened by a violent oscillation (one thinks of Verlaine oscillating between the church and the brothel) until it sinks in on that Whole where the contraries are united, the antinomies resolved.

ERNEST FENOLLOSA

The Chinese Written Character as a Medium for Poetry

One of the most noteworthy characteristics of modern poetics is the serious introduction of Oriental techniques into Western literature. As a philologist and literary theorist, Fenollosa suggested a study of Chinese as a means of developing new methods for the European and American poet. The Chinese language is fundamentally pictorial in the construction of words, whereas the European alphabetical languages tend toward the creation of abstractions. In Chinese an idea is acted out, as it were, in a highly sophisticated form of picture-writing usually called the ideogram. Fenollosa's discussions of the ideogram influenced Ezra Pound and other contemporary poets to attempt a new poetic method in which clusters of images and ideas (similar to a Chinese written character) would take the place of the old logic and sequence of European poetics.

The note at the beginning of this essay gives the background of its authorship and publication.

[*This essay was practically finished by the late Ernest Fenollosa; I have done little more than remove a few repetitions and shape a few sentences.*

We have here not a bare philological discussion, but a study of the fundamentals of all æsthetics. In his search through unknown art Fenollosa, coming upon unknown motives and principles unrecognized in the West, was already led into many modes of thought since fruitful in "new" western painting and poetry. He was a forerunner without knowing it and without being known as such.

*He discerned principles of writing which he had scarcely time to put into practice. In Japan he restored, or greatly helped to restore, a respect for the native art. In America and Europe he cannot be looked upon as a mere searcher after exotics. His mind was constantly filled with parallels and comparisons between eastern and western art. To him the exotic was always a means of fructification. He looked to an American renaissance. The vitality of his outlook can be judged from the fact that although this essay was written some time before his death in 1908 I have not had to change the allusions to western conditions. The later movements in art have corroborated his theories.—*Ezra Pound.]

*T*his twentieth century not only turns a new page in the book of the world, but opens another and a startling chapter. Vistas of strange futures unfold for man, of world-embracing cultures half weaned from Europe, of hitherto undreamed responsibilities for nations and races.

The Chinese problem alone is so vast that no nation can′ afford to ignore it. We in America, especially, must face it across the Pacific, and master it or it will master us. And the only way to master it is to strive with patient sympathy to understand the best, the most hopeful and the most human elements in it.

It is unfortunate that England and America have so long ignored or mistaken the deeper problems of Oriental culture. We have misconceived the Chinese for a materialistic people, for a debased and worn-out race. We have belittled the Japanese as a nation of copyists. We have stupidly assumed that Chinese history affords no glimpse of change in social evolution, no salient epoch of moral and spiritual crisis. We have denied the essential humanity of these peoples; and we have toyed with their ideals as if they were no better than comic songs in an "opera bouffe."

The duty that faces us is not to batter down their forts or to exploit their markets, but to study and to come to sympathize with their humanity and their generous aspirations. Their type of cultivation has been high. Their harvest of recorded experience doubles our own. The Chinese have been idealists, and experimenters in the making of great principles; their history opens a world of lofty aim and achievement, parallel to that of the ancient Mediterranean peoples. We need their best ideals to supplement our own—ideals enshrined in their art, in their literature and in the tragedies of their lives.

We have already seen proof of the vitality and practical value of oriental painting for ourselves and as a key to the eastern soul. It may be worth while to approach their literature, the intensest part of it, their poetry, even in an imperfect manner.

I feel that I should perhaps apologize* for presuming to follow that series of brilliant scholars, Davis, Legge, St. Denys and Giles, who have treated the subject of Chinese poetry with a wealth of erudition to which

---

* [The apology was unnecessary, but Professor Fenollosa saw fit to make it, and I therefore transcribe his words.—E. P.]

I can proffer no claim. It is not as a professional linguist nor as a sinologue that I humbly put forward what I have to say. As an enthusiastic student of beauty in Oriental culture, having spent a large portion of my years in close relation with Orientals, I could not but breathe in something of the poetry incarnated in their lives.

I have been for the most part moved to my temerity by personal considerations. An unfortunate belief has spread both in England and in America that Chinese and Japanese poetry are hardly more than an amusement, trivial, childish, and not to be reckoned in the world's serious literary performance. I have heard well-known sinologues state that, save for the purposes of professional linguistic scholarship, these branches of poetry are fields too barren to repay the toil necessary for their cultivation.

Now my own impression has been so radically and diametrically opposed to such a conclusion, that a sheer enthusiasm of generosity has driven me to wish to share with other Occidentals my newly discovered joy. Either I am pleasingly self-deceived in my positive delight, or else there must be some lack of æsthetic sympathy and of poetic feeling in the accepted methods of presenting the poetry of China. I submit my causes of joy.

Failure or success in presenting any alien poetry in English must depend largely upon poetic workmanship in the chosen medium. It was perhaps too much to expect that aged scholars who had spent their youth in gladiatorial combats with the refractory Chinese characters should succeed also as poets. Even Greek verse might have fared equally ill had its purveyors been perforce content with provincial standards of English rhyming. Sinologues should remember that the purpose of poetical translation is the poetry, not the verbal definitions in dictionaries.

One modest merit I may, perhaps, claim for my work: it represents for the first time a Japanese school of study in Chinese culture. Hitherto Europeans have been somewhat at the mercy of contemporary Chinese scholarship. Several centuries ago China lost much of her creative self, and of her insight into the causes of her own life, but her original spirit still lives, grows, interprets, transferred to Japan in all its original freshness. The Japanese to-day represent a stage of culture roughly corresponding to that of China under the Sung dynasty. I have been fortunate in studying for many years as a private pupil under Professor Kainan Mori, who is probably the greatest living authority on Chinese poetry. He has recently been called to a chair in the Imperial University of Tokio.

My subject is poetry, not language, yet the roots of poetry are in language. In the study of a language so alien in form to ours as is Chinese in its written character, it is necessary to inquire how those universal elements of form which constitute poetics can derive appropriate nutriment.

In what sense can verse, written in terms of visible hieroglyphics, be reckoned true poetry? It might seem that poetry, which like music is a *time art,* weaving its unities out of successive impressions of sound, could with difficulty assimilate a verbal medium consisting largely of semi-pictorial appeals to the eye.

Contrast, for example, Gray's line:

The curfew tolls the knell of parting day

with the Chinese line:

Moon   Rays   Like   Pure   Snow

Moon rays like pure snow.

Unless the sound of the latter be given, what have they in common? It is not enough to adduce that each contains a certain body of prosaic meaning; for the question is, how can the Chinese line imply, *as form,* the very element that distinguishes poetry from prose?

On second glance, it is seen that the Chinese words, though visible, occur in just as necessary an order as the phonetic symbols of Gray. All that poetic form requires is a regular and flexible sequence, as plastic as thought itself. The characters may be seen and read, silently by the eye, one after the other:

Moon rays like pure snow.

Perhaps we do not always sufficiently consider that thought is successive, not through some accident or weakness of our subjective operations but because the operations of nature are successive. The transferences of force from agent to object which constitute natural phenomena, occupy time. Therefore, a reproduction of them in imagination requires the same temporal order.*

Suppose that we look out of a window and watch a man. Suddenly he turns his head and actively fixes his attention upon something. We look ourselves and see that his vision has been focussed upon a horse. We saw, first, the man before he acted; second, while he acted; third, the object toward which his action was directed. In speech we split up the rapid continuity of this action and of its picture into its three essential parts or joints in the right order, and say:

Man sees horse.

It is clear that these three joints, or words, are only three phonetic symbols, which stand for the three terms of a natural process. But we

---

* [Style, that is to say, limpidity, as opposed to rhetoric.—E. P.]

could quite as easily denote these three stages of our thought by symbols equally arbitrary, *which had no basis in sound;* for example, by three Chinese characters:

Man   Sees   Horse

If we all knew *what division* of this mental horse-picture each of these signs stood for, we could communicate continuous thought to one another as easily by drawing them as by speaking words. We habitually employ the visible language of gesture in much this same manner.

But Chinese notation is something much more than arbitrary symbols. It is based upon a vivid shorthand picture of the operations of nature. In the algebraic figure and in the spoken word there is no natural connection between thing and sign: all depends upon sheer convention. But the Chinese method follows natural suggestion. First stands the man on his two legs. Second, his eye moves through space: a bold figure represented by running legs under an eye, a modified picture of an eye, a modified picture of running legs but unforgettable once you have seen it. Third stands the horse on his four legs.

The thought picture is not only called up by these signs as well as by words but far more vividly and concretely. Legs belong to all three characters: they are *alive.* The group holds something of the quality of a continuous moving picture.

The untruth of a painting or a photograph is that, in spite of its concreteness, it drops the element of natural succession.

Contrast the Laocoon statue with Browning's lines:

> "I sprang to the saddle, and Jorris, and he
>
> .   .   .   .   .   .
>
> And into the midnight we galloped abreast."

One superiority of verbal poetry as an art rests in its getting back to the fundamental reality of *time.* Chinese poetry has the unique advantage of combining both elements. It speaks at once with the vividness of painting, and with the mobility of sounds. It is, in some sense, more objective than either, more dramatic. In reading Chinese we do not seem to be juggling mental counters, but to be watching *things* work out their own fate.

Leaving for a moment the form of the sentence, let us look more closely at this quality of vividness in the structure of detached Chinese words. The earlier forms of these characters were pictorial, and their hold upon the imagination is little shaken, even in later conventional modifications. It is not so well known, perhaps, that the great number of these ideographic roots carry in them a *verbal idea of action*. It might be thought that a picture is naturally the picture of a *thing*, and that therefore the root ideas of Chinese are what grammar calls nouns.

But examination shows that a large number of the primitive Chinese characters, even the so-called radicals, are shorthand pictures of actions or processes.

For example, the ideograph meaning "to speak" is a mouth with two words and a flame coming out of it. The sign meaning "to grow up with difficulty" is grass with a twisted root. But this concrete *verb* quality, both in nature and in the Chinese signs, becomes far more striking and poetic when we pass from such simple, original pictures to compounds. In this process of compounding, two things added together do not produce a third thing but suggest some fundamental relation between them. For example, the ideograph for a "mess-mate" is a man and a fire.

A true noun, an isolated thing, does not exist in nature. Things are only the terminal points, or rather the meeting points of actions, cross-sections cut through actions, snap-shots. Neither can a pure verb, an abstract motion, be possible in nature. The eye sees noun and verb as one: things in motion, motion in things, and so the Chinese conception tends to represent them.

The sun underlying the bursting forth of plants = spring.

The sun sign tangled in the branches of the tree sign = east.

"Rice-field" plus "struggle" = male.

"Boat" plus "water," boat-water, a ripple.

Let us return to the form of the sentence and see what power it adds to the verbal units from which it builds. I wonder how many people have asked themselves why the sentence form exists at all, why it seems so universally necessary *in all languages?* Why *must* all possess it, and what is the normal type of it? If it be so universal it ought to correspond to some primary law of nature.

I fancy the professional grammarians have given but a lame response to this inquiry. Their definitions fall into two types: one, that a sentence expresses a "complete thought"; the other, that in it we bring about a union of subject and predicate.

The former has the advantage of trying for some natural objective standard, since it is evident that a thought can not be the test of its own completeness. But in nature there is *no* completeness. On the one hand, practical completeness may be expressed by a mere interjection, as "Hi! there!", or "Scat!", or even by shaking one's fist. No sentence is needed to make one's meaning more clear. On the other hand, no full sentence really completes a thought. The man who sees and the horse which is seen will not stand still. The man was planning a ride before he looked. The horse kicked when the man tried to catch him. The truth is that acts are successive, even continuous; one causes or passes into another. And though we may string never so many clauses into a single compound sentence, motion leaks everywhere, like electricity from an exposed wire. All processes in nature are inter-related; and thus there could be no complete sentence (according to this definition) save one which it would take all time to pronounce.

In the second definition of the sentence, as "uniting a subject and a predicate," the grammarian falls back on pure subjectivity. We do it all; it is a little private juggling between our right and left hands. The subject is that about which I am going to talk; the predicate is that which I am going to say about it. The sentence according to this definition is not an attribute of nature but an accident of man as a conversational animal.

If it were really so, then there could be no possible test of the truth of a sentence. Falsehood would be as specious as verity. Speech would carry no conviction.

Of course this view of the grammarians springs from the discredited, or rather the useless, logic of the middle ages. According to this logic, thought deals with abstractions, concepts drawn out of things by a sifting process. These logicians never inquired how the "qualities" which they pulled out of things came to be there. The truth of all their little checker-board juggling depended upon the natural order by which these powers or properties or qualities were folded in concrete things, yet they despised the "thing" as a mere "particular," or pawn. It was as if Botany should reason from the leaf-patterns woven into our table-cloths. Valid scientific thought consists in following as closely as may be the actual and entangled lines of forces as they pulse through things. Thought deals with no bloodless concepts but watches *things move* under its microscope.

The sentence form was forced upon primitive men by nature itself. It was not we who made it; it was a reflection of the temporal order in causation. All truth has to be expressed in sentences because all truth is the *transference of power*. The type of sentence in nature is a flash of lightning. It passes between two terms, a cloud and the earth. No unit of natural process can be less than this. All natural processes are, in their units, as much as this. Light, heat, gravity, chemical affinity, human will have this in common, that they redistribute force. Their unit of process can be represented as:

term	transference	term
from	of	to
which	force	which

If we regard this transference as the conscious or unconscious act of an agent we can translate the diagram into:

agent	act	object

In this the act is the very substance of the fact denoted. The agent and the object are only limiting terms.

It seems to me that the normal and typical sentence in English as well as in Chinese expresses just this unit of natural process. It consists of three necessary words; the first denoting the agent or subject from which the act starts; the second embodying the very stroke of the act; the third pointing to the object, the receiver of the impact. Thus:

Farmer   pounds   rice.

The form of the Chinese transitive sentence, and of the English (omitting particles) exactly corresponds to this universal form of action in nature. This brings language close to *things,* and in its strong reliance upon verbs it erects all speech into a kind of dramatic poetry.

A different sentence order is frequent in inflected languages like Latin, German or Japanese. This is because they are inflected, i.e., they have little tags and word-endings, or labels to show which is the agent, the object, etc. In uninflected languages, like English and Chinese, there is nothing but the order of the words to distinguish their functions. And this order would be no sufficient indication, were it not the *natural order*—that is, the order of cause and effect.

It is true that there are, in language, intransitive and passive forms, sentences built out of the verb "to be," and, finally, negative forms. To grammarians and logicians these have seemed more primitive than the transitive, or at least exceptions to the transitive. I had long suspected that these apparently exceptional forms had grown from the transitive or worn away from it by alteration or modification. This view is confirmed by Chinese examples, wherein it is still possible to watch the transformation going on.

The intransitive form derives from the transitive by dropping a generalized, customary, reflexive or cognate object. "He runs (a race)." "The sky reddens (itself)." "We breathe (air)." Thus we get weak and incomplete sentences which suspend the picture and lead us to think of some verbs as denoting states rather than acts. Outside grammar the word "state" would hardly be recognized as scientific. Who can doubt that when we say, "The wall shines," we mean that it actively reflects light to our eye?

The beauty of Chinese verbs is that they are all transitive or intransitive at pleasure. There is no such thing as a naturally intransitive verb. The passive form is evidently a correlative sentence, which turns about and makes the object into a subject. That the object is not in itself passive, but contributes some positive force of its own to the action, is in harmony both with scientific law and with ordinary experience. The English passive voice with "is" seemed at first an obstacle to this hypothesis, but one suspected that the true form was a generalized transitive verb meaning something like "receive," which had degenerated into an auxiliary. It was a delight to find this the case in Chinese.

In nature there are no negations, no possible transfers of negative force. The presence of negative sentences in language would seem to corroborate the logicians' view that assertion is an arbitrary subjective act. *We* can assert a negation, though nature can not. But here again science comes to our aid against the logician: all apparently negative or disruptive movements bring into play other positive forces. It requires great effort to annihilate. Therefore we should suspect that, if we could follow back the history of all negative particles, we should find that they also are sprung from transitive verbs. It is too late to demonstrate such derivations in the Aryan languages, the clue has been lost, but in Chinese we can still watch positive verbal conceptions passing over into so-called negatives. Thus in Chinese the sign meaning "to be lost in the forest" relates to a state of non-existence. English "not" = the Sanskrit *na*, which may come from the root *na*, to be lost, to perish.

Lastly comes the infinitive which substitutes for a specific colored verb the universal copula "is," followed by a noun or an adjective. We do not say a tree "greens itself," but "the tree is green"; not that "monkeys bring forth live young," but that "the monkey is a mammal." This is an ultimate weakness of language. It has come from generalizing all intransitive words into one. As "live," "see," "walk," "breathe," are generalized into states by dropping their objects, so these weak verbs are in turn reduced to the abstractest state of all, namely, bare existence.

There is in reality no such verb as a pure copula, no such original conception, our very word *exist* means "to stand forth," to show oneself by a definite act. "Is" comes from the Aryan root *as*, to breathe. "Be" is from *bhu*, to grow.

In Chinese the chief verb for "is" not only means actively "to have," but shows by its derivation that it expresses something even more concrete, namely, "to snatch from the moon with the hand." Here the baldest symbol of prosaic analysis is transformed by magic into a splendid flash of concrete poetry.

I shall not have entered vainly into this long analysis of the sentence if I have succeeded in showing how poetical is the Chinese form and how close to nature. In translating Chinese, verse especially, we must hold as closely as possible to the concrete force of the original, eschewing adjectives, nouns and intransitive forms wherever we can, and seeking instead strong and individual verbs.

Lastly we notice that the likeness of form between Chinese and English sentences renders translation from one to the other exceptionally easy. The genius of the two is much the same. Frequently it is possible by omitting English particles to make a literal word-for-word translation which will be not only intelligible in English, but even the strongest and most poetical English. Here, however, one must follow closely what is said, not merely what is abstractly meant.

Let us go back from the Chinese sentence to the individual written word. How are such words to be classified? Are some of them nouns by nature, some verbs and some adjectives? Are there pronouns and prepositions and conjunctions in Chinese as in good Christian languages?

One is led to suspect from an analysis of the Aryan languages that such differences are not natural, and that they have been unfortunately invented by grammarians to confuse the simple poetic outlook on life. All nations have written their strongest and most vivid literature before they invented a grammar. Moreover, all Aryan etymology points back to roots which are the equivalents of simple Sanskrit verbs, such as we find tabulated at the back of our Skeat. Nature herself has no grammar.* Fancy picking up a man and telling him that he is a noun, a dead thing rather than a bundle of functions! A "part of speech" is only *what it does.* Frequently our lines of cleavage fail, one part of speech acts for another. They *act for* one another because they were originally one and the same.

Few of us realize that in our own language these very differences once grew up in living articulation; that they still retain life. It is only when the difficulty of placing some odd term arises or when we are forced to translate into some very different language, that we attain for a moment the inner heat of thought, a heat which melts down the parts of speech to recast them at will.

One of the most interesting facts about the Chinese language is that in it we can see, not only the forms of sentences, but literally the parts of speech growing up, budding forth one from another. Like nature, the Chinese words are alive and plastic, because *thing* and *action* are not formally separated. The Chinese language naturally knows no grammar. It is only lately that foreigners, European and Japanese, have begun to torture this vital speech by forcing it to fit the bed of their definitions. We import into our reading of Chinese all the weakness of our own formalisms. This is especially sad in poetry, because the one necessity, even in our own poetry, is to keep words as flexible as possible, as full of the sap of nature.

Let us go further with our example. In English we call "to shine" a *verb in the infinitive,* because it gives the abstract meaning of the verb without conditions. If we want a corresponding adjective we take a different word, "bright." If we need a noun we say "luminosity," which is abstract, being derived from an adjective.† To get a tolerably concrete noun, we have to leave behind the verb and adjective roots, and light upon a thing arbitrarily cut off from its power of action, say "the sun" or "the moon." Of course there is nothing in nature so cut off, and therefore this nounizing is itself an abstraction. Even if we did have a common word underlying at once the verb "shine," the adjective "bright" and the noun "sun," we should probably call it an "infinitive

---

* [Even Latin, living Latin had not the network of rules they foist upon unfortunate school-children. These are borrowed sometimes from Greek grammarians, even as I have seen English grammars borrowing oblique cases from Latin grammars. Sometimes they sprang from the grammatizing or categorizing passion of pedants. Living Latin had only the feel of the cases: the ablative and dative emotion.—E. P.]

† [A good writer would use "shine" (i.e., to shine), shining, and "the shine" or "sheen," possibly thinking of the German *"schöne"* and *"Schönheit";* but this does not invalidate Prof. Fenollosa's next contention.—E. P.]

of the infinitive." According to our ideas, it should be something extremely abstract, too intangible for use.

The Chinese have one word, *ming* or *mei*. Its ideograph is the sign of the sun together with the sign of the moon. It serves as verb, noun, adjective. Thus you write literally, "the sun and moon of the cup" for "the cup's brightness." Placed as a verb, you write "the cup sun-and-moons," actually "cup sun-and-moon," or in a weakened thought, "is like sun," i.e., shines. "Sun-and-moon cup" is naturally a bright cup. There is no possible confusion of the real meaning, though a stupid scholar may spend a week trying to decide what "part of speech" he should use in translating a very simple and direct thought from Chinese to English.

The fact is that almost every written Chinese word is properly just such an underlying word, and yet it is *not* abstract. It is not exclusive of parts of speech, but comprehensive; not something which is neither a noun, verb, or adjective, but something which is all of them at once and at all times. Usage may incline the full meaning now a little more to one side, now to another, according to the point of view, but through all cases the poet is free to deal with it richly and concretely, as does nature.

In the derivation of nouns from verbs, the Chinese language is forestalled by the Aryan. Almost all the Sanskrit roots, which seem to underlie European languages, are primitive verbs, which express characteristic actions of visible nature. The verb must be the primary fact of nature, since motion and change are all that we can recognize in her. In the primitive transitive sentence, such as "Farmer pounds rice," the agent and the object are nouns only in so far as they limit a unit of action. "Farmer" and "rice" are mere hard terms which define the extremes of the pounding. But in themselves, apart from this sentence-function, they are naturally verbs. The farmer is one who tills the ground, and the rice is a plant which grows in a special way. This is indicated in the Chinese characters. And this probably exemplifies the ordinary derivation of nouns from verbs. In all languages, Chinese included, a noun is originally "that which does something," that which performs the verbal action. Thus the moon comes from the root *ma,* and means "the measurer." The sun means that which begets.

The derivation of adjectives from the verb need hardly be exemplified. Even with us, to-day, we can still watch participles passing over into adjectives. In Japanese the adjective is frankly part of the inflection of the verb, a special mood, so that every verb is also an adjective. This brings us close to nature, because everywhere the quality is only a power of action regarded as having an abstract inherence. Green is only a certain rapidity of vibration, hardness a degree of tenseness in cohering. In Chinese the adjective always retains a substratum of verbal meaning. We should try to render this in translation, not be content with some bloodless adjectival abstraction plus "is."

Still more interesting are the Chinese "prepositions," they are often post-positions. Prepositions are so important, so pivotal in European speech only because we have weakly yielded up the force of our intransitive verbs. We have to add small supernumerary words to bring back the original power. We still say "I see a horse," but with the weak verb "look," we have to add the directive particle "at" before we can restore the natural transitiveness.*

Prepositions represent a few simple ways in which incomplete verbs complete themselves. Pointing toward nouns as a limit they bring force to bear upon them. That is to say, they are naturally verbs, of generalized or condensed use. In Aryan languages it is often difficult to trace the verbal origins of simple prepositions. Only in *"off"* do we see a fragment of the thought "to throw off." In Chinese the preposition is frankly a verb, specially used in a generalized sense. These verbs are often used in their specially verbal sense, and it greatly weakens an English translation if they are systematically rendered by colorless prepositions.

Thus in Chinese: By = to cause; to = to fall toward; in = to remain, to dwell; from = to follow; and so on.

Conjunctions are similarly derivative, they usually serve to mediate actions between verbs, and therefore they are necessarily themselves actions. Thus in Chinese: Because = to use; and = to be included under one; another form of "and" = to be parallel; or = to partake; if = to let one do, to permit. The same is true of a host of other particles, no longer traceable in the Aryan tongues.

Pronouns appear a thorn in our evolution theory, since they have been taken as unanalyzable expressions of personality. In Chinese even they yield up their striking secrets of verbal metaphor. They are a constant source of weakness if colorlessly translated. Take, for example, the five forms of "I." There is the sign of a "spear in the hand" = a very emphatic I; five and a mouth = a weak and defensive I, holding off a crowd by speaking; to conceal = a selfish and private I; self (the cocoon sign) and a mouth = an egoistic I, one who takes pleasure in his own speaking; the self presented is used only when one is speaking to one's self.

I trust that this digression concerning parts of speech may have justified itself. It proves, first, the enormous interest of the Chinese language in throwing light upon our forgotten mental processes, and thus furnishes a new chapter in the philosophy of language. Secondly, it is indispensable for understanding the poetical raw material which the Chinese language affords. Poetry differs from prose in the concrete colors of its diction. It is not enough for it to furnish a meaning to philosophers. It must appeal to emotions with the charm of direct impression, flashing through regions where the intellect can only grope.† Poetry must render what is said,

---

* [This is a bad example. We can say "I look a fool," "look," transitive, now means resemble. The main contention is however correct. We tend to abandon specific words like *resemble* and substitute, for them, vague verbs with prepositional directors, or riders.—E. P.]

† [*Cf.* principle of Primary apparition, "Spirit of Romance."—E. P.]

not what is merely meant. Abstract meaning gives little vividness, and fullness of imagination gives all. Chinese poetry demands that we abandon our narrow grammatical categories, that we follow the original text with a wealth of concrete verbs.

But this is only the beginning of the matter. So far we have exhibited the Chinese characters and the Chinese sentence chiefly as vivid short-hand pictures of actions and processes in nature. These embody true poetry as far as they go. Such actions are *seen*, but Chinese would be a poor language and Chinese poetry but a narrow art, could they not go on to represent also what is unseen. The best poetry deals not only with natural images but with lofty thoughts, spiritual suggestions and obscure relations. The greater part of natural truth is hidden in processes too minute for vision and in harmonies too large, in vibrations, cohesions and in affinities. The Chinese compass these also, and with great power and beauty.

You will ask, how could the Chinese have built up a great intellectual fabric from mere picture writing? To the ordinary western mind, which believes that thought is concerned with logical categories and which rather condemns the faculty of direct imagination, this feat seems quite impossible. Yet the Chinese language with its peculiar materials has passed over from the seen to the unseen by exactly the same process which all ancient races employed. This process is metaphor, the use of material images to suggest immaterial relations.*

The whole delicate substance of speech is built upon substrata of metaphor. Abstract terms, pressed by etymology, reveal their ancient roots still embedded in direct action. But the primitive metaphors do not spring from arbitrary subjective processes. They are possible only because they follow objective lines of relations in nature herself. Relations are more real and more important than the things which they relate. The forces which produce the branch-angles of an oak lay potent in the acorn. Similar lines of resistance, half curbing the out-pressing vitalities, govern the branching of rivers and of nations. Thus a nerve, a wire, a roadway, and a clearing-house are only varying channels which communication forces for itself. This is more than analogy, it is identity of structure. Nature furnishes her own clues. Had the world not been full of homologies, sympathies, and identities, thought would have been starved and language chained to the obvious. There would have been no bridge whereby to cross from the minor truth of the seen to the major truth of the unseen. Not more than a few hundred roots out of our large vocabularies could have dealt directly with physical processes. These we can fairly well identify in primitive Sanskrit. They are, almost without exception, vivid verbs. The wealth of European speech grew, following slowly the intricate maze of nature's suggestions and affinities. Metaphor was piled upon metaphor in quasi-geological strata.

Metaphor, the revealer of nature, is the very substance of poetry. The

---

* [Compare Aristotle's *Poetics*.—E. P.]

known interprets the obscure, the universe is alive with myth. The beauty and freedom of the observed world furnish a model, and life is pregnant with art. It is a mistake to suppose, with some philosophers of æsthetics, that art and poetry aim to deal with the general and the abstract. This misconception has been foisted upon us by mediæval logic. Art and poetry deal with the concrete of nature, not with rows of separate "particulars," for such rows do not exist. Poetry is finer than prose because it gives us more concrete truth in the same compass of words. Metaphor, its chief device, is at once the substance of nature and of language. Poetry only does consciously* what the primitive races did unconsciously. The chief work of literary men in dealing with language, and of poets especially, lies in feeling back along the ancient lines of advance.† He must do this so that he may keep his words enriched by all their subtle undertones of meaning. The original metaphors stand as a kind of luminous background, giving color and vitality, forcing them closer to the concreteness of natural processes. Shakespeare everywhere teems with examples. For these reasons poetry was the earliest of the world arts; poetry, language and the care of myth grew up together.

I have alleged all this because it enables me to show clearly why I believe that the Chinese written language has not only absorbed the poetic substance of nature and built with it a second world of metaphor, but has, through its very pictorial visibility, been able to retain its original creative poetry with far more vigor and vividness than any phonetic tongue. Let us first see how near it is to the heart of nature in its metaphors. We can watch it passing from the seen to the unseen, as we saw it passing from verb to pronoun. It retains the primitive sap, it is not cut and dried like a walking-stick. We have been told that these people are cold, practical, mechanical, literal, and without a trace of imaginative genius. That is nonsense.

Our ancestors built the accumulations of metaphor into structures of language and into systems of thought. Languages to-day are thin and cold because we think less and less into them. We are forced, for the sake of quickness and sharpness, to file down each word to its narrowest edge of meaning. Nature would seem to have become less like a paradise and more and more like a factory. We are content to accept the vulgar misuse of the moment. A late stage of decay is arrested and embalmed in the dictionary. Only scholars and poets feel painfully back along the thread of our etymologies and piece together our diction, as best they may, from forgotten fragments. This anemia of modern speech is only too well encouraged by the feeble cohesive force of our phonetic symbols.

---

* [Vide also an article on "Vorticism" in the *Fortnightly Review* for September, 1914. "The language of exploration" now in my "Gaudier-Brzeska."—E. P.]

† [I would submit in all humility that this applies in the rendering of ancient texts. The poet in dealing with his own time, must also see to it that language does not petrify on his hands. He must prepare for new advances along the lines of true metaphor that is interpretative metaphor, or image, as diametrically opposed to untrue, or ornamental metaphor.—E. P.]

There is little or nothing in a phonetic word to exhibit the embryonic stages of its growth. It does not bear its metaphor on its face. We forget that personality once meant, not the soul, but the soul's mask. This is the sort of thing one can not possibly forget in using the Chinese symbols.

In this Chinese shows its advantage. Its etymology is constantly visible. It retains the creative impulse and process, visible and at work. After thousands of years the lines of metaphoric advance are still shown, and in many cases actually retained in the meaning. Thus a word, instead of growing gradually poorer and poorer as with us, becomes richer and still more rich from age to age, almost consciously luminous. Its uses in national philosophy and history, in biography and in poetry, throw about it a nimbus of meanings. These centre about the graphic symbol. The memory can hold them and use them. The very soil of Chinese life seems entangled in the roots of its speech. The manifold illustrations which crowd its annals of personal experience, the lines of tendency which converge upon a tragic climax, moral character as the very core of the principle—all these are flashed at once on the mind as reinforcing values with an accumulation of meaning which a phonetic language can hardly hope to attain. Their ideographs are like blood-stained battle flags to an old campaigner. With us, the poet is the only one for whom the accumulated treasures of the race-words are real and active. Poetic language is always vibrant with fold on fold of overtones, and with natural affinities, but in Chinese the visibility of the metaphor tends to raise this quality to its intensest power.

I have mentioned the tyranny of mediæval logic. According to this European logic thought is a kind of brickyard. It is baked into little hard units or concepts. These are piled in rows according to size and then labeled with words for future use. This use consists in picking out a few bricks, each by its convenient label, and sticking them together into a sort of wall called a sentence by the use either of white mortar for the positive copula "is," or of black mortar for the negative copula "is not." In this way we produce such admirable propositions as "A ringtailed baboon is not a constitutional assembly."

Let us consider a row of cherry trees. From each of these in turn we proceed to take an "abstract," as the phrase is, a certain common lump of qualities which we may express together by the name cherry or cherryness. Next we place in a second table several such characteristic concepts: cherry, rose, sunset, iron-rust, flamingo. From these we abstract some further common quality, dilutation or mediocrity, and label it "red" or "redness." It is evident that this process of abstraction may be carried on indefinitely and with all sorts of material. We may go on forever building pyramids of attenuated concept until we reach the apex "being."

But we have done enough to illustrate the characteristic process. At the base of the pyramid lie *things*, but stunned, as it were. They can never know themselves for things until they pass up and down among the layers of the pyramids. The way of passing up and down the pyramid may be exemplified as follows: We take a concept of lower attenuation, such as "cherry"; we see that it is contained under one higher, such as "redness." Then we are permitted to say in sentence form, "Cherryness is contained under redness," or for short, "(the) cherry is red." If, on the other hand, we do not find our chosen subject under a given predicate we use the black copula and say, for example, "(The) cherry is not liquid."

From this point we might go on to the theory of the syllogism, but we refrain. It is enough to note that the practised logician finds it convenient to store his mind with long lists of nouns and adjectives, for these are naturally the names of classes. Most text-books on language begin with such lists. The study of verbs is meagre, for in such a system there is only one real working verb, to-wit, the quasi-verb "is." All other verbs can be transformed into participles and gerunds. For example, "to run" practically becomes a case of "running." Instead of thinking directly, "The man runs," our logician makes two subjective equations, namely: The individual in question is contained under the class "man"; and the class "man" is contained under the class of "running things."

The sheer loss and weakness of this method is apparent and flagrant. Even in its own sphere it can not think half of what it wants to think. It has no way of bringing together any two concepts which do not happen to stand one under the other and in the same pyramid. It is impossible to represent change in this system or any kind of growth. This is probably why the conception of evolution came so late in Europe. *It could not make way until it was prepared to destroy the inveterate logic of classification.*

Far worse than this, such logic can not deal with any kind of interaction or with any multiplicity of function. According to it, the function of my muscles is as isolated from the function of my nerves, as from an earthquake in the moon. For it the poor neglected things at the bases of the pyramids are only so many particulars or pawns.

Science fought till she got at the things. All her work has been done from the base of the pyramids, not from the apex. She has discovered how functions cohere in things. She expresses her results in grouped sentences which embody no nouns or adjectives but verbs of special character. The true formula for thought is: The cherry tree is all that it does. Its correlated verbs compose it. At bottom these verbs are transitive. Such verbs may be almost infinite in number.

In diction and in grammatical form science is utterly opposed to logic. Primitive men who created language agreed with science and not with logic. Logic has abused the language which they left to her mercy. Poetry agrees with science and not with logic.

The moment we use the copula, the moment we express subjective inclusions, poetry evaporates. The more concretely and vividly we express the interactions of things the better the poetry. We need in poetry thousands of active words, each doing its utmost to show forth the motive and vital forces. We can not exhibit the wealth of nature by mere summation, by the piling of sentences. Poetic thought works by suggestion, crowding maximum meaning into the single phrase pregnant, charged, and luminous from within.

In Chinese character each work accumulated this sort of energy in itself.

Should we pass formally to the study of Chinese poetry, we should warn ourselves against logicianized pitfalls. We should beware of modern narrow utilitarian meanings ascribed to the words in commercial dictionaries. We should try to preserve the metaphoric overtones. We should beware of English grammar, its hard parts of speech, and its lazy satisfaction with nouns and adjectives. We should seek and at least bear in mind the verbal undertone of each noun. We should avoid "is" and bring in a wealth of neglected English verbs. Most of the existing translations violate all of these rules.*

The development of the normal transitive sentence rests upon the fact that one action in nature promotes another; thus the agent and the object are secretly verbs. For example, our sentence, "Reading promotes writing," would be expressed in Chinese by three full verbs. Such a form is the equivalent of three expanded clauses and can be drawn out into adjectival, participial, infinitive, relative or conditional members. One of many possible examples is, "If one reads it teaches him how to write." Another is, "One who reads becomes one who writes." But in the first condensed form a Chinese would write, "Read promote write." The dominance of the verb and its power to obliterate all other parts of speech give us the model of terse fine style.

I have seldom seen our rhetoricians dwell on the fact that the great strength of our language lies in its splendid array of transitive verbs, drawn both from Anglo-Saxon and from Latin sources. These give us the most individual characterizations of force. Their power lies in their recognition of nature as a vast storehouse of forces. We do not say in English that things seem, or appear, or eventuate, or even that they are; but that they *do*. Will is the foundation of our speech.† We catch the Demiurge in the act. I had to discover for myself why Shakespeare's English was so immeasurably superior to all others. I found that it was his persistent, natural, and magnificent use of hundreds of transitive verbs. Rarely will you find an "is" in his sentences. "Is" weakly lends itself to the uses of our rhythm, in the unaccented syllables; yet he sternly discards it. A study of Shakespeare's verbs should underlie all exercises in style.

We find in poetical Chinese a wealth of transitive verbs, in some way

---

* [These precautions should be broadly conceived. It is not so much their letter, as the underlying feeling of objectification and activity, that matters.—E. P.]

† [Compare Dante's definition of "rectitudo" as the direction of the will, probably taken from Aquinas.—E. P.]

greater even than in the English of Shakespeare. This springs from their power of combining several pictorial elements in a single character. We have in English no verb for what two things, say the sun and moon, both do together. Prefixes and affixes merely direct and qualify. In Chinese the verb can be more minutely qualified. We find a hundred variants clustering about a single idea. Thus "to sail a boat for purposes of pleasure" would be an entirely different verb from "to sail for purposes of commerce." Dozens of Chinese verbs express various shades of grieving, yet in English translations they are usually reduced to one mediocrity. Many of them can be expressed only by periphrasis, but what right has the translator to neglect the overtones? There are subtle shadings. We should strain our resources in English.

It is true that the pictorial clue of many Chinese ideographs can not now be traced, and even Chinese lexicographers admit that combinations frequently contribute only a phonetic value. But I find it incredible that any such minute subdivision of the idea could have ever existed alone as abstract sound without the concrete character. It contradicts the law of evolution. Complex ideas arise only gradually, as the power of holding them together arises. The paucity of Chinese sound could not so hold them. Neither is it conceivable that the whole list was made at once, as commercial codes of cipher are compiled. Therefore we must believe that the phonetic theory is in large part unsound. The metaphor once existed in many cases where we can not now trace it. Many of our own etymologies have been lost. It is futile to take the ignorance of the Han dynasty for omniscience.* It is not true, as Legge said, that the original picture characters could never have gone far in building up abstract thought. This is a vital mistake. We have seen that our own languages have all sprung from a few hundred vivid phonetic verbs by figurative derivation. A fabric more vast could have been built up in Chinese by metaphorical composition. No attenuated idea exists which it might not have reached more vividly and more permanently than we could have been expected to reach with phonetic

---

* [Professor Fenollosa is well borne out by chance evidence. The vorticist sculptor Gaudier-Brzeska sat in my room before he went off to the war. He was able to read the Chinese radicals and many compound signs almost at pleasure. He was of course, used to consider all life and nature in the terms of planes and of bounding lines. Nevertheless he had spent only a fortnight in the museum studying the Chinese characters. He was amazed at the stupidity of lexicographers who could not discern for all their learning the pictorial values which were to him perfectly obvious and apparent. Curiously enough, a few weeks later Edmond Dulac, who is of a totally different tradition, sat here, giving an impromptu panegyric on the elements of Chinese art, on the units of composition, drawn from the written characters. He did not use Professor Fenollosa's own words, he said "bamboo" instead of "rice." He said the essence of the bamboo is in a certain way it grows, they have this in their sign for bamboo, all designs of bamboo proceed from it. Then he went on rather to disparage vorticism, on the grounds that it could not hope to do for the Occident, in one life-time, what had required centuries of development in China.—E. P.]

roots. Such a pictorial method, whether the Chinese exemplified it or not, would be the ideal language of the world.

Still, is it not enough to show that Chinese poetry gets back near to the processes of nature by means of its vivid figure, its wealth of such figure? If we attempt to follow it in English we must use words highly charged, words whose vital suggestion shall interplay as nature interplays. Sentences must be like the mingling of the fringes of feathered banners, or as the colors of many flowers blended into the single sheen of a meadow.

The poet can never see too much or feel too much. His metaphors are only ways of getting rid of the dead white plaster of the copula. He resolves its indifference into a thousand tints of verb. His figures flood things with jets of various light, like the sudden up-blaze of fountains. The prehistoric poets who created language discovered the whole harmonious framework of nature, they sang out her processes in their hymns. And this diffused poetry which they created, Shakespeare has condensed into a more tangible substance. Thus in all poetry a word is like a sun, with its corona and chromosphere; words crowd upon words, and enwrap each other in their luminous envelopes until sentences become clear, continuous light-bands.

Now we are in condition to appreciate the full splendor of certain lines of Chinese verse. Poetry surpasses prose especially in that the poet selects for juxtaposition those words whose overtones blend into a delicate and lucid harmony. All arts follow the same law; refined harmony lies in the delicate balance of overtones. In music the whole possibility and theory of harmony is based on the overtones. In this sense poetry seems a more difficult art.

How shall we determine the metaphorical overtones of neighboring words? We can avoid flagrant breaches like mixed metaphor. We can find the concord or harmonizing at its intensest, as in Romeo's speech over the dead Juliet.

Here also the Chinese ideography has its advantage, in even a simple line, for example, "The sun rises in the east."

The overtones vibrate against the eye. The wealth of composition in characters makes possible a choice of words in which a single dominant overtone colors every plane of meaning. That is perhaps the most conspicuous quality of Chinese poetry. Let us examine our line. The

Sun   Rises   (in the)   East

sun, the shining, on one side, on the other the sign of the east, which is the sun entangled in the branches of a tree. And in the middle sign, the verb "rise," we have further homology; the sun is above the horizon, but beyond that the single upright line is like the growing trunk-line of the tree sign. This is but a beginning, but it points a way to the method, and to the method of intelligent reading.

WALLACE STEVENS

from

Adagia

The following epigrammatic notes were published in Wallace Stevens' posthumous works. Stevens, although an American, was a conscious follower of the French Symbolist school. In his epigrams one can trace the conflict in his own work and thought between "Romantic" and "Classicist" doctrine. Stevens is quite clearly an adherent of the latter school, both in his poetry and in his criticism, yet in these jottings he sometimes veers sharply toward the Romantic statement.

*T*o give a sense of the freshness or vividness of life is a valid purpose for poetry. A didactic purpose justifies itself in the mind of the teacher; a philosophical purpose justifies itself in the mind of the philosopher. It is not that one purpose is as justifiable as another but that some purposes are pure, others impure. Seek those purposes that are purely the purposes of the pure poet.

.   .   .   .   .

Literature is the better part of life. To this it seems inevitably necessary to add, provided life is the better part of literature.

.   .   .   .   .

After one has abandoned a belief in god, poetry is that essence which takes its place as life's redemption.

Art, broadly, is the form of life or the sound or color of life. Considered as form (in the abstract) it is often indistinguishable from life itself.

The poet seems to confer his identity on the reader. It is easiest to recognize this when listening to music—I mean this sort of thing: the transference.

Accuracy of observation is the equivalent of accuracy of thinking.

· · · · ·

The loss of a language creates confusion or dumbness.

The collecting of poetry from one's experience as one goes along is not the same thing as merely writing poetry.

The relation of art to life is of the first importance especially in a skeptical age since, in the absence of a belief in God, the mind turns to its own creations and examines them, not alone from the aesthetic point of view, but for what they reveal, for what they validate and invalidate, for the support that they give.

A grandiose subject is not an assurance of a grandiose effect but, most likely, of the opposite.

Art involves vastly more than the sense of beauty.

Life is the reflection of literature.

As life grows more terrible, its literature grows more terrible.

Poetry and materia poetica are interchangeable terms.

· · · · ·

The imagination wishes to be indulged.

A new meaning is the equivalent of a new word.

Poetry is not personal.

· · · · ·

A dead romantic is a falsification.

The romantic cannot be seen through: it is for the moment willingly not seen through.

Poetry is a means of redemption.

Poetry is a form of melancholia. Or rather, in melancholy, it is one of the *"aultres choses solatieuses."*

· · · · ·

The real is only the base. But it is the base.

· · · · ·

The poem reveals itself only to the ignorant man.

The relation between the poetry of experience and the poetry of rhetoric is not the same thing as the relation between the poetry of reality and that of the imagination. Experience, at least in the case of a poet of any scope, is much broader than reality.

To a large extent, the problems of poets are the problems of painters, and poets must often turn to the literature of painting for a discussion of their own problems.

· · · ·

Abstraction is a part of idealism. It is in that sense that it is ugly.

In poetry at least the imagination must not detach itself from reality.

Not all objects are equal. The vice of imagism was that it did not recognize this.

· · · ·

All poetry is experimental poetry.

The bare image and the image as a symbol are the contrast: the image without meaning and the image as meaning. When the image is used to suggest something else, it is secondary. Poetry as an imaginative thing consists of more than lies on the surface.

· · · ·

In poetry, you must love the words, the ideas and the images and rhythms with all your capacity to love anything at all.

· · · ·

It is the belief and not the god that counts.

· · · ·

What we see in the mind is as real to us as what we see by the eye.

Poetry must be irrational.

The purpose of poetry is to make life complete in itself.

Poetry increases the feeling for reality.

The mind is the most powerful thing in the world.

There is nothing in life except what one thinks of it.

There is nothing beautiful in life except life.

There is no wing like meaning.

Consider: I. That the whole world is material for poetry; II. That there is not a specifically poetic material.

One reads poetry with one's nerves.

· · · ·

Sentimentality is a failure of feeling.

The imagination is the romantic.

Poetry is not the same thing as the imagination taken alone. Nothing is itself taken alone. Things are because of interrelations or interactions.

The final belief is to believe in a fiction, which you know to be a fiction, there being nothing else. The exquisite truth is to know that it is a fiction and that you believe in it willingly.

. . . . .

Wine and music are not good until afternoon. But poetry is like prayer in that it is most effective in solitude and in the times of solitude as, for example, in the earliest morning.

. . . . .

Poetry is a poetic conception, however expressed. A poem is poetry expressed in words. But in a poem there is a poetry of words. Obviously, a poem may consist of several poetries.

. . . . .

Ethics are no more a part of poetry than they are of painting.

. . . . .

As the reason destroys, the poet must create.

. . . . .

It is not every day that the world arranges itself in a poem.

. . . . .

The aesthetic order includes all other orders but is not limited to them.

Religion is dependent on faith. But aesthetics is independent of faith. The relative positions of the two might be reversed. It is possible to establish aesthetics in the individual mind as immeasurably a greater thing than religion. Its present state is the result of the difficulty of establishing it except in the individual mind.

. . . . .

Poetry is a purging of the world's poverty and change and evil and death. It is a present perfecting, a satisfaction in the irremediable poverty of life.

Poetry is the scholar's art.

. . . . .

To study and to understand the fictive world is the function of the poet.

. . . . .

God is a symbol for something that can as well take other forms, as, for example, the form of high poetry.

The time will come when poems like Paradise will seem like very *triste* contraptions.

. . . . .

Reality is a vacuum.

All men are murderers.

The word must be the thing it represents; otherwise, it is a symbol. It is a question of identity.

. . . . .

In dramatic poetry the imagination attaches itself to a heightened reality.

. . . . .

There must be something of the peasant in every poet.

. . . . .

The poet is the priest of the invisible.

. . . . .

Metaphor creates a new reality from which the original appears to be unreal.

. . . . .

Romanticism is to poetry what the decorative is to painting.

. . . . .

A poem is a café. (Restoration.)

Poets acquire humanity.

Thought tends to collect in pools.

. . . . .

Life is not free from its forms.

. . . . .

We have made too much of life. A journal of life is rarely a journal of happiness.

. . . . .

Poetry sometimes crowns the search for happiness. It is itself a search for happiness.

. . . . .

Esthetique is the measure of a civilization: not the sole measure, but a measure.

Poetry must resist the intelligence almost successfully.

The romantic exists in precision as well as in imprecision.

. . . . .

A change of style is a change of subject.

. . . . .

The romantic is the first phase of (a non-pejorative) lunacy.

. . . . .

The poet is a god, or, the young poet is a god. The old poet is a tramp.

. . . . .

I have no life except in poetry. No doubt that would be true if my whole life was free for poetry.

. . . . .

Nothing could be more inappropriate to American literature than its English source since the Americans are not British in sensibility.

. . . . .

French and English constitute a single language.

. . . . .

The momentum of the mind is all toward abstraction.

In the long run the truth does not matter.

. . . . .

Poetry creates a fictitious existence on an exquisite plane. This definition must vary as the plane varies, an exquisite plane being merely illustrative.

Keys to Modern Romanticism

THE ROMANTIC MYSTIQUE OF UNITY

WALT WHITMAN

preface to

LEAVES OF GRASS

As the poetry of Poe and Baudelaire forms the basic example of a Classical poetics, so does Whitman's *Leaves of Grass* provide the most outspoken example for a Romantic poetics. Whitman's exaltation of man and of popular government and the ideal of human progress is the opposite of the traditionalist and pessimistic philosophy of Hulme, Eliot, Pound, and Yeats, as well as of Baudelaire and Poe. *Leaves of Grass* says everything Whitman had to say about the "divinity" of man, and the Preface restates in prose his creed of man's greatness and America as the promised land of humanity liberated from tradition and from the morality of the past.

*A*merica does not repel the past or what it has produced under its forms or amid other politics or the idea of castes or the old religions . . . accepts the lesson with calmness . . . is not so impatient as has been supposed that the slough still sticks to opinions and manners and literature while the life which served its requirements has passed into the new life of the new forms . . . perceives that the corpse is slowly borne from the eating and sleeping rooms of the house . . . perceives that it waits a little while in the door . . . that it was fittest for its days . . . that its action has descended to the stalwart and wellshaped heir who approaches . . . and that he shall be fittest for his days.

The Americans of all nations at any time upon the earth have probably the fullest poetical nature. The United States themselves are essentially the greatest poem. In the history of the earth hitherto the largest
and most stirring appear tame and orderly to their ampler largeness and
stir. Here at last is something in the doings of man that corresponds with
the broadcast doings of the day and night. Here is not merely a nation
but a teeming nation of nations. Here is action untied from strings
necessarily blind to particulars and details magnificently moving in vast
masses. Here is the hospitality which forever indicates heroes. . . .
Here are the roughs and beards and space and ruggedness and nonchalance that the soul loves. Here the performance disdaining the
trivial unapproached in the tremendous audacity of its crowds and
groupings and the push of its perspective spreads with crampless and
flowing breadth and showers its prolific and splendid extravagance.
One sees it must indeed own the riches of the summer and winter, and
need never be bankrupt while corn grows from the ground or the
orchards drop apples or the bays contain fish or men beget children upon
women.
     Other states indicate themselves in their deputies . . . but the
genius of the United States is not best or most in its executives or
legislatures, nor in its ambassadors or authors or colleges or churches or
parlors, nor even in its newspapers or inventors . . . but always most in
the common people. Their manners speech dress friendships—the freshness and candor of their physiognomy—the picturesque looseness of
their carriage . . . their deathless attachment to freedom—their aver-
sion to anything indecorous or soft or mean—the practical acknowledgment of the citizens of one state by the citizens of all other states—the
fierceness of their roused resentment—their curiosity and welcome of
novelty—their self-esteem and wonderful sympathy—their susceptibility
to a slight—the air they have of persons who never knew how it felt to
stand in the presence of superiors—the fluency of their speech—their
delight in music, the sure symptom of manly tenderness and native
elegance of soul . . . their good temper and openhandedness—the
terrible significance of their elections—the President's taking off his hat
to them not they to him—these too are unrhymed poetry. It awaits the
gigantic and generous treatment worthy of it.
     The largeness of nature of the nation were monstrous without a
corresponding largeness and generosity of the spirit of the citizen. Not
nature nor swarming states nor streets and steamships nor prosperous
business nor farms nor capital nor learning may suffice for the ideal of
man . . . nor suffice the poet. No reminiscences may suffice either. A
live nation can always cut a deep mark and can have the best authority
the cheapest . . . namely from its own soul. This is the sum of the
profitable uses of individuals or states and of present action and grandeur and of the subjects of poets.—As if it were necessary to trot back
generation after generation to the eastern records! As if the beauty and
sacredness of the demonstrable must fall behind that of the mythical!

As if men do not make their mark out of any times! As if the opening of the western continent by discovery and what has transpired since in North and South America were less than the small theatre of the antique or the aimless sleepwalking of the middle ages! The pride of the United States leaves the wealth and finesse of the cities and all returns of commerce and agriculture and all the magnitude of geography or shows of exterior victory to enjoy the breed of fullsized men or one fullsized man unconquerable and simple.

The American poets are to enclose old and new for America is the race of races. Of them a bard is to be commensurate with a people. To him the other continents arrive as contributions . . . he gives them reception for their sake and his own sake. His spirit responds to his country's spirit . . . he incarnates its geography and natural life and rivers and lakes. Mississippi with annual freshets and changing chutes, Missouri and Columbia and Ohio and Saint Lawrence with the falls and beautiful masculine Hudson, do not embouchure where they spend themselves more than they embouchure into him. The blue breadth over the inland sea of Virginia and Maryland and the sea off Massachusetts and Maine and over Manhattan bay and over Champlain and Erie and over Ontario and Huron and Michigan and Superior, and over the Texan and Mexican and Floridian and Cuban seas and over the seas off California and Oregon, is not tallied by the blue breadth of the waters below more than the breadth of above and below is tallied by him. When the long Atlantic coast stretches longer and the Pacific coast stretches longer he easily stretches with them north or south. He spans between them also from east to west and reflects what is between them. On him rise solid growths that offset the growths of pine and cedar and hemlock and liveoak and locust and chestnut and cypress and hickory and limetree and cottonwood and tuliptree and cactus and wildvine and tamarind and persimmon . . . and tangles as tangled as any canebrake or swamp . . . and forests coated with transparent ice and icicles hanging from the boughs and crackling in the wind . . . and sides and peaks of mountains . . . and pasturage sweet and free as savannah or upland or prairie . . . with flights and songs and screams that answer those of the wildpigeon and highhold and orchardoriole and coot and surf-duck and redshouldered-hawk and fish-hawk and white-ibis and indian-hen and cat-owl and water-pheasant and quabird and pied-sheldrake and blackbird and mockingbird and buzzard and condor and night-heron and eagle. To him the hereditary countenance descends both mother's and father's. To him enter the essences of the real things and past and present events—of the enormous diversity of temperature and agriculture and mines—the tribes of red aborigines—the weatherbeaten vessels entering new ports or making landings on rocky coasts—the first settlements north or south—the rapid stature and muscle—the haughty defiance of '76, and the war and peace and formation of the constitution . . . the union always surrounded by blatherers and always calm and impregnable—the perpetual coming of immigrants—

the wharfhem'd cities and superior marine—the unsurveyed interior—
the loghouses and clearings and wild animals and hunters and trappers
. . . the free commerce—the fisheries and whaling and gold-digging—
the endless gestation of new states—the convening of Congress every
December, the members duly coming up from all climates and the uttermost parts . . . the noble character of the young mechanics and of all
free American workmen and workwomen . . . the general ardor and
friendliness and enterprise—the perfect equality of the female with the
male . . . the large amativeness—the fluid movement of the popula-
tion—the factories and mercantile life and laborsaving machinery—the
Yankee swap—the New-York firemen and the target excursion—the
southern plantation life—the character of the northeast and of the north-
west and southwest—slavery and the tremulous spreading of hands to
protect it, and the stern opposition to it which shall never cease till it
ceases or the speaking of tongues and the moving of lips cease. For such
the expression of the American poet is to be transcendent and new. It
is to be indirect and not direct or descriptive or epic. Its quality goes
through these to much more. Let the age and wars of other nations be
chanted and their eras and characters be illustrated and that finish the
verse. Not so the great psalm of the republic. Here the theme is creative and has vista. Here comes one among the wellbeloved stonecutters
and plans with decision and science and sees the solid and beautiful
forms of the future where there are now no solid forms.

Of all nations the United States with veins full of poetical stuff
most need poets and will doubtless have the greatest and use them the
greatest. Their Presidents shall not be their common referee so much
as their poets shall. Of all mankind the great poet is the equable man.
Not in him but off from him things are grotesque or eccentric or fail of
their sanity. Nothing out of its place is good and nothing in its place is
bad. He bestows on every object or quality its fit proportions neither
more nor less. He is the arbiter of the diverse and he is the key. He is
the equalizer of his age and land . . . he supplies what wants supply-
ing and checks what wants checking. If peace is the routine out of him
speaks the spirit of peace, large, rich, thrifty, building vast and populous
cities, encouraging agriculture and the arts and commerce—lighting the
study of man, the soul, immortality—federal, state or municipal government, marriage, health, freetrade, intertravel by land and sea . . .
nothing too close, nothing too far off . . . the stars not too far off. In
war he is the most deadly force of the war. Who recruits him recruits
horse and foot . . . he fetches parks of artillery the best that engineer
ever knew. If the time becomes slothful and heavy he knows how to
arouse it . . . he can make every word he speaks draw blood. Whatever stagnates in the flat of custom or obedience or legislation he never
stagnates. Obedience does not master him, he masters it. High up out
of reach he stands turning a concentrated light . . . he turns the pivot
with his finger . . . he baffles the swiftest runners as he stands and
easily overtakes and envelops them. The time straying toward infidelity

and confections and persiflage he withholds by his steady faith . . . he spreads out his dishes . . . he offers the sweet firmfibred meat that grows men and women. His brain is the ultimate brain. He is no arguer . . . he is judgment. He judges not as the judge judges but as the sun falling around a helpless thing. As he sees the farthest he has the most faith. His thoughts are the hymns of the praise of things. In the talk on the soul and eternity and God off of his equal plane he is silent. He sees eternity less like a play with a prologue and denouement . . . he sees eternity in men and women . . . he does not see men and women as dreams or dots. Faith is the antiseptic of the soul . . . it pervades the common people and preserves them . . . they never give up be-lieving and expecting and trusting. There is that indescribable freshness and unconsciousness about an illiterate person that humbles and mocks the power of the noblest expressive genius. The poet sees for a cer-tainty how one not a great artist may be just as sacred and perfect as the greatest artist. . . . The power to destroy or remould is freely used by him but never the power of attack. What is past is past. If he does not expose superior models and prove himself by every step he takes he is not what is wanted. The presence of the greatest poet conquers . . . not parleying or struggling or any prepared attempts. Now he has passed that way see after him! there is not left any vestige of despair or misanthropy or cunning or exclusiveness or the ignominy of a nativity or color or delusion of hell or the necessity of hell . . . and no man thenceforward shall be degraded for ignorance or weakness or sin.

The greatest poet hardly knows pettiness or triviality. If he breathes into any thing that was before thought small it dilates with the grandeur and life of the universe. He is a seer . . . he is individual . . . he is complete in himself . . . the others are as good as he, only he sees it and they do not. He is not one of the chorus . . . he does not stop for any regulations . . . he is the president of regulation. What the eyesight does to the rest he does to the rest. Who knows the curious mystery of the eyesight? The other senses corroborate themselves, but this is removed from any proof but its own and foreruns the identities of the spiritual world. A single glance of it mocks all the investigations of man and all the instruments and books of the earth and all reason-ing. What is marvellous? what is unlikely? what is impossible or base-less or vague? after you have once just opened the space of a peachpit and given audience to far and near and to the sunset and had all things enter with electric swiftness softly and duly without confusion or jostling or jam.

The land and sea, the animals fishes and birds, the sky of heaven and the orbs, the forest mountains and rivers, are not small themes . . . but folks expect of the poet to indicate more than the beauty and dignity which always attach to dumb real objects . . . they expect him to indicate the path between reality and their souls. Men and women per-ceive the beauty well enough . . . probably as well as he. The pas-sionate tenacity of hunters, woodmen, early risers, cultivators of gardens and orchards and fields, the love of healthy women for the manly form, seafaring persons, drivers of horses, the passion for light and the open air, all is an old varied sign of the unfailing perception of beauty and of a residence of the poetic in outdoor people. They can never be assisted by poets to perceive . . . some may but they never can. The poetic quality is not marshalled in rhyme or uniformity or abstract addresses to things nor in melancholy complaints or good precepts, but is the life of these and much else and is in the soul. The profit of rhyme is that it drops seeds of a sweeter and more luxuriant rhyme, and of uniformity that it conveys itself into its own roots in the ground out of sight. The rhyme and uniformity of perfect poems show the free growth of metrical laws and bud from them as unerringly and loosely as lilacs or roses on a bush, and take shapes as compact as the shapes of chestnuts and oranges and melons and pears, and shed the perfume impalpable to form. The fluency and ornaments of the finest poems or music or orations or recitations are not independent but dependent. All beauty comes from beautiful blood and a beautiful brain. If the greatnesses are in conjunction in a man or woman it is enough . . . the fact will prevail through the universe . . . but the gaggery and gilt of a million years will not prevail. Who troubles himself about his ornaments or fluency is lost. This is what you shall do: Love the earth and sun and the animals, despise riches, give alms to every one that asks, stand up for the stupid and crazy, devote your income and labor to others, hate tyrants, argue not concerning God, have patience and indulgence toward the people, take off your hat to nothing known or unknown or to any man or number of men, go freely with powerful uneducated persons and with the young and with the mothers of families, read these leaves in the open air every season of every year of your life, re-examine all you have been told at school or church or in any book, dismiss whatever insults your own soul, and your very flesh shall be a great poem and have the richest fluency not only in its words but in the silent lines of its lips and face and between the lashes of your eyes and in every motion and joint of your body. . . . The poet shall not spend his time in unneeded work. He shall know that the ground is always ready ploughed and manured . . . others may not know it but he shall. He shall go directly to the creation. His trust shall master the trust of everything he touches . . . and shall master all attachment.

The known universe has one complete lover and that is the greatest poet. He consumes an eternal passion and is indifferent which chance happens and which possible contingency of fortune or misfortune and persuades daily and hourly his delicious pay. What balks or breaks others is fuel for his burning progress to contact and amorous joy. Other proportions of the reception of pleasure dwindle to nothing to his proportions. All expected from heaven or from the highest he is rapport with in the sight of the daybreak or a scene of the winter woods or the presence of children playing or with his arm round the neck of a man or woman. His love above all love has leisure and expanse . . . he leaves room ahead of himself. He is no irresolute or suspicious lover . . . he is sure . . . he scorns intervals. His experience and the showers and thrills are not for nothing. Nothing can jar him . . . suffering and darkness cannot—death and fear cannot. To him complaint and jealousy and envy are corpses buried and rotten in the earth . . . he saw them buried. The sea is not surer of the shore or the shore of the sea than he is of the fruition of his love and of all perfection and beauty.

The fruition of beauty is no chance of hit or miss . . . it is inevitable as life . . . it is exact and plumb as gravitation. From the eyesight proceeds another eyesight and from the hearing proceeds another hearing and from the voice proceeds another voice eternally curious of the harmony of things with man. To these respond perfections not only in the committees that were supposed to stand for the rest but in the rest themselves just the same. These understand the law of perfection in masses and floods . . . that its finish is to each for itself and onward from itself . . . that it is profuse and impartial . . . that there is not a minute of the light or dark nor an acre of the earth or sea without it —nor any direction of the sky nor any trade or employment nor any turn of events. This is the reason that about the proper expression of beauty there is precision and balance . . . one part does not need to be thrust above another. The best singer is not the one who has the most lithe and powerful organ . . . the pleasure of poems is not in them that take the handsomest measure and similes and sound.

Without effort and without exposing in the least how it is done the greatest poet brings the spirit of any or all events and passions and scenes and persons some more and some less to bear on your individual character as you hear or read. To do this well is to compete with the laws that pursue and follow time. What is the purpose must surely be there and the clue of it must be there . . . and the faintest indication is the indication of the best and then becomes the clearest indication. Past and present and future are not disjoined but joined. The greatest poet forms the consistence of what is to be from what has been and is. He drags the dead out of their coffins and stands them again on their feet . . . he says to the past, Rise and walk before me that I may realize you. He learns the lesson . . . he places himself where the future becomes present. The greatest poet does not only dazzle his rays over character and scenes and passions . . . he finally ascends and finishes all . . . he exhibits the pinnacles that no man can tell what they are for or what is beyond . . . he glows a moment on the extremest verge. He is most wonderful in his last half-hidden smile or frown . . . by that flash of the moment of parting the one that sees it shall be encouraged or terrified afterwards for many years. The greatest poet does not moralize or make applications of morals . . . he knows the soul. The soul has that measureless pride which consists in never acknowledging any lessons but its own. But it has sympathy as measureless as its pride and the one balances the other and neither can stretch too far while it stretches in company with the other. The inmost secrets of art sleep with the twain. The greatest poet has lain close betwixt both and they are vital in his style and thoughts.

The art of art, the glory of expression and the sunshine of the light of letters is simplicity. Nothing is better than simplicity . . . nothing can make up for excess or for the lack of definiteness. To carry on the heave of impulse and pierce intellectual depths and give all subjects their articulations are powers neither common nor very uncommon. But to speak in literature with the perfect rectitude and insouciance of the movements of animals and the unimpeachableness of the sentiment of trees in the woods and grass by the roadside is the flawless triumph of art. If you have looked on him who has achieved it you have looked on one of the masters of the artists of all nations and times. You shall not contemplate the flight of the graygull over the bay or the mettlesome action of the blood horse or the tall leaning of sunflowers on their stalk or the appearance of the sun journeying through heaven or the appearance of the moon afterward with any more satisfaction than you shall contemplate him. The greatest poet has less a marked style and is more the channel of thoughts and things without increase or diminution, and is the free channel of himself. He swears to his art, I will not be meddlesome, I will not have in my writing any elegance or effect or originality to hang in the way between me and the rest like curtains. I will have nothing hang in the way, not the richest curtains. What I tell I tell for precisely what it is. Let who may exalt or startle or fascinate or soothe I will have purposes as health or heat or snow has and be as regardless of observation. What I experience or portray shall go from my composition without a shred of my composition. You shall stand by my side and look in the mirror with me.

The old red blood and stainless gentility of great poets will be proved by their unconstraint. A heroic person walks at his ease through and out of that custom or precedent or authority that suits him not. Of the traits of the brotherhood of writers savans musicians inventors and artists nothing is finer than silent defiance advancing from new free forms. In the need of poems philosophy politics mechanism science behaviour, the craft of art, an appropriate native grand-opera, shipcraft, or any craft, he is greatest forever and forever who contributes the greatest original practical example. The cleanest expression is that which finds no sphere worthy of itself and makes one.

The messages of great poets to each man and woman are, Come to us on equal terms, Only then can you understand us, We are no better than you, What we enclose you enclose, What we enjoy you may enjoy. Did you suppose there could be only one Supreme? We affirm there can be unnumbered Supremes, and that one does not countervail another any more than one eyesight countervails another . . . and that men can be good or grand only of the consciousness of their supremacy within them. What do you think is the grandeur of storms and dismemberments and the deadliest battles and wrecks and the wildest fury of the elements and the power of the sea and the motion of nature and of the throes of human desires and dignity and hate and love? It is that something in the soul which says, Rage on, Whirl on, I tread master here and everywhere, Master of the spasms of the sky and of the shatter of the sea, Master of nature and passion and death, And of all terror and all pain.

The American bards shall be marked for generosity and affection and for encouraging competitors . . . They shall be kosmos . . . without monopoly or secrecy . . . glad to pass any thing to any one . . . hungry for equals night and day. They shall not be careful of riches and privilege . . . they shall be riches and privilege . . . they shall perceive who the most affluent man is. The most affluent man is he that confronts all the shows he sees by equivalents out of the stronger wealth of himself. The American bard shall delineate no class of persons nor one or two out of the strata of interests nor love most nor truth most nor the soul most nor the body most . . . and not be for the eastern states more than the western or the northern states more than the southern.

Exact science and its practical movements are no checks on the greatest poet but always his encouragement and support. The outset and remembrance are there . . . there the arms that lifted him first and brace him best . . . there he returns after all his goings and comings. The sailor and traveler . . . the anatomist chemist astronomer geologist phrenologist spiritualist mathematician historian and lexicographer are not poets, but they are the lawgivers of poets and their construction underlies the structure of every perfect poem. No matter what rises or is uttered they sent the seed of the conception of it . . . of them and by them stand the visible proofs of souls . . . always of their father-stuff must be begotten the sinewy races of bards. If there shall be love and content between the father and the son and if the greatness of the son is the exuding of the greatness of the father there shall be love between the poet and the man of demonstrable science. In the beauty of poems are the tuft and final applause of science.

Great is the faith of the flush of knowledge and of the investigation of the depths of qualities and things. Cleaving and circling here swells the soul of the poet yet is president of itself always. The depths are fathomless and therefore calm. The innocence and nakedness are resumed . . . they are neither modest nor immodest. The whole theory of the special and supernatural and all that was twined with it or educed out of it departs as a dream. What has ever happened . . . what happens and whatever may or shall happen, the vital laws enclose all . . . they are sufficient for any case and for all cases . . . none to be hurried or retarded . . . any miracle of affairs or persons inadmissable in the vast clear scheme where every motion and every spear of grass and the frames and spirits of men and women and all that concerns them are unspeakably perfect miracles all referring to all and each distinct and in its place. It is also not consistent with the reality of the soul to admit that there is anything in the known universe more divine than men and women.

Men and women and the earth and all upon it are simply to be taken as they are, and the investigation of their past and present and future shall be unintermitted and shall be done with perfect candor. Upon this basis philosophy speculates ever looking toward the poet, ever regarding the eternal tendencies of all toward happiness never inconsistent with what is clear to the senses and to the soul. For the eternal tendencies of all toward happiness make the only point of sane philosophy. Whatever comprehends less than that . . . whatever is less than the laws of light and of astronomical motion . . . or less than the laws that follow the thief the liar the glutton and the drunkard through this life and doubtless afterward . . . or less than vast stretches of time or the slow formation of density or the patient upheaving of strata— is of no account. Whatever would put God in a poem or system of philosophy as contending against some being or influence is also of no account. Sanity and ensemble characterise the great master . . . spoilt in one principle all is spoilt. The great master has nothing to do with miracles. He sees health for himself in being one of the mass . . . he sees the hiatus in singular eminence. To the perfect shape comes common ground. To be under the general law is great for that is to correspond with it. The master knows that he is unspeakably great and that all are unspeakably great . . . that nothing for instance is greater than to conceive children and bring them up well . . . that to be is just as great as to perceive or tell.

In the make of the great masters the idea of political liberty is indispensable. Liberty takes the adherence of heroes wherever men and women exist . . . but never takes any adherence or welcome from the rest more than from poets. They are the voice and exposition of liberty. They out of ages are worthy the grand idea . . . to them it is confided and they must sustain it. Nothing has precedence of it and nothing can warp or degrade it. The attitude of great poets is to cheer up slaves and horrify despots. The turn of their necks, the sound of their feet, the motions of their wrists, are full of hazard to the one and hope to the other. Come nigh them awhile and though they neither speak or advise you shall learn the faithful American lesson. Liberty is poorly served by men whose good intent is quelled from one failure or two failures or any number of failures, or from the casual indifference or ingratitude of the people, or from the sharp show of the tushes of power, or the bringing to bear soldiers and cannon or any penal statutes. Liberty relies upon itself, invites no one, promises nothing, sits in calmness and light, is positive and composed, and knows no discouragement. The battle rages with many a loud alarm and frequent advance and retreat . . . the enemy triumphs . . . the prison, the handcuffs, the iron necklace and anklet, the scaffold, garrote and leadballs do their work . . . the cause is asleep . . . the strong throats are choked with their own blood . . .

the young men drop their eyelashes toward the ground when they pass each other . . . and is liberty gone out of that place? No never. When liberty goes it is not the first to go nor the second or third to go . . . it waits for all the rest to go . . . it is the last . . . When the memories of the old martyrs are faded utterly away . . . when the large names of patriots are laughed at in the public halls from the lips of the orators . . . when the boys are no more christened after the same but christened after tyrants and traitors instead . . . when the laws of the free are grudgingly permitted and laws for informers and bloodmoney are sweet to the taste of the people . . . when I and you walk abroad upon the earth stung with compassion at the sight of numberless brothers answering our equal friendship and calling no man master—and when we are elated with noble joy at the sight of slaves . . . when the soul retires in the cool communion of the night and surveys its experience and has much extasy over the word and deed that put back a helpless innocent person into the gripe of the gripers or into any cruel inferiority . . . when those in all parts of these states who could easier realize the true American character but do not yet—when the swarms of cringers, suckers, doughfaces, lice of politics, planners of sly involutions for their own preferment to city offices or state legislatures or the judiciary or congress or the presidency, obtain a response of love and natural deference from the people whether they get the offices or no . . . when it is better to be a bound booby and rogue in office at a high salary than the poorest free mechanic or farmer with his hat unmoved from his head and firm eyes and a candid and generous heart . . . and when servility by town or state or the federal government or any oppression on a large scale or small scale can be tried on without its own punishment following duly after in exact proportion against the smallest chance of escape . . . or rather when all life and all the souls of men and women are discharged from any part of the earth—then only shall the instinct of liberty be discharged from that part of the earth.

As the attributes of the poets of the kosmos concentre in the real body and soul and in the pleasure of things they possess the superiority of genuineness over all fiction and romance. As they emit themselves facts are showered over with light . . . the daylight is lit with more volatile light . . . also the deep between the setting and rising sun goes deeper many fold. Each precise object or condition or combination or process exhibits a beauty . . . the multiplication table its—old age its— the carpenter's trade its—the grand-opera its . . . the hugehulled clean-shaped New-York clipper at sea under steam or full sail gleams with unmatched beauty . . . the American circles and large harmonies of government gleam with theirs . . . and the commonest definite intentions and actions with theirs. The poets of the kosmos advance through all interpositions and coverings and turmoils and stratagems to first principles. They are of use . . . they dissolve poverty from its need and riches from its conceit. You large proprietor they say shall not realize or perceive more than any one else. The owner of the library is not he who holds a legal title to it having bought and paid for it. Any one and every one is owner of the library who can read the same through all the varieties of tongues and subjects and styles, and in whom they enter with ease and take residence and force toward paternity and maternity, and make supple and powerful and rich and large. . . . These American states strong and healthy and accomplished shall receive no pleasure from violations of natural models and must not permit them. In paintings or mouldings or carvings in mineral or wood, or in the illustrations of books or newspapers, or in any comic or tragic prints, or in the patterns of woven stuffs or any thing to beautify rooms or furniture or costumes, or to put upon cornices or monuments or on the prows or sterns of ships, or to put anywhere before the human eye indoors or out, that which distorts honest shapes or which creates unearthly beings or places or contingencies is a nuisance and revolt. Of the human form especially it is so great it must never be made ridiculous. Of ornaments to a work nothing outre can be allowed . . . but those ornaments can be allowed that conform to the perfect facts of the open air and that flow out of the nature of the work and come irrepressibly from it and are necessary to the completion of the work. Most works are most beautiful without ornament. . . . Exaggerations will be revenged in human physiology. Clean and vigorous children are jetted and conceived only in those communities where the models of natural forms are public every day. . . Great genius and the people of these states must never be demeaned to romances. As soon as histories are properly told there is no more need of romances.

The great poets are also to be known by the absence in them of tricks and by the justification of perfect personal candor. Then folks echo a new cheap joy and a divine voice leaping from their brains: How beautiful is candor! All faults may be forgiven of him who has perfect candor. Henceforth let no man of us lie, for we have seen that openness wins the inner and outer world and that there is no single exception, and that never since our earth gathered itself in a mass have deceit or subterfuge or prevarication attracted its smallest particle of the faintest tinge of a shade—and that through the enveloping wealth and rank of a state or the whole republic of states a sneak or sly person shall be discovered and despised . . . and that the soul has never been once fooled and never can be fooled . . . and thrift without the loving nod of the soul is only a foetid puff . . . and there never grew up in any of the continents of the globe nor upon any planet or satellite or star, nor upon the asteroids, nor in any part of ethereal space, nor in the midst of density, nor under the fluid wet of the sea, nor in that condition which precedes the birth of babes, nor at any time during the changes of life, nor in that condition that follows what we term death, nor in any stretch of abeyance or action afterward of vitality, nor in any process of formation or reformation anywhere, a being whose instinct hated the truth.

Extreme caution or prudence, the soundest organic health, large hope and comparison and fondness for women and children, large alimentive-

ness and destructiveness and causality, with a perfect sense of the oneness of nature and the propriety of the same spirit applied to human
affairs . . . these are called up of the float of the brain of the world
to be parts of the greatest poet from his birth out of his mother's womb
and from her birth out of her mother's. Caution seldom goes far enough.
It has been thought that the prudent citizen was the citizen who applied himself to solid gains and did well for himself and his family and
completed a lawful life without debt or crime. The greatest poet sees
and admits these economies as he sees the economies of food and sleep,
but has higher notions of prudence than to think he gives much when
he gives a few slight attentions at the latch of the gate. The premises of
the prudence of life are not the hospitality of it or the ripeness and
harvest of it. Beyond the independence of a little sum laid aside for
burial-money, and of a few clapboards around and shingles overhead
on a lot of American soil owned, and the easy dollars that supply the
year's plain clothing and meals, the melancholy prudence of the abandonment of such a great being as a man is to the toss and pallor of years
of moneymaking with all their scorching days and icy nights and all
their stifling deceits and underhanded dodgings, or infinitesimals of
parlors, or shameless stuffing while others starve . . . and all the loss
of the bloom and odor of the earth and of the flowers and atmosphere
and of the sea and of the true taste of the women and men you pass or
have to do with in youth or middle age, and the issuing sickness and
desperate revolt at the close of a life without elevation or naivete, and
the ghastly chatter of a death without serenity or majesty, is the great
fraud upon modern civilization and forethought, blotching the surface
and system which civilization undeniably drafts, and moistening with
tears the immense features it spreads and spreads with such velocity
before the reached kisses of the soul . . . Still the right explanation
remains to be made about prudence. The prudence of the mere wealth
and respectability of the most esteemed life appears too faint for the
eye to observe at all when little and large alike drop quietly aside at the
thought of the prudence suitable for immortality. What is wisdom that
fills the thinness of a year or seventy or eighty years to wisdom spaced
out by ages and coming back at a certain time with strong reinforce-
ments and rich presents and the clear faces of wedding-guests as far as
you can look in every direction running gaily toward you? Only the
soul is of itself . . . all else has reference to what ensues. All that a
person does or thinks is of consequence. Not a move can a man or
woman make that affects him or her in a day or a month or any part
of the direct lifetime or the hour of death but the same affects him or
her onward afterward through the indirect lifetime. The indirect is
always as great and real as the direct. The spirit receives from the body
just as much as it gives to the body. Not one name of word or deed
. . . not of venereal sores or discolorations . . . not the privacy of the
onanist . . . not of the putrid veins of gluttons or rumdrinkers . . .
not peculation or cunning or betrayal or murder . . . no serpentine

poison of those that seduce women . . . not the foolish yielding of
women . . . not prostitution . . . not of any depravity of young men
. . . not of the attainment of gain by discreditable means . . . not any
nastiness of appetite . . . not any harshness of officers to men or judges
to prisoners or fathers to sons or sons to fathers or husbands to wives
or bosses to their boys . . . not of greedy looks or malignant wishes
. . . nor any of the wiles practised by people upon themselves . . . ever
is or ever can be stamped on the programme but it is duly realized and
returned, and that returned in further performances . . . and they
returned again. Nor can the push of charity or personal force ever be
any thing else than the profoundest reason, whether it brings arguments
to hand or no. No specification is necessary . . . to add or subtract or
divide is in vain. Little or big, learned or unlearned, white or black,
legal or illegal, sick or well, from the first inspiration down the wind-
pipe to the last expiration out of it, all that a male or female does that
is vigorous and benevolent and clean is so much sure profit to him or her
in the unshakable order of the universe and through the whole scope of
it forever. If the savage or felon is wise it is well . . . if the greatest
poet or savan is wise it is simply the same . . . if the President or chief
justice is wise it is the same . . . if the young mechanic or farmer is
wise it is no more or less . . . if the prostitute is wise it is no more
nor less. The interest will come round . . . all will come round. All
the best actions of war and peace . . . all help given to relatives and
strangers and the poor and old and sorrowful and young children and
widows and the sick, and to all shunned persons . . . all furtherance of
fugitives and of the escape of slaves . . . all the self-denial that stood
steady and aloof on wrecks and saw others take the seats of the boats
. . . all offering of substance or life for the good old cause, or for a
friend's sake or opinion's sake . . . all pains of enthusiasts scoffed at
by their neighbors . . . all the vast sweet love and precious suffering
of mothers . . . all honest men baffled in strifes recorded or unrecorded
. . . all the grandeur and good of the few ancient nations whose fragments of annals we inherit . . . and all the good of the hundreds of far
mightier and more ancient nations unknown to us by name or date or
location . . . all that was ever manfully begun, whether it succeeded
or not . . . all that has at any time been well suggested out of the
divine heart of man or by the divinity of his mouth or by the shaping
of his great hands . . . and all that is well thought or done this day on
any part of the surface of the globe . . . or on any of the wandering
stars or fixed stars by those there as we are here . . . or that is henceforth to be well thought or done by you whoever you are, or by any
one—these singly and wholly inured at their time and inure now and
will inure always to the identities from which they sprung or shall
spring . . . Did you guess any of them lived only its moment? The
world does not so exist . . . no parts palpable or impalpable so exist
. . . no result exists now without being from its long antecedent
result, and that from its antecedent, and so backward without the

farthest mentionable spot coming a bit nearer the beginning than any other spot. . . . Whatever satisfies the soul is truth. The prudence of the greatest poet answers at last the craving and glut of the soul, is not contemptuous of less ways of prudence if they conform to its ways, puts off nothing, permits no let-up for its own case or any case, has no particular sabbath or judgment-day, divides not the living from the dead or the righteous from the unrighteous, is satisfied with the present, matches every thought or act by its correlative, knows no possible forgiveness or deputed atonement . . . knows that the young man who composedly periled his life and lost it has done exceeding well for himself, while the man who has not periled his life and retains it to old age in riches and ease has perhaps achieved nothing for himself worth mentioning . . . and that only that person has no great prudence to learn who has learnt to prefer real longlived things, and favors body and soul the same, and perceives the indirect assuredly following the direct, and what evil or good he does leaping onward and waiting to meet him again—and who in his spirit in any emergency whatever neither hurries or avoids death.

The direct trial of him who would be the greatest poet is today. If he does not flood himself with the immediate age as with vast oceanic tides . . . and if he does not attract his own land body and soul to himself and hang on its neck with incomparable love and plunge his semitic muscle into its merits and demerits . . . and if he be not himself the age transfigured . . . and if to him is not opened the eternity which gives similitude to all periods and locations and processes and animate and inanimate forms, and which is the bond of time, and rises up from its inconceivable vagueness and infiniteness in the swimming shape of today, and is held by the ductile anchors of life, and makes the present spot the passage from what was to what shall be, and commits itself to the representation of this wave of an hour and this one of the sixty beautiful children of the wave—let him merge in the general run and wait his development. . . . Still the final test of poems or any character or work remains. The prescient poet projects himself centuries ahead and judges performer or performance after the changes of time. Does it live through them? Does it still hold on untired? Will the same style and the direction of genius to similar points be satisfactory now? Has no new discovery in science or arrival at superior planes of thought and judgment and behaviour fixed him or his so that either can be looked down upon? Have the marches of tens and hundreds and thousands of years made willing detours to the right hand and the left hand for his sake? Is he beloved long and long after he is buried? Does the young man think often of him? and the young woman think often of him? and do the middleaged and the old think of him?

A great poem is for ages and ages in common and for all degrees and complexions and all departments and sects and for a woman as much as a man and a man as much as a woman. A great poem is no finish to a man or woman but rather a beginning. Has any one fancied he could sit at last under some due authority and rest satisfied with ex-

planations and realize and be content and full? To no such terminus
does the greatest poet bring . . . he brings neither cessation or sheltered
fatness and ease. The touch of him tells in action. Whom he takes he
takes with firm sure grasp into live regions previously unattained . . .
thenceforward is no rest . . . they see the space and ineffable sheen
that turn the old spots and lights into dead vacuums. The companion
of him beholds the birth and progress of stars and learns one of the
meanings. Now there shall be a man cohered out of tumult and chaos
. . . the elder encourages the younger and shows him how . . . they
two shall launch off fearlessly together till the new world hits an orbit
for itself and looks unabashed on the lesser orbits of the stars and sweeps
through the ceaseless rings and shall never be quiet again.

There will soon be no more priests. Their work is done. They may
wait awhile . . . perhaps a generation or two . . . dropping off by
degrees. A superior breed shall take their place . . . the gangs of kosmos
and prophets en masse shall take their place. A new order shall arise
and they shall be the priests of man, and every man shall be his own
priest. The churches built under their umbrage shall be the churches
of men and women. Through the divinity of themselves shall the kosmos
and the new breed of poets be interpreters of men and women and of all
events and things. They shall find their inspiration in real objects today,
symptoms of the past and future. . . . They shall not deign to defend
immortality or God or the perfection of things or liberty or the exquisite
beauty and reality of the soul. They shall arise in America and be
responded to from the remainder of the earth.

The English language befriends the grand American expression . . .
it is brawny enough and limber and full enough. On the tough stock of
a race who through all change of circumstances was never without the
idea of political liberty, which is the animus of all liberty, it has attracted the terms of daintier and gayer and subtler and more elegant
tongues. It is the powerful language of resistance . . . it is the dialect
of common sense. It is the speech of the proud and melancholy races
and of all who aspire. It is the chosen tongue to express growth faith
self-esteem freedom justice equality friendliness amplitude prudence
decision and courage. It is the medium that shall well nigh express the
inexpressible.

No great literature nor any like style of behaviour or oratory or social
intercourse or household arrangements or public institutions or the treatment by bosses of employed people, nor executive detail or detail of the
army or navy, nor spirit of legislation or courts or police or tuition or
architecture or songs or amusements or the costumes of young men, can
long elude the jealous and passionate instinct of American standards.
Whether or no the sign appears from the mouths of the people, it throbs
a live interrogation in every freeman's and freewoman's heart after that
which passes by or this built to remain. Is it uniform with my country?
Are its disposals without ignominious distinctions? Is it for the ever-
growing communes of brothers and lovers, large, well-united, proud be-

yond the old models, generous beyond all models? Is it something grown fresh out of the fields or drawn from the sea for use to me today here? I know that what answers for me an American must answer for any individual or nation that serves for a part of my materials. Does this answer? or is it without reference to universal needs? or sprung of the needs of the less developed society of special ranks? or old needs of pleasure overlaid by modern science and forms? Does this acknowledge liberty with audible and absolute acknowledgement, and set slavery at nought for life and death? Will it help breed one goodshaped and well-hung man, and a woman to be his perfect and independent mate? Does it improve manners? Is it for the nursing of the young of the republic? Does it solve readily with the sweet milk of the nipples of the breasts of the mother of many children? Has it too the old ever-fresh forbearance and impartiality? Does it look with the same love on the last born and on those hardening toward stature, and on the errant, and on those who disdain all strength of assault outside of their own?

The poems distilled from other poems will probably pass away. The coward will surely pass away. The expectation of the vital and great can only be satisfied by the demeanor of the vital and great.

The swarms of the polished deprecating and reflectors and the polite float off and leave no remembrance. America prepares with composure and goodwill for the visitors that have sent word. It is not intellect that is to be their warrant and welcome. The talented, the artist, the ingenious, the editor, the statesman, the erudite . . . they are not un-appreciated . . . they fall in their place and do their work. The soul of the nation also does its work. No disguise can pass on it . . . no disguise can conceal from it. It rejects none, it permits all. Only toward as good as itself and toward the like of itself will it advance half-way. An individual is as superb as a nation when he has the qualities which make a superb nation. The soul of the largest and wealthiest and proudest nation may well go half-way to meet that of its poets. The signs are effectual. There is no fear of mistake. If the one is true the other is true. The proof of a poet is that his country absorbs him as affectionately as he has absorbed it.

JAMES E. MILLER, JR.

from

"Song of Myself" as Inverted Mystical Experience

For obvious reasons, modern Classicist criticism has ignored Whitman, and it is only recently that scholars have begun to examine his poetry in its formal aspects. The following two excerpts from *A Critical Guide to "Leaves of Grass"* bring to light for the first time in our century the *mystique* of Whitman and the formal organization of his poems. James Miller's widely acclaimed study joins the argument of Romantic and Classicist—the natural versus the cultured man. The identification of Whitman as mystic goes a long way to clarify his poetry and reverse the stock opinion of this nineteenth-century poet as professional American and *poseur*.

"Song of Myself" has long been considered a loosely organized, perhaps even chaotic, poem held together, if at all, by the robust personality of Walt Whitman. Whitman himself may have contributed to this concept of the poem. Untitled when it appeared in the first edition of *Leaves of Grass* in 1855, it was called "Poem of Walt Whitman, an American" in the 1856 edition, "Walt Whitman" in the 1860 edition, and was given its present title in the 1881 edition. This frequent change of title, together with the many revisions made in the numbering of the sections and in the text itself, suggests two possibilities: either Whitman was uncertain, perhaps confused, as to the basic nature of what he was writing; or he was struggling to perfect a work of art the execution of which had fallen short of the conception. Too frequently the critics have assumed as self-evident the first of these possibilities. Inability to find a structure in "Song of Myself" has resulted from a failure to find a center of relevancy, an "informing idea," to which the parts of the poem may be related.

"Song of Myself" is the dramatic representation of a mystical experience. The term "dramatic representation" indicates an important distinction: the poem is not necessarily a transcript of an actual mystical experience but rather a work of art in which such an experience, conceived in the imagination, is represented dramatically, with the author assuming the main role. The mystical experience is dramatically represented in the sense that the poet portrays his preparation for and his entry into a state of mystical consciousness (sections 1–5), his progressively significant and meaningful experience while in this state (sections 6–49), and finally his emergence from the mystical state (sections 50–52).

The central portion of the poem, sections 6–49, may be related, step by step, to the "Mystic Way," as described by Evelyn Underhill in her valuable study *Mysticism*.[1] In what she herself labels an "arbitrary classification," she analyzes five "phases of the mystical life": (1) the awakening of self; (2) the purification of self; (3) illumination; (4) the dark night of the soul; (5) union. These phases, Miss Underhill insists, answer only "loosely and generally to experiences which seldom present themselves in so rigid and unmixed a form."[2] "Song of Myself" conforms in framework remarkably well to these five stages, but with some significant differences from the traditional mystical concepts or attitudes. These differences, central to the poet's meaning and intention, represent an inversion of some of the steps in the mystic way or a reversal of values held by the traditional mystic.

"Song of Myself," considered as the dramatic representation of an inverted mystical experience, may be analyzed as follows:

I. SECTIONS 1–5: Entry into the mystical state
II. SECS. 6–16: Awakening of self
III. SECS. 17–32: Purification of self
IV. SECS. 33–37: Illumination and the dark night of the soul
V. SECS. 38–43: Union (faith and love)
VI. SECS. 44–49: Union (perception)
VII. SECS. 50–52: Emergence from the mystical state

The third and fourth stages in the mystic way (illumination and the dark night of the soul) have been combined in sections 33–37; Miss Underhill indicates that, in reality, the fourth phase sometimes accompanies, intermittently, the third and that her separation of the two is somewhat arbitrary. Each of the two parts of "Song of Myself" devoted to the fifth stage of the mystic way is concerned with separate, distinct characteristics of union as described by Miss Underhill.

Portrayal of the entry into and emergence from the mystical state of consciousness in sections 1–5 and 50–52 conforms to the popular concept of the behavior of the mystic, his "going into" and "coming out of" the mystic trance. This portrayal represents what William James called the "sporadic type" of mystical experience in which the individual gains sudden, fleeting insight or transcendent knowledge. But, between the beginning and the end of this trancelike state, the poet portrays the laborious steps of the traditional mystic in his efforts to achieve union with the Transcendent. The poet not only fuses the two kinds of mystical experience into one but also, for poetic economy and dramatic intensity, portrays the five stages of the mystic way as following one another immediately in time, whereas in reality the mystic might take years to reach his goal of union. Justification for

---

[1] Evelyn Underhill, *Mysticism: A Study in the Nature and Development of Man's Spiritual Consciousness* (11th ed.; London: Methuen & Co., Ltd., 1926).
[2] *Ibid.*, p. 205.

this departure from reality may be found in the requirements of a work of art: "Song of Myself" is a poem, not a historical, philosophical, or religious document.

JAMES E. MILLER, JR.

America's Epic

𝒟id Whitman write the epic for modern America? There have been many who contend that *Leaves of Grass* is merely a collection of lyric poetry, some good, some 'bad, all of it of a peculiarly personal nature that disqualifies its attitudes and philosophy generally. There have been others who have defended Whitman's book as the embodiment of the American reality and ideal, as a superb fulfilment of all the genuine requirements of the national epic.

What did Whitman believe? The answer may be found in a number of prose works, beginning with the 1855 Preface. It is clear in this early work that Whitman desired *Leaves of Grass* to bear a unique relationship with America: "Here [in America] at last is something in the doings of man that corresponds with the broadcast doings of the day and night. . . . It awaits the gigantic and generous treatment worthy of it." It is generally recognized that the entire Preface is a veiled account of Whitman's concept of his own role as poet. Certainly he includes himself in the category when he asserts: "The poets of the kosmos advance through all interpositions and coverings and turmoils and stratagems to first principles." Although Whitman does not use the term, it is clear throughout the 1855 Preface that he believes his book to have the basic nature and general scope of the traditional national epic.

In *Democratic Vistas,* in the same indirect manner, Whitman again reveals his concept of the nature of his poetry: "Never was anything more wanted than, to-day, and here in the States, the poet of the modern is wanted, or the great literatus of the modern. At all times, perhaps, the central point in any nation, and that whence it is itself really sway'd the most and whence it sways others, is its national literature, especially its archetypal poems" (V, 54–55). Whitman was by this time (1871) acutely aware that America had not accepted his book as he had planned and hoped. There can be little doubt that he conceived *Leaves of Grass* as an "archetypal" poem produced and offered to America at its "central point"—a book "sway'd" by the nation and written to sway others. Such a work as Whitman calls for in *Democratic*

Vistas is surely the epic of America. And, basically, it is his own work which he desires to be recognized as such.

In "A Backward Glance o'er Travel'd Roads" (1888), summing up the contribution of his own work, Whitman again emphasizes the need of the nation for a commensurate poetry. But no longer is he evasive; his claim is direct: "As America fully and fairly construed is the legitimate result and evolutionary outcome of the past, so I would dare to claim for my verse." The Old World, as the poet points out, "has had the poems of myths, fictions, feudalism, conquest, caste, dynastic wars, and splendid exceptional characters," but the "New World needs the poems of realities and science and of the democratic average and basic equality." And, instead of the "splendid exceptional characters" of the Old World epics, the New World epic will portray simply—man: "In the centre of all, and object of all, stands the Human Being, towards whose heroic and spiritual evolution poems and everything directly or indirectly tend, Old World or New" (V, 54).

Should there be any doubts about the ambition of Whitman to write America's epic, the opening pages of *Leaves of Grass* should dispel them. In "Inscriptions" and "Starting from Paumanok" there are innumerable indications of the epic nature of the work. In the very opening poem, Whitman uses the construction, "I Sing," characteristic of the epic in introducing themes—"One's-Self I Sing," "The Female equally with the Male I sing," "The Modern Man I sing." In this first poem, too, the Muse is mentioned—"Not physiognomy alone nor brain alone is worthy for the Muse, I say the Form complete is worthier far"; but it is not until the second poem, "As I Ponder'd in Silence," that the Muse is invoked, addressed, and reassured. As the poet considers his work, he is visited by the Old World Muse:

> A Phantom arose before me with distrustful aspect,
> Terrible in beauty, age, and power,
> The genius of poets of old lands [I, 1].

This Muse is skeptical, for all past epics countenanced by the "haughty shade" have had as their subject the "theme of War, the fortune of battles,/The making of perfect soldiers." The poet welcomes the challenge and assures the Muse that he, too, sings of "war, and a longer and greater one than any." In the poet's war, the field is the world, the battle "For life and death, for the Body and for the eternal Soul." The central point of this key "Inscriptions" poem is that the poet's book qualifies as an epic, even under the Old World definition, if sufficient liberality is allowed in interpreting the terms.

There are other instances in *Leaves of Grass* in which Whitman calls attention to the epic nature of his book. In "Starting from Paumanok" he outlines his plan for encompassing in his poetry the entire nation— "Solitary, singing in the West, I strike up for a New World." The poems of *Leaves of Grass* are to constitute "a programme of chants" for "Americanos." The poet advises:

Take my leaves America, take them South and take them North,
Make welcome for them everywhere, for they are your own offspring
[I, 18].

Whitman's insistence on an intimate and unique relation between his
book and his country appears no more frequently than his appeal to
the Muse. In "Song of the Exposition," the form is epic if the tone is
comic:

> Come Muse migrate from Greece and Ionia,
> Cross out please those immensely overpaid accounts [I, 238].

If in this poem the Muse loses some of her dignity as the poet instals
her amid the drainpipes, artificial fertilizers, and the kitchen ware, in
"By Blue Ontario's Shore" the Muse is transfigured into a "Phantom
gigantic superb, with stern visage," who commands the poet:

Chant me the poem, *it said,* that comes from the soul of America, chant
   me the carol of victory,
And strike up the marches of Libertad, marches more powerful yet,
And sing me before you go the song of the throes of Democracy [II, 107].

It is characteristic of Whitman that he would reverse the Old World
epic practice by which the poet called upon the Muse for help and
would place the Muse in the position of pleading with the poet to continue his writing so that vital themes would not go unsung.

It is clear from both external and internal evidence that Whitman
thought of his work in epic terms. The extent to which he fulfilled
his epic ambitions, however, may be measured only in terms of his
final achievement. The answer that achievement provides is impressive.

For the hero of his epic, Whitman created the archetypal personality for the New World (the modern man of "One's-Self I Sing"),
a man both individual and of the mass. This hero, unlike the hero of
past epics, discovers his heroic qualities not in superman characteristics
but in the *selfhood* common to every man. Every man in America,
according to Whitman, is potentially an epic hero, if he is sufficiently
aware of the potentiality of his selfhood, if he celebrates his vital pro-
creative role, and if he is capable of depth of feeling in spiritually complex attachments. In doing and being all these things, the New World
epic hero sings the song of himself, acknowledges the parentage of Adam,
and finds spiritual fulfilment in "Calamus" comradeship. He accepts,
moreover, his New World place in space and position in time. He
relishes his home on the rolling earth, and he finds that his appointed
position in the unfolding of mystic evolution places him where all time
past converges and all time future originates.

Having created his epic hero by broad, free strokes in the first part
of *Leaves of Grass,* Whitman next engages him in the usual trial of
strength in a great and crucial war on which the national destiny depends. As Whitman's modern man of the New World represents above
all a reconciliation of the paradoxically opposed ideals of democracy—

individuality and equality (separateness and "en-masse")—so his epic hero paradoxically exemplifies both traits in war. "Drum-Taps" demonstrates the triumph of the American epic hero "en-masse." No individual is singled out from the rest for heroic deeds, but, throughout, the emphasis is on the ranks, the large mass of men welded together in comradeship and a common national purpose. The poet at one point asserts that America has too long "learn'd from joys and prosperity only":

But now, ah now, to learn from crises of anguish, advancing, grappling with direst fate and recoiling not,
And now to conceive and show to the world what your children en-masse really are,
(For who except myself has yet conceiv'd what your children en-masse really are?) [II, 77].

But, as the Civil War proved the heroic quality on an epic scale of America's "children en-masse," the same national crisis also demonstrated democracy's ability to produce individuality of epic proportions. "Drum-Taps" gives way to "Memories of President Lincoln" and that magnificent threnody, "When Lilacs Last in the Dooryard Bloom'd." But the traits of this epic hero are not different from but similar to the traits of the soldiers "en-masse." He is the "powerful western fallen star"; he is the captain of the ship whose loss is universally mourned; he is the "dear commander" of the soldiers; but he is above all the "departing comrade" who possessed an infinite capacity for love.

In the latter part of *Leaves of Grass,* the mythological background of the epic hero of the New World is completed as he is related to the "resistless gravitation of spiritual law." The entire section of the book from "Proud Music of the Storm" through "Whispers of Heavenly Death" not only presents the New World hero with "religious" convictions and impresses him with the reality of the spiritual world but also provides him with his immortality. Even the gods (like the heroes) in this New World epic are conceived in democratic terms. At the climactic point in "Passage to India" the poet exclaims:

Surrounded, copest, frontest God, yieldest, the aim attain'd,
As fill'd with friendship, love complete, the Elder Brother found,
The Younger melts in fondness in his arms [II, 196].

God is the "final" comrade, the perfect embodiment of those ideal traits earlier invested in the New World epic hero. The relationship to God is not the relationship of a subject to his superior but the relationship of the ideal brotherhood, the perfectly fulfilled comradeship.

In a very complicated way, Whitman's epic embodies at the same time that it creates America's image of itself—the American dream, the American vision, as it reached its climactic elaboration during the nineteenth century. If in retrospect Whitman's faith in science and democracy seems naïve, we must remember that our perspective is a bit jaded. And Whitman's faith was the American faith, his naïveté the American naïveté. In insisting on being the poet of science and democracy and, above all, of "religion," Whitman was not clinging to personal attitudes but was rather defining the nineteenth century's view of the universe and itself and reflecting it in his epic, as the epic poets of the past— Homer, Vergil, Dante, and Milton—reflected their own times in order to become epic spokesmen for their ages. Whitman embraced the modern "myth" of science, democracy, religion, and much more. The question of the "truth" of these nineteenth-century beliefs and attitudes is as irrelevant as the question of the "truth" of Homer's gods or Milton's devils. The relevant fact is that these views were held by an entire culture and the people lived and acted in the simple faith that their beliefs were true.

Leaves of Grass has just claim as America's epic. No attempt before it (and there were many) succeeded in becoming more than awkward imitations of the epics of the past. No book after it can ever again achieve its unique point of view. Coming shortly after the birth of the nation, embodying the country's first terrible trial by fire, prophesying the greatness to be thrust upon these states, Leaves of Grass possesses a position of intimate relationship with America that no other work can now ever assume. For better or worse, Leaves of Grass is America's, a reflection of her character and of her soul and of her achievements and her aspirations. If Leaves of Grass transfigures what it reflects, that is because its poet wanted to dwell not on the reality but on the ideal. If Leaves of Grass has its shortcomings and defects, so, surely, does the culture it attempted to embody. But after all the reservations are stated and the qualifications noted, we must confess that the book does measure up. If Whitman's vision exceeded his achievement, the scope of his achievement was still sufficient to win him just claim to the title of America's epic poet.

ARTHUR RIMBAUD

from

A SEASON IN HELL

Along with Whitman, Rimbaud is the chief hero of modern "Romanticism." Rimbaud is unique in world literature—a master poet who composed all his work between the ages of fourteen and eighteen, and then abandoned literature in disgust. Rimbaud created a myth of youthful revolt which is even today one of the moving forces of poetry. (The "Beat" poets, like many similar groups, all but worship him.)

The present excerpt is from Rimbaud's "prose poem" called *A Season in Hell*. His is not a hell of guilt, like Baudelaire's or Eliot's, but the hell caused by suppression—suppression by parental authority, church authority, state authority. Rimbaud escapes from these suppressions by diving into the world of hallucination in which he satisfies his dreams of liberation and revenge, and invents the modern world in which every human absurdity comes to life.

II. Alchemy of the Word

*N*ow for me! The story of one of my follies.

For a long time I boasted of possessing every possible landscape and held in derision the celebrities of modern painting and poetry.

I loved maudlin paintings, decorative panels, stage-sets, the backdrops of mountebanks, old inn signs, popular prints; old-fashioned literature, church Latin, erotic books innocent of all spelling, the novels of our ancestors, fairytales, children's storybooks, antiquated operas, inane refrains and artless rhythms.

I dreamed crusades, unrecorded voyages of discovery, republics without a history, religious wars hushed up, revolutions of customs, the displacements of races and continents: I believed in sorcery of every sort.

I invented the color of vowels!—*A* black, *E* white, *I* red, *O* blue, *U* green.—I regulated the form and the movement of every consonant, and with instinctive rhythms I prided myself on inventing a poetic language accessible some day to all the senses. I reserved all rights of translation.

At first it was an experiment. I wrote silences, I wrote the night. I recorded the inexpressible. I fixed frenzies in their flight.

.   .   .   .   .

Poetic quaintness played a large part in my alchemy of the word.

I became an adept at simple hallucination: in place of a factory I really saw a mosque, a school of drummers composed of angels, carriages on the highways of the sky, a drawing-room at the bottom of a lake; monsters, mysteries; the title of a melodrama would raise horrors before me.

Then I would explain my magic sophisms with the hallucination of words!

Finally I came to regard as sacred the disorder of my mind. I was idle, full of a sluggish fever: I envied the felicity of beasts, caterpillars that represent the innocence of limbo, moles, the sleep of virginity!

My temper soured. In kinds of ballads I said farewell to the world:*

* [This passage is followed by one of Rimbaud's more conventional poems. —Ed.]

LEWIS CARROLL

from

THROUGH THE LOOKING GLASS

Lewis Carroll's "Alice" books are among the most famous children's books in the world, but the effect of the Alice books reaches far beyond what their author intended. Carroll (whose real name was Dodgson) was a mathematics professor at Oxford. He made up his stories for children alone, and especially the child named Alice, but he inadvertently contributed to the modern novel and poem by using hallucination as his technique, like Rimbaud. The famous "Jabberwocky" poem, presented in the first chapter of *Through the Looking Glass,* is a parody of poetry and simultaneously an example of literary hallucination. Rimbaud used hallucination as an escape from his situation; Carroll also considered the established world insane and the "insanity" of the looking-glass or dream world a better version of reality.

Carroll's upside-down world is virtually the same thing as Rimbaud's revolutionary world: the hero-victim is the child. In Lewis Carroll's books the child always triumphs. At the end of the horrendous and comic adventures of Alice in Wonderland, she points her finger at her accusers and says contemptuously, "Why, you are nothing but a pack of cards!"—a sweeping condemnation of societies, empires, and cultural systems built upon pasteboard.

"Now, if you'll only attend, Kitty, and not talk so much, I'll tell you all my ideas about Looking-glass House. First, there's the room you can see through the glass—that's just the same as our drawing-room, only the things go the other way. I can see all of it when I get upon a chair—all but the bit just behind the fireplace. Oh! I do so wish I could see *that* bit! I want so much to know whether they've a fire in the winter: you never *can* tell, you know, unless our fire smokes, and then smoke comes up in that room too—but that may be only pretense, just to make it look as if they had a fire. Well then, the books are something like our books, only the words go the wrong way; I know that because I've held up one of our books to the glass, and then they hold up one in the other room.

"How would you like to live in Looking-glass House, Kitty? I wonder if they'd give you milk in there? Perhaps Looking-glass milk isn't good to drink—But oh, Kitty! now we come to the passage. You can just see a little *peep* of the passage in Looking-glass House, if you leave the door of our drawing-room wide open: and it's very like our passage as far as you can see, only you know it may be quite different on beyond. Oh, Kitty! how nice it would be if we only could get through into Looking-glass House! I'm sure it's got, oh! such beautiful things in it! Let's pretend there's a way of getting through into it, somehow, Kitty. Let's pretend the glass has got all soft like gauze, so that we can get through. Why, it's turning into a sort of mist now, I declare! It'll be easy enough to get through—" She was up on the chimney-piece while she said this, though she hardly knew how she had got there. And certainly the glass *was* beginning to melt away, just like a bright silvery mist.

In another moment Alice was through the glass, and jumped lightly down into the Looking-glass room. The very first thing she did was to look whether there was a fire in the fireplace, and she was quite pleased to find that there was a real one, blazing away as brightly as the one she had left behind. "So I shall be as warm here as I was in the old room," thought Alice: "warmer, in fact, because there'll be no one here to scold me away from the fire. Oh, what fun it'll be, when they see me through the glass in here, and can't get at me!"

Then she began looking about and noticed that what could be seen from the old room was quite common and uninteresting, but that all the rest was as different as possible. For instance, the pictures on the wall next the fire seemed to be all alive, and the very clock on the chimney-piece (you know you can only see the back of it in the looking-glass) had got the face of a little old man, and grinned at her.

"They don't keep this room so tidy as the other," Alice thought to herself, as she noticed several of the chessmen down in the hearth among the cinders: but in another moment, with a little "Oh!" of surprise, she was down on her hands and knees watching them. The chessmen were walking about two and two.

"Here are the Red King and the Red Queen," Alice said (in a whisper, for fear of frightening them) "and there are the White King and the White Queen sitting on the edge of the shovel—and here are two castles walking arm in arm—I don't think they can hear me," she went on as she put her head closer down, "and I'm nearly sure they can't see me. I feel somehow as if I were invisible—"

Here something began squeaking on the table behind Alice, and made her turn her head just in time to see one of the White Pawns roll over and begin kicking; she watched it with great curiosity to see what would happen next.

"It is the voice of my child!" the White Queen cried out, as she rushed past the King, so violently that she knocked him among the cinders.

"My precious Lily! My imperial kitten!" and she began scrambling wildly up the side of the fender.

"Imperial fiddlestick!" said the King, rubbing his nose, which had been hurt by the fall. He had a right to be a *little* annoyed with the Queen, for he was covered with ashes from head to foot.

Alice was very anxious to be of use, and, as the poor little Lily was nearly screaming herself into a fit, she hastily picked up the Queen and set her on the table by the side of her noisy little daughter.

The Queen gasped, and sat down: the rapid journey through the air had quite taken away her breath, and for a minute or two she could do nothing but hug the little Lily in silence. As soon as she recovered her breath a little, she called out to the White King, who was sitting sulkily among the ashes, "Mind the volcano!"

"What volcano?" said the King, looking up anxiously into the fire, as if he thought that was the most likely place to find one.

"Blew—me—up," panted the Queen, who was still a little out of breath. "Mind you come up—the regular way—don't get blown up!"

Alice watched the White King as he slowly struggled up from bar to bar, till at last she said:

"Why, you'll be hours and hours getting to the table, at that rate. I'd far better help you, hadn't I?" But the King took no notice of the question; it was quite clear that he could neither hear her nor see her.

So Alice picked him up very gently, and lifted him across more slowly than she had lifted the Queen, that she mightn't take his breath away; but before she put him on the table, she thought she might as well dust him a little, he was so covered with ashes.

She said afterward that she had never seen in all her life such a face as the King made, when he found himself held in the air by an invisible hand, and being dusted; and he was far too much astonished to cry out, but his eyes and his mouth went on getting larger and larger and rounder and rounder, till her hand shook so with laughter that she nearly let him drop upon the floor.

"Oh! *please* don't make such faces, my dear!" she cried out, quite forgetting that the King couldn't hear her. "You make me laugh so that I can hardly hold you! And don't keep your mouth so wide open! All the ashes will get into it—there, now I think you're tidy enough!" she added, as she smoothed his hair, and set him upon the table near the Queen.

The King immediately fell flat on his back, and lay perfectly still; and Alice was a little alarmed at what she had done, and went round the room to see if she could find any water to throw over him. However, she could find nothing but a bottle of ink, and when she got back with it she found he had recovered, and he and the Queen were talking together in a frightened whisper—so low, that Alice could hardly hear what they said.

The King was saying, "I assure you, my dear, I turned cold to the very ends of my whiskers!"

To which the Queen replied, "You haven't got any whiskers."

"The horror of that moment," the King went on, "I shall never, *never* forget!"

"You will, though," the Queen said, "if you don't make a memorandum of it."

Alice looked on with great interest as the King took an enormous memorandum-book out of his pocket, and began writing. A sudden thought struck her, and she took hold of the end of the pencil, which came some way over his shoulder, and began writing for him.

The poor King looked puzzled and unhappy, and struggled with the pencil for some time without saying anything; but Alice was too strong for him, and at last he panted out, "My dear! I really *must* get a thinner pencil. I can't manage this one a bit; it writes all manner of things that I don't intend—"

"What manner of things?" said the Queen, looking over the book (in which Alice had put *'The White Knight is sliding down the poker. He balances very badly'*). "That's not a memorandum of *your* feelings!"

There was a book lying near Alice on the table, and while she sat watching the White King (for she was still a little anxious about him, and had the ink all ready to throw over him, in case he fainted again), she turned over the leaves, to find some part that she could read, "for it's all in some language I don't know," she said to herself.

It was like this.

JABBERWOCKY

'Twas brillig, and the slithy toves
Did gyre and gimble in the wabe;
All mimsy were the borogoves,
And the mome raths outgrabe.

She puzzled over this for some time, but at last a bright thought struck her. "Why, it's a looking-glass-book, of course! And if I hold it up to a glass, the words will all go the right way again."

This was the poem that Alice read.

JABBERWOCKY

'Twas brillig, and the slithy toves
   Did gyre and gimble in the wabe;
All mimsy were the borogoves,
   And the mome raths outgrabe.

"Beware the Jabberwock, my son!
   The jaws that bite, the claws that catch!
Beware the Jubjub bird, and shun
   The frumious Bandersnatch!"

He took his vorpal sword in hand:
   Long time the manxome foe he sought—
So rested he by the Tumtum tree,
   And stood awhile in thought.

And as in uffish thought he stood,
   The Jabberwock, with eyes of flame,
Came whiffling through the tulgey wood,
   And burbled as it came!

> One, two! One, two! And through and through
> The vorpal blade went snicker-snack!
> He left it dead, and with its head
> He went galumphing back.
>
> "And hast thou slain the Jabberwock?
> Come to my arms, my beamish boy!
> O frabjous day! Callooh! Callay!"
> He chortled in his joy.
>
> 'Twas brillig, and the slithy toves
> Did gyre and gimble in the wabe;
> All mimsy were the borogoves,
> And the mome raths outgrabe.

"It seems very pretty," she said when she had finished it, "but it's *rather* hard to understand!" (You see she didn't like to confess, even to herself, that she couldn't make it out at all.) "Somehow it seems to fill my head with ideas—only I don't exactly know what they are! However, *somebody* killed *something*: that's clear, at any rate—"

GERARD MANLEY HOPKINS

preface to

POEMS

Gerard Manley Hopkins, a convert to Catholicism in Victorian England, is one of the most vital poets of the twentieth century. He was not appreciated or understood as a poet in his lifetime, and it was not until 1918 that his poems were published and acclaimed.

Any attempt to classify Hopkins as a Classicist or a Romantic will reveal the essential absurdity of these terms. He is included here among the Romantics, however, because of his revolutionary theory of versification ("sprung rhythm") and because of his poetic explorations into the "inscapes" and "instresses" of nature. It is significant to note that the modern Classicists hold strong reservations about Hopkins' "excessive" style and his rich love of all natural things.

The poems in this book are written some in Running Rhythm, the common rhythm in English use, some in Sprung Rhythm, and some in a mixture of the two. And those in the common rhythm are some counterpointed, some not.

Common English rhythm, called Running Rhythm above, is measured by feet of either two or three syllables and (putting aside the imperfect feet at the beginning and end of lines and also some unusual measures, in which feet seem to be paired together and double or composite feet to arise) never more or less.

Every foot has one principal stress or accent, and this or the syllable it falls on may be called the Stress of the foot and the other part, the one or two unaccented syllables, the Slack. Feet (and the rhythms made out of them) in which the stress comes first are called Falling Feet and Falling Rhythms, feet and rhythm in which the slack comes first are called Rising Feet and Rhythms, and if the stress is between two slacks there will be Rocking Feet and Rhythms. These distinctions are real and true to nature; but for purposes of scanning it is a great convenience to follow the example of music and take the stress always first, as the accent or the chief accent always comes first in a musical bar. If this is done there will be in common English verse only two possible feet—the so-called accentual Trochee and Dactyl, and correspondingly only two possible uniform rhythms, the so-called Trochaic and Dactylic. But they may be mixed and then what the Greeks called a Logaoedic Rhythm arises. These are the facts and according to these the scanning of ordinary regularly-written English verse is very simple indeed and to bring in other principles is here unnecessary.

But because verse written strictly in these feet and by these principles will become same and tame the poets have brought in licences and departures from rule to give variety, and especially when the natural rhythm is rising, as in the common ten-syllable or five-foot verse, rhymed or blank. These irregularities are chiefly Reversed Feet and Reversed or Counterpoint Rhythm, which two things are two steps or degrees of licence in the same kind. By a reversed foot I mean the putting the stress where, to judge by the rest of the measure, the slack should be and the slack where the stress, and this is done freely at the beginning of a line and, in the course of a line, after a pause; only scarcely ever in the second foot or place and never in the last, unless when the poet designs some extraordinary effect; for these places are characteristic and sensitive and cannot well be touched. But the reversal of the first foot and of some middle foot after a strong pause is a thing so natural that our poets have generally done it, from Chaucer down, without remark and it commonly passes unnoticed and cannot be said to amount to a formal change of rhythm, but rather is that irregularity which all natural growth and motion shews. If however the reversal is repeated in two feet running, especially so as to include the sensitive second foot, it must be due either to great want of ear or else is a calculated effect, the superinducing or *mounting* of a new rhythm upon the old; and since the new or mounted rhythm is actually heard and at the same time the mind naturally supplies the natural or standard foregoing rhythm, for we do not forget what the rhythm is that by rights we should be hearing, two rhythms are in some manner running at once and we have something answerable to counterpoint in music, which is two or more strains of tune going on together, and this is Counterpoint Rhythm. Of this kind of verse Milton is the great master and the choruses of *Samson Agonistes* are written throughout in it—but with the disadvantage that he does not let the reader clearly know what the ground-rhythm is meant to be and so they have struck most readers as merely irregular. And in fact if you counterpoint throughout, since one only of the counter rhythms is actually heard, the other is really destroyed or cannot come to exist, and what is written is one rhythm only and probably Sprung Rhythm, of which I now speak.

Sprung Rhythm, as used in this book, is measured by feet of from one to four syllables, regularly, and for particular effects any number of weak or slack syllables may be used. It has one stress, which falls on the only syllable, if there is only one, or, if there are more, then scanning as above, on the first, and so gives rise to four sorts of feet, a monosyllable and the so-called accentual Trochee, Dactyl, and the First Paeon. And there will be four corresponding natural rhythms; but nominally the feet are mixed and any one may follow any other. And hence Sprung Rhythm differs from Running Rhythm in having or being only one nominal rhythm, a mixed or 'logaoedic' one, instead of three, but on the other hand in having twice the flexibility of foot, so that any two stresses may either follow one another running or be divided by one, two, or three slack syllables. But strict Sprung Rhythm cannot be counterpointed. In Sprung Rhythm, as in logaoedic rhythm generally, the feet are assumed to be equally long or strong and their seeming inequality is made up by pause or stressing.

Remark also that it is natural in Sprung Rhythm for the lines to be *rove over*, that is for the scanning of each line immediately to take up that of the one before, so that if the first has one or more syllables at its end the other must have so many the less at its beginning; and in fact the scanning runs on without break from the beginning, say, of a stanza to the end and all the stanza is one long strain, though written in lines asunder.

Two licences are natural to Sprung Rhythm. The one is rests, as in music; but of this an example is scarcely to be found in this book, unless in the *Echos,* second line. The other is *hangers* or *outrides,* that is one, two, or three slack syllables added to a foot and not counting in the nominal scanning. They are so called because they seem to hang below the line or ride forward or backward from it in another dimension than the line itself, according to a principle needless to explain here. These outriding half feet or hangers are marked by a loop underneath them, and plenty of them will be found.

The other marks are easily understood, namely accents, where the reader might be in doubt which syllable should have the stress; slurs, that is loops *over* syllables, to tie them together into the time of one; little loops at the end of a line to shew that the rhyme goes on to the first letter of the next line; what in music are called pauses ⌒, to shew that the syllable should be dwelt on; and twirls ~, to mark reversed or counter-pointed rhythm.

Note on the nature and history of Sprung Rhythm—Sprung Rhythm is the most natural of things. For (1) it is the rhythm of common speech and of written prose, when rhythm is perceived in them. (2) It is the rhythm of all but the most monotonously regular music, so that in the words of choruses and refrains and in songs written closely to music it arises. (3) It is found in nursery rhymes, weather saws, and so on; because, however these may have been once made in running rhythm, the terminations having dropped off by the change of language, the stresses come together and so the rhythm is sprung. (4) It arises in common verse when reversed or counterpointed, for the same reason.

But nevertheless in spite of all this and though Greek and Latin lyric verse, which is well known, and the old English verse seen in *Pierce Ploughman* are in sprung rhythm, it has in fact ceased to be used since the Elizabethan age, Greene being the last writer who can be said to have recognised it. For perhaps there was not, down to our days, a single, even short, poem in English in which sprung rhythm is employed—not for single effects or in fixed places—but as the governing principle of the scansion. I say this because the contrary has been asserted: if it is otherwise the poem should be cited.

Some of the sonnets in this book are in five-foot, some in six-foot or Alexandrine lines.

Nos. 13 and 22 are Curtal-Sonnets, that is they are constructed in proportions resembling those of the sonnet proper, namely 6 + 4 instead of 8 + 6, with however a halfline tailpiece (so that the equation is rather $12\frac{1}{2} + \frac{1}{2} = 2\frac{1}{2} = 10\frac{1}{2}$).

GERARD MANLEY HOPKINS

from his notebooks
Inscape and Instress

1871

*E*nd of March and beginning of April—This is the time to study inscape* in the spraying of trees, for the swelling buds carry

---

* [W. A. M. Peters, S.J., in his *Gerard Manley Hopkins*, gives the following definition: "I infer that '*in*-scape' is the outward reflection of the *inner* nature of a thing, or a sensible copy or presentation of its individual essence. . . ."—Ed.]

them to a pitch which the eye could not else gather—for out of much much more, out of little not much, out of nothing nothing: in these sprays at all events there is a new world of inscape. The male ashes are very boldly jotted with the heads of the bloom which tuft the outer ends of the branches. The staff of each of these branches is closely knotted with the places where buds are or have been, so that it is something like a finger which has been tied up with string and keeps the marks. They are in knops of a pair, one on each side, and the knops are set alternately, at crosses with the knops above and the knops below, the bud of course is a short smoke-black pointed nail-head or beak pieced of four lids or nippers. Below it, like the hollow below the eye or the piece between the knuckle and the root of the nail, is a half-moon-shaped sill as if once chipped from the wood and this gives the twig its quaining in the outline. When the bud breaks at first it shews a heap of fruity purplish anthers looking something like unripe elder-berries but these push open into richly-branched tree-pieces coloured buff and brown, shaking out loads of pollen, and drawing the tuft as a whole into peaked quains—mainly four, I think, two bigger and two smaller

.   .   .   .   .

April 27. . . . Mesmerised a duck with chalk lines drawn from her beak sometimes level and sometimes forwards on a black table. They explain that the bird keeping the abiding offscape of the hand grasping her neck fancies she is still held down and cannot lift her head as long as she looks at the chalk line, which she associates with the power that holds her. This duck lifted her head at once when I put it down on the table without chalk. But this seems inadequate. It is most likely the fascinating instress* of the straight white stroke

.   .   .   .   .

June 13. A beautiful instance of inscape sided on the slide, that is successive sidings of one inscape, is seen in the behaviour of the flag flower from the shut bud to the full blowing: each term you can distinguish is beautiful in itself and of course if the whole 'behaviour' were gathered up and so stalled it would have a beauty of all the higher degree

.   .   .   .   .

1872

Feb. 23. A lunar halo: I looked at it from the upstairs library window. It was a grave grained sky, the strands rising a little from left to right.

---

* [Peters gives this definition: "The original meaning of instress then is that stress or energy of being by which 'all things are upheld' and strive after continued existence. Placing 'instress' by the side of 'inscape' we note that the instress will strike the poet as the force that holds the inscape together; it is for him the power that ever actualizes the inscape."—Ed.]

The halo was not quite round, for in the first place it was a little pulled and drawn below, by the refraction of the lower air perhaps, but what is more it fell in on the nether left hand side to rhyme the moon itself, which was not quite at full. I could not but strongly feel in my fancy the odd instress of this, the moon leaning on her side, as if fallen back, in the cheerful light floor within the ring, after with magical rightness and success tracing round her the ring the steady copy of her own outline. But this sober grey darkness and pale light was happily broken through by the orange of the pealing of Mitton bells

Another night from the gallery window I saw a brindled heaven, the moon just marked by a blue spot pushing its way through the darker cloud, underneath and on the skirts of the rack bold long flakes whitened and swaled like feathers, below the garden with the heads of the trees and shrubs furry grey: I read a broad careless inscape flowing throughout

At the beginning of March they were felling some of the ashes in our grove

.   .   .   .   .

July 19. The ovary of the blown foxglove surrounded by the green calyx is perhaps that conventional flower in Pointed and other floriated work which I could not before identify. It might also be St. John's-wort

Stepped into a barn of ours, a great shadowy barn, where the hay had been stacked on either side, and looking at the great rudely arched timber-frames—principals(?) and tie-beams, which make them look like bold big *A*'s with the cross-bar high up—I thought how sadly beauty of inscape was unknown and buried away from simple people and yet how near at hand it was if they had eyes to see it and it could be called out everywhere again. . . .

After the examinations we went for our holiday out to Douglas in the Isle of Man Aug. 3. At this time I had first begun to get hold of the copy of Scotus on the Sentences in the Baddely library and was flush with a new stroke of enthusiasm. It may come to nothing or it may be a mercy from God. But just then when I took in any inscape of the sky or sea I thought of Scotus

.   .   .   .   .

Dec. 12. A Blandyke.[1] Hard frost, bright sun, a sky of blue 'water.' On the fells with Mr. Lucas. Parlick Pike and that ridge ruddy with fern and evening light. Ground sheeted with taut tattered streaks of crisp gritty snow. Green-white tufts of long bleached grass like heads of hair or the crowns of heads of hair, each a whorl of slender curves, one tuft taking up another—however these I might have noticed any day. I saw the inscape though freshly, as if my eye were still growing, though with a companion the eye and the ear are for the most part shut and instress cannot come. We started pheasants and a grouse with flickering

---

[1] Stonyhurst word for a monthly holiday.

wings. On the slope of the far side under the trees the fern looked ginger-coloured over the snow. When there was no snow and dark greens about, as I saw it just over the stile at the top of the Forty-Acre the other day, It made bats and splinters of smooth caky road-rut-colour

. . . . .

1873

April 8. The ashtree growing in the corner of the garden was felled. It was lopped first: I heard the sound and looking out and seeing it maimed there came at that moment a great pang and I wished to die and not to see the inscapes of the world destroyed any more

. . . . .

July 22. Very hot, though the wind, which was south, dappled very sweetly on one's face and when I came out I seemed to put it on like a gown as a man puts on the shadow he walks into and hoods or hats himself with the shelter of a roof, a penthouse, or a copse of trees, I mean it rippled and fluttered like light linen, one could feel the folds and braids of it—and indeed a floating flag is like wind visible and what weeds are in a current; it gives it thew and fires it and bloods it in.— Thunderstorm in the evening, first booming in gong-sounds, as at Aosta, as if high up and so not reechoed from the hills; the lightning very slender and nimble and as if playing very near but after supper it was so bright and terrible some people said they had never seen its like. People were killed, but in other parts of the country it was more violent than with us. Flashes lacing two clouds above or the cloud and the earth started upon the eyes in live veins of rincing or riddling liquid white, inched and jagged as if it were the shivering of a bright riband string which had once been kept bound round a blade and danced back into its pleatings. Several strong thrills of light followed the flash but a grey smother of darkness blotted the eyes if they had seen the fork, also dull furry thickened scapes of it were left in them

. . . . .

1874

July 12. I noticed the smell of the big cedar, not just in passing it but always at a patch of sunlight on the walk a little way off. I found the bark smelt in the sun and not in the shade and I fancied too this held even of the smell it shed in the air.

July 13. The comet—I have seen it at bedtime in the west, with head to the ground, white, a soft well-shaped tail, not big: I felt a certain awe and instress, a feeling of strangeness, flight (it hangs like a shuttlecock at the height, before it falls), and of threatening.

5

THE ROMANTIC VOYAGER

WILFRED OWEN

preface to

POEMS

One of the literary results of the First World War was the birth
of a powerful antiwar poetry and the death of the sentimental,
patriotic literature. Owen, an officer in the British Army and a
hero of battle, wrote some of the most powerful antiwar poetry in
literature. Owen was killed a few days before the Armistice, but his
poetry and the little unfinished Preface became a kind of manifesto for the poets of the generation of Auden, Spender, Day
Lewis, and MacNeice.

*T*his book is not about heroes. English Poetry is not yet fit to
speak of them.

Nor is it about deeds, or lands, nor anything about glory, honour,
might, majesty, dominion, or power, except War.

Above all I am not concerned with Poetry.

My subject is War, and the pity of War.

The Poetry is in the pity.

Yet these elegies are to this generation in no sense consolatory. They
may be to the next. All a poet can do to-day is warn. That is why the
true Poets must be truthful.

(If I thought the letter of this book would last, I might have used
proper names; but if the spirit of it survives—survives Prussia—my am-

bition and those names will have achieved themselves fresher fields than
Flanders. . . .)

W. H. AUDEN

from THE ENCHAFED FLOOD

The Artist as Don Quixote

Auden has been one of the most articulate spokesmen for the
Romantic position in modern poetry. In the following notes, taken
from a prose work defining the nature of the Romantic artist, he
describes the Romantic as a poet accursed by society and by his
own nature. Auden's Romanticism is complicated by his eventual
surrender to the Classical religious position and the belief that
dogma is once again a necessity for the poet. Thus he rejoins Eliot
and Eliot's school after a long career as anti-Classicist.

*T*o understand the romantic identification of sin with consciousness, we must take it together with two other romantic characteristics, the romantic image of the hero as a mariner, an explorer of
novelty, and the romantic contempt for the bourgeois and respectable,
the churl who lives by conventional custom and habit. Is not this
nostalgia for innocence precisely the characteristic of the man whose
dedicated career is the exploration of the hitherto unknown and unconscious, who is by the very nature of his voyage travelling farther
and farther away from unconsciousness; and would not the same man
despise most those who have started, cannot go back, yet dare not go
forward?

In earlier ages it was the business of the artist to record the great acts
and thoughts of others. Hector and Achilles are the heroes; Homer
records them. Later the hero might be Truth, and the poet's business to
set down what has oft been thought but ne'er so well expressed. The
contribution of the poet, that is, was his gift for language.

The characteristic of the Romantic period is that the artist, the maker
himself, becomes the epic hero, the daring thinker, whose deeds he has
to record. Between about 1770 and 1914 the great heroic figures are
not men of action but individual geniuses, both artists and, of course,
scientists (but they are not our province) with a religious dedication to
furthering knowledge, and the kind of knowledge the artist could

obtain was chiefly from himself. Characteristically, the subtitle of Wordsworth's epic poem is "The Growth of the Poet's Mind." Faust, Don Juan, Captain Ahab are not really the heroes of their respective books, but the imaginative projections of their creators, i.e., what they do is not really done as a man of action acts for the sake of the act, but in order to know what it feels like to act. Ahab is, so to speak, what it feels like to be Ishmael the recorder. The artist who has thus to be at once the subject of his experiment and the recorder enjoys excitement and suffers terrors hardly known before. He ceases to have an identity and becomes like the Baker, who cannot remember his name and no longer bakes but hunts. He used to bake bridecake, i.e., his recording of glorious deeds and thoughts strengthened the bonds of community. Now he is a nomad explorer, whose one virtue is his courage that can

> "joke with hyaenas returning their stare
> With an impudent wag of the head."

Further, to become so dedicated to a lonely task, done not for the public but for the sake of the truth, mere talent is insufficient. The romantic artist is a *poète maudit*, i.e., an individual marked out by some catastrophe like Ahab's which supplies the driving passion to go ever forward, to the limits of exhaustion.

Nothing was not to be known, nothing: hysteria, debauchery, disorder, grief, nor despair.

What Rimbaud said of himself in *Une Saison en Enfer* before bidding good-bye to art is true, more or less, one way or another, of them all.

Je m'habituai à l'hallucination simplex: je voyais très franchement une mosquée à la place d'une usine, une école de tambours faite par les anges, des calèches sur les routes du ciel, un salon au fond d'un lac; les monstres, les mystères; un titre de vaudeville dressait des épouvantes devant moi. Puis j'expliquai mes sophismes magiques avec l'hallucination des mots! Je finis par trouver sacré le desordre de mon esprit. J'étais oisif, en proie à une lourde fièvre: j'enviais la félicité des bêtes,—les chenilles, qui représentent l'innocence des limbes, les taupes, le sommeil de la virginité.
(Une Saison en Enfer) *

Small wonder then if their capacity for experience was burned out quite early, like Wordsworth's, or if the ability to express vanished in a welter of feelings, like Coleridge's, or if the man himself suffered from spleen, like Baudelaire. More remarkable is the realisation by some of them that the artist is not, as he had thought, Don Quixote, the Religious Hero, but only Ishmael, the explorer of possibility, for whom the Button-Moulder and the Boojum are waiting at the next cross-roads where they will be asked to prove whether or no they have become their actual selves.

Thus Melville:

---

* [See p. 187 for translation.]

Round the world! There is much in that sound to inspire proud feelings; but whereto does all that circumnavigation lead? Only through numberless perils to the very point whence we started, where those that we left behind secure were all the time before us.

Thus Rimbaud:

"I! I who called myself magus or angel, dispensed with all morality, I am cast back to the soil, with a duty to seek, and enough actuality to grasp! Peasant!—I will ask pardon for having nourished myself on lies. And now, let us go."

(Une Saison en Enfer)

We live in a new age in which the artist neither can have such a unique heroic importance nor believes in the Art-God enough to desire it, an age, for instance, when the necessity of dogma is once more recognised, not as the contradiction of reason and feeling but as their ground and foundation, in which the heroic image is not the nomad wanderer through the desert or over the ocean, but the less exciting figure of the builder, who renews the ruined walls of the city. Our temptations are not theirs. We are less likely to be tempted by solitude into Promethean pride: we are far more likely to become cowards in the face of the tyrant who would compel us to lie in the service of the False City. It is not madness we need to flee but prostitution. Let us, reading the logs of their fatal but heroic voyages, remember their courage.

Melville once wrote a Requiem for soldiers lost in ocean transports, which seems to me no less fitting a requiem for him and his brethren in France, England and America.

> All creatures joying in the morn,
> Save them forever from joyance torn,
>   Whose bark was lost where now the dolphins play;
> Save them that by the fabled shore,
>   Down the pale stream are washed away,
> Far to the reef of bones are borne;
>   And never revisits them the light,
> Nor sight of long-sought land and pilot more;
>   Nor heed they now the lone bird's flight
> Round the lone spar where mid-sea surges pour.

WILLIAM CARLOS WILLIAMS

from

IN THE AMERICAN GRAIN

Williams' sketches of the great American heroes are frequently negative. Benjamin Franklin's worship of thrift, for instance, is interpreted by Williams as a doctrine of smugness which would turn into a national worship of Security. The more practical Franklin became, the less beautiful were the results of his practicality. His "meddling" with the lightning, as Williams puts it, is a desecration of the American spirit and of nature itself.

Williams stands against Eliot in modern poetry as the most energetic influence for a truly national American poetry based upon trial and error, spontaneity, use of the American language, and for an unremitting honesty and self-criticism of the American situation.

*H*e's sort of proud of his commonness, isn't he?"

He was the balancer full of motion without direction, the gyroscope which by its large spinning kept us, at that early period of our fate, upon an even keel.

The greatest winner of his day, he represents a voluptuousness of omnivorous energy brought to a dead stop by the rock of New World inopportunity. His energy never attained to a penetrant gist; rather it was stopped by and splashed upon the barrier, like a melon. His "good" was scattered about him. This is what is called being "practical." At such "success" we smile to see Franklin often so puffed up.

In the sheer mass of his voluptuous energy lies his chief excuse—a trait he borrowed without recognition from the primitive profusion of his surroundings.

Relaxed in a mass of impedimenta he found opportunity for thought.

Franklin, along with all the responsible aristocrats of his period, shows the two major characteristics of a bulky, crude energy, something in proportion to the continent, and a colossal restraint equalizing it. The result must have been a complete cancellation, frustration or descent to a low plane for release, which latter alternative he chose shiningly.

He played with lightning and the French court.

The great force (which was in him the expression of the New World) must have had not only volume but a quality, the determination of which will identify him. It was in Franklin, as shown characteristically in this letter, a scattering to reconnoitre.

Poor Richard's Almanac was as important in founding the nation as Paine's *Age of Reason*—he adaged them into a kind of pride in possession.

By casting scorn at men merely of birth while stressing the foundation of estates which should be family strongholds he did the service of discouraging aristocracy and creating it—the qualifying condition being that he repelled that which was foreign and supported that which was native—on a lower level FOR THE TIME BEING. He sparred for time: he was a diplomat of distinction with positive New World characteristics.

His mind was ALL out of the New World. Feeling a strength, a backing which was the New itself, he could afford to be sly with France, England or any nation; since, to live, he had to be sly with the massive strength of that primitive wilderness with whose conditions he had been bred to battle: thus, used to a mass EQUAL to them, he could swing them too. So again he asserted his nativity.

Strong and New World in innate strength, he is without beauty. The force of the New World is never in these men open; it is sly, covert, almost cringing. It is the mass that forces them into praise of mediocrity to escape its compulsions: so there is a kind of nastiness in his TOUCHING the hand of the Marchioness, in his meddling with the lightning, a resentment against his upstart bumptiousness in advising London how to light its stupidly ill-lit streets.

There has not yet appeared in the New World any one with sufficient strength for the open assertion. So with Franklin, the tone is frightened and horribly smug—at his worst; it flames a little in de Soto; it is necessary to Boone to lose himself in the wilds; there are no women— Houston's bride is frightened off; the New Englanders are the clever bone-men. Nowhere the open, free assertion save in the Indian: this is the quality. Jones has to leave the American navy, we feel, to go to Russia, for release.

It is necessary in appraising our history to realize that the nation was the offspring of the desire to huddle, to protect—of terror—superadded to a new world of great beauty and ripest blossom that well-nigh no man of distinction saw save Boone.

Franklin is the full development of the timidity, the strength that denies itself.

Such is his itch to serve science.

"Education" represented to these pioneers an *obscure* knowledge of the great beauty that was denied them, but of the great beauty under their feet no man seems to have been conscious, to appreciable degree; the foundation they must *first* appraise.

Nowhere does the full assertion come through save as a joke, jokingly, that masks the rest.

The terrible beauty of the New World attracts men to their ruin. Franklin did not care to be ruined—he only wanted to touch.

"I wish he hadn't gone fooling with lightning; I wish he'd left it alone—the old fool." Sure enough, he didn't dare let it go in at the top of his head and out at his toes, that's it; he *had* to fool with it. He sensed the power and knew only enough to want to run an engine with it. His fingers itched to be meddling, to do the little concrete thing—the barrier against a flood of lightning that would inundate him. Of course he was the most useful, "the most industrious citizen that Philadelphia or America had ever known." He was the dike keeper, keeping out the wilderness with his wits. Fear drove his curiosity.

Do something, anything, to keep the fingers busy—not to realize—the lightning. Be industrious, let money and comfort increase; money is like a bell that keeps the dance from terrifying, as it would if it were silent and we could hear the grunt,—thud—swish. It is small, hard; it keeps the attention fixed so that the eyes shall not see. And such is humor: pennies—that see gold come of copper by adding together, shrewd guesses hidden under the armament of an humble jest.

Poor Richard.

Don't offend.

His mighty answer to the New World's offer of a great embrace was THRIFT. Work night and day, build up, penny by penny, a wall against that which is threatening, the terror of life, poverty. Make a fort to be secure in.

The terrific energy of the new breed is its first character; the second is its terror before the NEW.

As a boy, he had tentatively loosed himself once to love, to curiosity perhaps, which was the birth of his first son. But the terror of that dare must have frightened the soul out of him. Having dared that once, his heart recoiled; his teaching must have smitten him. But Franklin, shrewd fellow, did not succumb to the benumbing judgment and go branded, repentant or rebellious. He trotted off gaily to Philly and noticed Bettsy in the shop on Arch Street, the first day.

He is our wise prophet of chicanery, the great buffoon, the face on the penny stamp.

The shock his youth got went into the fibre of the Constitution: he joked himself into a rich life—so he joked the country into a good alliance: to fortify, to buckle up—and reserve a will to be gay, to BE —(on the side).

Poor Richard: Save, be rich—and do as you please—might have been his motto, with an addendum: provided your house has strong walls and thick shutters.

Prince Richard in the lamb's skin: with a tongue in the cheek for aristocracy, humbly, arrogantly (that you may wish to imitate me) touching everything.

To want to touch, not to wish anything to remain clean, aloof—comes always of a kind of timidity, from fear.

The character they had (our pioneer statesmen, etc.) was that of giving their fine energy, as they must have done, to the smaller, narrower, protective thing and not to the great, New World. Yet they cannot quite leave hands off it but must TOUCH it, in a "practical" way, that is a joking, shy, nasty way, using "science" etc., not with the generosity of the savage or scientist but in a shameful manner. The sweep of the force was too horrible to them; it would have swept them into chaos. They HAD to do as they *could* but it can be no offense that their quality should be *named*. They could have been inspired by the new QUALITY about them to yield to loveliness in a fresh spirit.

It is the placing of his enthusiasm that characterizes the man.

It is not to mark Franklin, but to attempt to appraise the nature of the difficulties that molded him, the characteristic *weight of the mass;* how nearly all our national heroes have been driven back—and praised by reason of their shrewdness in making walls: not in bursting into flower.

To discover the NEW WORLD: that there is something there: what it has done to us, its quality, its weight, its prophets, its—horrible temper.

The niggardliness of our history, our stupidity, sluggishness of spirit, the falseness of our historical notes, the complete missing of the point. Addressed to the wrong head, the tenacity with which the fear still inspires laws, customs,—the suppression of the superb corn dance of the Chippewas, since it symbolizes the generative processes,—as if morals have but one character, and that,—sex: while morals are deformed in the name of PURITY; till, in the confusion, almost nothing remains of the great American New World but a memory of the Indians.

E. E. CUMMINGS

introduction to
POEMS 1923–1954

Cummings' Romantic "I" is usually written as lower case "i" and symbolizes his revolt against standardized society, whether democratic or socialistic. The small "i" is a protest against the artificial dream-world of science as well. Cummings considers the artist all but lost in the jungle of modern life, and he celebrates in bitter satire his contempt for the salesman, the politician, the physicist, and the traditional sentimental poet. His sometimes difficult technique represents a striving for the simplicity and freshness of the child, or the unspoiled individual who has not surrendered to the pressures of conformity.

*T*he poems to come are for you and for me and are not for mostpeople
—it's no use trying to pretend that mostpeople and ourselves are alike.

Mostpeople have less in common with ourselves than the squarerootof-minusone. You and I are human beings;mostpeople are snobs.

Take the matter of being born. What does being born mean to most-people? Catastrophe unmitigated. Socialrevolution. The cultured aristo-crat yanked out of his hyperexclusively ultravoluptuous superpalazzo,and dumped into an incredibly vulgar detentioncamp swarming with every conceivable species of undesirable organism. Mostpeople fancy a guaran-teed birthproof safetysuit of nondestructible selflessness. If mostpeople were to be born twice they'd improbably call it dying—

you and I are not snobs. We can never be born enough. We are human beings;for whom birth is a supremely welcome mystery,the mystery of growing:the mystery which happens only and whenever we are faithful to ourselves. You and I wear the dangerous looseness of doom and find it becoming. Life,for eternal us,is now;and now is much too busy being a little more than everything to seem anything,catastrophic included.

Life,for mostpeople,simply isn't. Take the socalled standardofliving. What do mostpeople mean by "living"? They don't mean living. They mean the latest and closest plural approximation to singular prenatal passivity which science,in its finite but unbounded wisdom,has succeeded in selling their wives. If science could fail,a mountain's a mammal. Most-people's wives can spot a genuine delusion of embryonic omnipotence immediately and will accept no substitutes

—luckily for us,a mountain is a mammal. The plusorminus movie to end moving,the strictly scientific parlourgame of real unreality,the tyranny conceived in misconception and dedicated to the proposition that every man is a woman and any woman a king,hasn't a wheel to stand on. What their most synthetic not to mention transparent majesty,mrsandmr collective foetus,would improbably call a ghost is walking. He isn't an undream of anaesthetized impersons,or a cosmic comfortstation,or a tran-scendentally sterilized lookiesoundiefeelietastiesmellie. He is a healthily complex,a naturally homogeneous,citizen of immortality. The now of his each pitying free imperfect gesture,his any birth or breathing,insults per-fected inframortally millenniums of slavishness. He is a little more than everything,he is democracy;he is alive:he is ourselves.

Miracles are to come. With you I leave a remembrance of mira-cles:they are by somebody who can love and who shall be con-tinually reborn,a human being;somebody who said to those near him, when his fingers would not hold a brush "tie it into my hand"—

nothing proving or sick or partial. Nothing false,nothing difficult or easy or small or colossal. Nothing ordinary or extraordinary,nothing emptied or filled,real or unreal;nothing feeble and known or clumsy and guessed. Everywhere tints childrening,innocent spontaneous,true. No-where possibly what flesh and impossibly such a garden,but actually flowers which breasts are among the very mouths of light. Nothing believed or doubted;brain over heart,surface:nowhere hating or to fear; shadow,mind without soul. Only how measureless cool flames of making; only each other building always distinct selves of mutual entirely opening;

only alive. Never the murdered finalities of wherewhen and yesno,impo-
tent nongames of wrongright and rightwrong;never to gain or pause,never
the soft adventure of undoom,greedy anguishes and cringing ecstasies of
inexistence;never to rest and never to have:only to grow.

Always the beautiful answer who asks a more beautiful question

6

ROMANTIC SELF-CRITICISM

ROBINSON JEFFERS

the dregs of romanticism—foreword to

SELECTED POETRY OF ROBINSON JEFFERS

The defeat of the Romantic position in the twentieth century has resulted in some cases in an almost suicidal philosophy of human despair. The poetry of Robinson Jeffers affords the best example: the failure of man to realize his own greatness causes Jeffers to turn upon the human race itself and to depict it in all its sadistic violence and corruption. This is inverted Romanticism, so to speak, and it borders on absurdity. Drawing heavily upon modern psychology and the German pessimistic philosophers (such as Schopenhauer), the Greek tragedians, and even the Marquis de Sade, Jeffers constructs a world-view which is virtually nihilistic to man.

*T*his book presents in one volume about half of my published work. In making the selection it was easy to eliminate the poems published in 1912 and 1916, which were only preparatory exercises, to say the best for them; and it was easy to omit a number of shorter poems from later volumes. After that the selection became more or less arbitrary. Several of the longer poems had to be omitted, for I have no desire to publish a "collected works" at this time, but there appears little reason to choose among them. *The Women at Point Sur* seems to me—in spite of grave faults—the most inclusive, and poetically the most intense, of any of my poems; it is omitted from this selection because it is the least understood and least liked, and because it is the longest. *Dear Judas* also was not liked and is therefore omitted, though I think it has value, if any of these poems has. *Such Counsels You Gave to Me* is omitted in order to make room for a number of shorter pieces from the same volume. The omission of *Cawdor* is purely arbitrary and accidental; I had finally to choose between this and *Thurso's Landing;* and there was no ground for choice; I simply drew lots in my mind.

The arrangement of the book is merely chronological; the long poems are presented in the order of their writing, the short ones in groups as they were first published. The earliest of the long poems was written, I think, in 1921 and 1922; the earliest of the short ones in 1917. This is *The Songs of the Dead Men to the Three Dancers*—choruses from a wartime play—reprinted here only as a sample of the metrical experiments that occupied my mind for awhile.

A good friend of mine, who is also my publisher, wants me to turn this foreword to some account; he says that a number of people have written pro and con about my verses, and it is high time for the author himself to say something. Very likely. But I do not wish to commend or defend them, though sufficiently attacked; and it seems to me that their meaning is not obscure. Perhaps a few notes about their origins may be of interest to anyone who is interested in the verses themselves.

Long ago, before anything included here was written, it became evident to me that poetry—if it was to survive at all—must reclaim some of the power and reality that it was so hastily surrendering to prose. The modern French poetry of that time, and the most "modern" of the English poetry, seemed to me thoroughly defeatist, as if poetry were in terror of prose, and desperately trying to save its soul from the victor by giving up its body. It was becoming slight and fantastic, abstract, unreal, eccentric; and was not even saving its soul, for these are generally anti-poetic qualities. It must reclaim substance and sense, and physical and psychological reality. This feeling has been basic in my mind since then. It led me to write narrative poetry, and to draw subjects from contemporary life; to present aspects of life that modern poetry had generally avoided; and to attempt the expression of philosophic and scientific ideas in verse. It was not in my mind to open new fields for poetry, but only to reclaim old freedom.

Still it was obvious that poetry and prose are different things; their provinces overlap, but must not be confused. Prose, of course, is free of all fields; it seemed to me, reading poetry and trying to write it, that poetry is bound to concern itself chiefly with permanent things and the permanent aspects of life. That was perhaps the great distinction between them, as regards subject and material. Prose can discuss matters of the moment; poetry must deal with things that a reader two thousand years away could understand and be moved by. This excludes much of the circumstance of modern life, especially in the cities. Fashions, forms of machinery, the more complex social, financial, political adjustments, and so forth, are all ephemeral, exceptional; they exist but will never exist again. Poetry must concern itself with (relatively) permanent things. These have poetic value; the ephemeral has only news value.

Another formative principle came to me from a phrase of Nietzsche's: "The poets? The poets lie too much." I was nineteen when the phrase stuck in my mind; a dozen years passed before it worked effectively, and I decided not to tell lies in verse. Not to feign any emotion that I did not feel; not to pretend to believe in optimism or pessimism, or unreversible progress; not to say anything because it was popular, or generally accepted, or fashionable in intellectual circles, unless I myself believed it; and not to believe easily. These negatives limit the field; I am not recommending them but for my own occasions.

Here are the principles that conditioned the verse in this book before it was written; but it would not have been written at all except for certain accidents that changed and directed my life. (Some kind of verse I should have written, of course, but not this kind.) The first of these accidents was my meeting with the woman to whom this book is dedicated, and her influence, constant since that time. My nature is cold and undiscriminating; she excited and focused it, gave it eyes and nerves and sympathies. She never saw any of my poems until they were finished and typed, yet by her presence and conversation she has co-authored every one of them. Sometimes I think there must be some value in them, if only for that reason. She is more like a woman in a Scotch ballad, passionate, untamed and rather heroic—or like a falcon —than like any ordinary person.

A second piece of pure accident brought us to the Monterey coast mountains, where for the first time in my life I could see people living —amid magnificent unspoiled scenery—essentially as they did in the Idyls or the Sagas, or in Homer's Ithaca. Here was life purged of its ephemeral accretions. Men were riding after cattle, or plowing the headland, hovered by white sea-gulls, as they have done for thousands of years, and will for thousands of years to come. Here was contemporary life that was also permanent life; and not shut from the modern world but conscious of it and related to it; capable of expressing its spirit, but unencumbered by the mass of poetically irrelevant details and complexities that make a civilization.

By this time I was nearing thirty, and still a whole series of accidents was required to stir my lazy energies to the point of writing verse that seemed to be—whether good or bad—at least my own voice.

So much for the book as a whole: a few notes may be added as to the origins of particular poems.

Tamar grew up from the biblical story, mixed with a reminiscence of Shelley's *Cenci,* and from the strange, introverted and storm-twisted beauty of Point Lobos. *Roan Stallion* originated from an abandoned cabin that we discovered in a roadless hollow of the hills. When later we asked about its history no one was able to tell us anything except that the place had been abandoned ever since its owner was killed by a stallion.

This is the only one of my poems of which I can remember clearly the moment of conception. I had just finished *The Tower Beyond Tragedy* and was looking about for another subject—which was to be contemporary, because I repented of using a Greek story when there were so many new ones at hand. I was quarrying granite under the sea-cliff to build our house with, and slacking on the job sat down on a wet rock to look at the sunset and think about my next poem. The stallion and the desolate cabin came to mind; then immediately, for persons of the drama, came the Indian woman and her white husband, real persons whom I had often seen driving through our village in a ramshackle buggy. The episode of the woman swimming her horse through a storm-swollen ford at night came also; it was part of her actual history. . . . So that when I stood up and began to handle stones again, the poem had already made itself in my mind.

The Tower Beyond Tragedy was suggested to me by the imposing personality of a Jewish actress who was our guest for a day or two. She was less than successful on the stage, being too tall, and tragic in the old-fashioned manner; but when she stood up in our little room under the low ceiling and recited a tragic ballad—"Edward, Edward"—for a few people gathered there, the experience made me want to build a heroic poem to match her formidable voice and rather colossal beauty. I thought these would be absurdly out of place in any contemporary story, so I looked back toward the feet of Aeschylus, and cast this woman for the part of Cassandra in my poem.

Apology for Bad Dreams originated from the episode of the woman and her sons torturing a horse, a thing which happened on our coast. Cruelty is a part of nature, at least of human nature, but it is the one thing that seems unnatural to us; the tension of the mind trying to recognize cruelty and evil as part of the sum of things is what made the poem. (This woman a few years later was killed by another horse: an unusual piece of justice.)

The story of *The Loving Shepherdess* was suggested by a footnote in one of the novels of Walter Scott, which I was reading aloud to our sons. I cannot remember which novel it was. The note tells about a half-insane girl who wandered up and down Scotland with a dwindling flock of sheep, that perished one by one.

The story of *Thurso's Landing* was suggested entirely, I think, by the savage beauty of the canyon and sea-cliff that are its scene, and by the long-abandoned lime-works there. I cannot remember planning the story at all. When we first saw this place, in 1914, the heavy steel cable was hanging across the sky of the canyon, still supporting a rusted skip. During the war it was taken down for scrap-iron.

The phrase "Give your heart to the hawks" swam about in my mind for several years as a good title for a poem; then one day I noticed the scene and farmhouse that seemed to fit the title, in Sycamore Canyon, just south of Big Sur; and between the title and the scene the poem unrolled itself.

At the Birth of an Age had a more calculated origin. I was considering the main sources of our civilization, and listed them roughly as Hebrew-Christian, Roman, Greek, Teutonic. Then it occurred to me that I had written something about the Hebrew-Christian source in *Dear Judas,* and that *The Tower Beyond Tragedy* might pass for a recognition of the Greek source. About the Roman source I should probably never write anything, for it is less sympathetic to me. Recognition of the Teutonic source might be an interesting theme for a new poem, I thought . . . and the Volsung Saga might serve for fable. Only as the poem progressed did the Teutonic element begin to warp and groan under the tension of Christian influence. The symbol of the self-tortured God, that closes the poem, had appeared to me long before in *Apology for Bad Dreams* and in *The Women at Point Sur*—Heauton-timoroumenos, the self-tormentor—but it stands most clearly in the self-hanged Odin of Norse mythology.

ALLEN TATE

Hart Crane

Allen Tate is the foremost literary Classicist in America, and it is from this standpoint that he writes about the Romantic Hart Crane. Tate and Crane were contemporaries and friends, despite their temperamental and doctrinal differences. The essay that follows is a closely reasoned argument against the attempt of Hart Crane to create an American epic poem. Tate pronounced the epical "The Bridge" a magnificent failure and concluded that Crane's heroic attempt to launch such a poem only proved its impossibility.

$\mathscr{T}$he career of Hart Crane will be written by future critics as a chapter in the neo-symbolist movement.[1] An historical view of his poetry at this time would be misleading and incomplete. Like most poets of his age in America, Crane discovered Rimbaud through Eliot and the Imagists; it is certain that long before he had done any of his best work he had come to believe himself the spiritual heir of the

---

[1] This essay is composed of two papers written several years apart, the one in 1932, a few months after Crane's death, the other in 1937 as a review of Philip Horton's *Hart Crane: The Life of an American Poet.*

French poet. He had an instinctive mastery of the fused metaphor of symbolism, but it is not likely that he ever knew more of the symbolist poets than he had got out of Pound's *Pavannes and Divisions*. Whether Crane's style is symbolistic, or should, in many instances, like the first six or seven stanzas of "The River," be called Elizabethan, is a question that need not concern us now.

Between "The Bridge" and "Une Saison d'Enfer" there is little essential affinity. Rimbaud achieved "disorder" out of implicit order, after a deliberate cultivation of "derangement," but in our age the disintegration of our intellectual systems is accomplished. With Crane the disorder is original and fundamental. That is the special quality of his mind that belongs peculiarly to our own time. His aesthetic problem, however, was more general; it was the historic problem of romanticism.

Harold Hart Crane, one of the great masters of the romantic movement, was born in Garretsville, Ohio, on July 21, 1899. His birthplace is a small town near Cleveland, in the old Western Reserve, a region which, as distinguished from the lower portions of the state, where people from the Southern up-country settled, was populated largely by New England stock. He seems to have known little of his ancestry, but he frequently said that his maternal forbears had given Hartford, Connecticut, its name, and that they went "back to Stratford-on-Avon" —a fiction surely, but one that gave him distinct pleasure. His formal education was slight. After the third year at high school, when he was fifteen, it ended, and he worked in his father's candy factory in Cleveland, where the family had removed in his childhood. He repeatedly told me that money had been set aside for his education at college, but that it had been used for other purposes. With the instinct of genius he read the great poets, but he never acquired an objective mastery of any literature, or even of the history of his country—a defect of considerable interest in a poet whose most ambitious work is an American epic.

In any ordinary sense Crane was not an educated man; in many respects he was an ignorant man. There is already a Crane legend, like the Poe legend—it should be fostered because it will help to make his poetry generally known—and the scholars will decide it was a pity that so great a talent lacked early advantages. It is probable that he was incapable of the formal discipline of a classical education, and probable, too, that the eclectic education of his time would have scattered and killed his talent. His poetry not only has defects of the surface, it has a defect of vision; but its great and peculiar value cannot be separated from its limitations. Its qualities are bound up with a special focus of the intellect and sensibility, and it would be folly to wish that his mind had been better trained or differently organized.

The story of his suicide is well known. The information that I have seems authentic, but it is incomplete and subject to excessive interpretation. Toward the end of April, 1932, he embarked on the S. S. *Orizaba* bound from Vera Cruz to New York. On the night of April 26 he got into a brawl with some sailors; he was severely beaten and robbed. At noon the next day, the ship being in the Caribbean a few hours out of Havana, he rushed from his stateroom clad in pajamas and overcoat, walked through the smoking-room out onto the deck, and then the length of the ship to the stern. There without hesitation he made a perfect dive into the sea. It is said that a life-preserver was thrown to him; he either did not see it or did not want it. By the time the ship had turned back he had disappeared. Whether he forced himself down —for a moment he was seen swimming—or was seized by a shark, as the captain believed, cannot be known. After a search of thirty-five minutes his body was not found, and the *Orizaba* put back into her course.

In the summer of 1930 he had written to me that he feared his most ambitious work, *The Bridge,* was not quite perfectly "realized," that probably his soundest work was in the shorter pieces of *White Buildings,* but that his mind, being once committed to the larger undertaking, could never return to the lyrical and more limited form. He had an extraordinary insight into the foundations of his work, and I think this judgment of it will not be refuted.

From 1922 to 1928—after that year I saw him and heard from him irregularly until his death—I could observe the development of his style from poem to poem; and his letters—written always in a pure and lucid prose—provide a valuable commentary on his career. This is not the place to bring all this material together for judgment. As I look back upon his work and its relation to the life he lived, a general statement about it comes to my mind that may throw some light on the dissatisfaction that he felt with his career. It will be a judgment upon the life and works of a man whom I knew affectionately for ten years as a friend.

Suicide was the sole act of will left to him short of a profound alteration of his character. I think the evidence of this is the locked-in sensibility, the insulated egoism, of his poetry—a subject that I shall return to. The background of his death was dramatically perfect: a large portion of his finest imagery was of the sea, chiefly the Caribbean:

> O minstrel galleons of Carib fire,
> Bequeath us to no earthly shore until
> Is answered in the vortex of our grave
> The seal's wide spindrift gaze towards paradise.

His verse is full of splendid images of this order, a rich symbolism for an implicit pantheism that, whatever may be its intrinsic merit, he had the courage to vindicate with death in the end.

His pantheism was not passive and contemplative; it rose out of the collision between his own locked-in sensibility and the ordinary forms of experience. Every poem is a thrust of that sensibility into the world: his defect lay in his inability to face out the moral criticism implied in the failure to impose his will upon experience.

The Bridge is presumably an epic. How early he had conceived the idea of the poem and the leading symbolism, it is difficult to know; certainly as early as February, 1923. Up to that time, with the exception of "For the Marriage of Faustus and Helen" (1922), he had written only short poems, but most of them, "Praise for an Urn," "Black Tambourine," "Paraphrase," and "Emblems of Conduct," [2] are among his finest work. It is a mistake then to suppose that all of *White Buildings* is early experimental writing; a large portion of that volume, and perhaps the least successful part of it, is made up of poems written after *The Bridge* was begun. "Praise for an Urn" was written in the spring of 1922—one of the finest elegies by an American poet—and although his later development gave us a poetry that the period would be much the less rich for not having, he never again had such perfect mastery of his subject—because he never again quite knew what his subject was.

Readers familiar with "For the Marriage of Faustus and Helen" admire it by passages, but the form of the poem, in its framework of symbol, is an abstraction empty of any knowable experience. The originality of the poem is in its rhythms, but it has the conventional diction that a young poet picks up in his first reading. Crane, I believe, felt that this was so; and he became so dissatisfied, not only with the style of the poem, which is heavily influenced by Eliot and Laforgue, but with the "literary" character of the symbolism, that he set about the greater task of writing *The Bridge*. He had looked upon his "Faustus and Helen" as an answer to the pessimism of the school of Eliot, and *The Bridge* was to be an even more complete answer.

There was a fundamental mistake in Crane's diagnosis of Eliot's problem. Eliot's "pessimism" grows out of an awareness of the decay of the individual consciousness and its fixed relations to the world; but Crane thought that it was due to something like pure "orneriness," an unwillingness "to share with us the breath released," the breath being a new kind of freedom that he identified emotionally with the age of the machine. This vagueness of purpose, in spite of the apparently concrete character of the Brooklyn Bridge, which became the symbol of his epic, he never succeeded in correcting. The "bridge" stands for no well-defined experience; it differs from the Helen and Faust symbols only in its unliterary origin. I think Crane was deceived by this difference, and by the fact that Brooklyn Bridge is "modern" and a fine piece of "mechanics." His more ambitious later project permitted him no greater mastery of formal structure than the more literary symbolism of his youth.

The fifteen parts of *The Bridge* taken as one poem suffer from the lack of a coherent structure, whether symbolic or narrative: the coherence of the work consists in the personal quality of the writing—in mood, feeling, and tone. In the best passages Crane has perfect mastery over the quality of his style; but the style lacks an objective pattern of ideas elaborate enough to carry it through an epic or heroic work. The

---

[2] It is now known that this poem is an elaboration of a "sonnet" entitled "Conduct" by Samuel Greenberg. See *Poems* by Samuel Greenberg, edited by Harold Holden and Jack McManis (New York, 1947).

single symbolic image, in which the whole poem centers, is at one moment the actual Brooklyn Bridge; at another, it is any bridge or "connection"; at still another, it is a philosophical pun and becomes the basis of a series of analogies.

In "Cape Hatteras," the aëroplane and Walt Whitman are analogous "bridges" to some transcendental truth. Because the idea is variously metaphor, symbol, and analogy, it tends to make the poem static. The poet takes it up, only to be forced to put it down again *when the poetic image of the moment is exhausted.* The idea does not, in short, fill the poet's mind; it is the starting point for a series of short flights, or inventions connected only in analogy—which explains the merely personal passages, which are obscure, and the lapses into sentimentality. For poetic sentimentality is emotion undisciplined by the structure of events or ideas of which it is ostensibly a part. The idea is not objective and articulate in itself; it lags after the poet's vision; it appears and disappears; and in the intervals Crane improvises, often beautifully, as in the flight of the aëroplane, sometimes badly, as in the passage on Whitman in the same poem.

In the great epic and philosophical works of the past, notably *The Divine Comedy,* the intellectual groundwork is not only simple philosophically; we not only know that the subject is personal salvation, just as we know that Crane's is the greatness of America: we are given also the complete articulation of the idea down to the slightest detail, and we are given it objectively apart from anything that the poet is going to say about it. When the poet extends his perception, there is a further extension of the groundwork ready to meet it and discipline it, and to compel the sensibility of the poet to stick to the subject. It is a game of chess; neither side can move without consulting the other. Crane's difficulty is that of modern poets generally: they play the game with half of the men, the men of sensibility, and because sensibility can make any move, the significance of all moves is obscure.

If we subtract from Crane's idea its periphery of sensation, we have left only the dead abstraction, the Greatness of America, which is capable of elucidation neither on the logical plane nor in terms of a generally known idea of America.

The theme of *The Bridge* is, in fact, an emotional over-simplification of a subject-matter that Crane did not, on the plane of narrative and idea, simplify at all. The poem is emotionally homogeneous and simple —it contains a single purpose; but because it is not structurally clarified it is emotionally confused. America stands for a passage into new truths. Is this the meaning of American history? The poet has every right to answer yes, and this he has done. But just what in America or about America stands for this? Which American history? The historical plot of the poem, which is the groundwork on which the symbolic bridge stands, is arbitrary and broken, where the poet would have gained an overwhelming advantage by choosing a single period or episode, a concrete event with all its dramatic causes, and by following it up minutely, and being bound to it. In short, he would have gained an advantage could he have found a subject to stick to.

Does American culture afford such a subject? It probably does not. After the seventeenth century the sophisticated history of the scholars came into fashion; our popular, legendary chronicles come down only from the remoter European past. It was a sound impulse on Crane's part to look for an American myth, some simple version of our past that lies near the center of the American consciousness; an heroic tale with just enough symbolism to give his mind both direction and play. The soundness of his purpose is witnessed also by the kind of history in the poem: it is inaccurate, and it will not at all satisfy the sticklers for historical fact. It is the history of the motion picture, of naïve patriotism. This is sound; for it ignores the scientific ideal of historical truth-in-itself, and looks for a cultural truth which might win the spontaneous allegiance of the people. It is on such simple integers of truth, not truth of fact but of religious necessity, that men unite. The American mind was formed by the eighteenth-century Enlightenment, which broke down the European "truths" and gave us a temper deeply hostile to the making of new religious truths of our own.

The impulse in *The Bridge* is religious, but the soundness of an impulse is no warrant that it will create a sound art form. The form depends on too many factors beyond the control of the poet. The age is scientific and pseudo-scientific, and our philosophy is Dewey's instrumentalism. And it is possibly this circumstance that has driven the religious attitude into a corner where it lacks the right instruments for its defense and growth, and where it is in a vast muddle about just what these instruments are. Perhaps this disunity of the intellect is responsible for Crane's unphilosophical belief that the poet, unaided and isolated from the people, can create a myth.

If anthropology has helped to destroy the credibility of myths, it has shown us how they rise: their growth is mysterious from the people as a whole. It is probable that no one man ever put myth into history. It is still a nice problem among higher critics, whether the authors of the Gospels were deliberate myth-makers, or whether their minds were simply constructed that way; but the evidence favors the latter. Crane was a myth-maker, and in an age favorable to myths he would have written a mythical poem in the act of writing an historical one.

It is difficult to agree with those critics who find his epic a single poem and as such an artistic success. It is a collection of lyrics, the best of which are not surpassed by anything in American literature. The writing is most distinguished when Crane is least philosophical, *when he writes from sensation.* "The River" has some blemishes towards the end, but by and large it is a masterpiece of order and style; it alone is enough to place Crane in the first rank of American poets, living or dead. Equally good but less ambitious are the "Proem: To Brooklyn Bridge," and "Harbor Dawn," and "The Dance" from the section called "Powhatan's Daughter."

These poems bear only the loosest relation to the symbolic demands of the theme; they contain allusions to the historical pattern or extend the slender structure of analogy running through the poem. They are primarily lyrical, and each has its complete form. The poem "Indiana," written presumably to complete the pattern of "Powhatan's Daughter," does not stand alone, and it is one of the most astonishing failures ever made by a poet of Crane's genius. "The Dance" gives us the American background for the coming white man, and "Indiana" carries the stream of history to the pioneer West. It is a nightmare of sentimentality. Crane is at his most "philosophical" in a theme in which he feels no poetic interest whatever.

The structural defect of *The Bridge* is due to this fundamental contradiction of purpose. In one of his best earlier poems, "The Wine Menagerie," he exclaims: "New thresholds, new anatomies!"—new sensation, but he could not subdue the new sensation to a symbolic form.

His pantheism is necessarily a philosophy of sensation without point of view. An epic is a judgment of human action, an implied evaluation of a civilization, a way of life. In *The Bridge* the civilization that contains the subway hell of the section called "The Tunnel" is the same civilization of the aëroplane that the poet apostrophizes in "Cape Hatteras": there is no reason why the subway should be a fitter symbol of damnation than the aëroplane: both were produced by the same mentality on the same moral plane. There is a concealed, meaningless analogy between, on the one hand, the height of the plane and the depth of the subway, and, on the other, "higher" and "lower" in the religious sense. At one moment Crane faces his predicament of blindness to any rational order of value, and knows that he is damned; but he cannot face it long, and he tries to rest secure upon the intensity of sensation.

To the vision of the abyss in "The Tunnel," a vision that Dante passed through midway of this mortal life, Crane had no alternative: when it became too harrowing he cried to his Pocahontas, a typically romantic and sentimental symbol:

Lie to us—dance us back our tribal morn!

It is probably the perfect word of romanticism in this century. When Crane saw that his leading symbol, the bridge, would not hold all the material of his poem, he could not sustain it ironically, in the classical manner, by probing its defects; nor in the personal sections, like "Quaker Hill," does he include himself in his Leopardian denunciation of life. He is the blameless victim of a world whose impurity violates the moment of intensity, which would otherwise be enduring and perfect. He is betrayed, not by a defect of his own nature, but by the external world; he asks of nature, perfection—requiring only of himself, intensity. The persistent, and persistently defeated, pursuit of a natural absolute places Crane at the center of his age.

Alternately he asserts the symbol of the bridge and abandons it, because fundamentally he does not understand it. The idea of bridge-ship is an elaborate blur leaving the inner structure of the poem confused.

Yet some of the best poetry of our generation is in *The Bridge*. Its inner confusion is a phase of the inner cross-purposes of the time. Crane was one of those men whom every age seems to select as the spokesmen of its spiritual life; they give the age away. The accidental features of their lives, their place in life, their very heredity, seem to fit them for their rôle; even their vices contribute to the preparation. Crane's biographer will have to study the early influences that confirmed him in narcissism, and thus made him typical of the rootless spiritual life of our time. The character formed by those influences represents an immense concentration, and becomes almost a symbol, of American life in this age.

Crane's poetry has incalculable moral value: it reveals our defects in their extremity. I have said that he knew little of the history of his country. It was not merely a defect of education, but a defect, in the spiritual sense, of the modern mind. Crane lacked the sort of indispensable understanding of his country that a New England farmer has who has never been out of his township. *The Bridge* attempts to include all American life, but it covers the ground with seven-league boots and, like a sightseer, sees nothing. With reference to its leading symbol, it has no subject-matter. The poem is the effort of a solipsistic sensibility to locate itself in the external world, to establish points of reference.

It seems to me that by testing out his capacity to construct a great objective piece of work, in which his definition of himself should have been articulated, he brought his work to an end. I think he knew that the structure of *The Bridge* was finally incoherent, and for that reason—as I have said—he could no longer believe even in his lyrical powers; he could not return to the early work and take it up where he had left off. Far from "refuting" Eliot, his whole career is a vindication of Eliot's major premise—that the integrity of the individual consciousness has broken down. Crane had, in his later work, no individual consciousness: the hard firm style of "Praise for an Urn," which is based upon a clear-cut perception of moral relations, and upon their ultimate inviolability, begins to disappear when the poet goes out into the world and finds that the simplicity of a child's world has no universal sanction. From then on, instead of the effort to define himself in the midst of almost overwhelming complications—a situation that might have produced a tragic poet—he falls back upon the intensity of consciousness, rather than the clarity, for his center of vision. And that is romanticism.

His world had no center, and the thrust into sensation is responsible for the fragmentary quality of his most ambitious work. This thrust took two directions—the blind assertion of the will, and the blind desire for self-destruction. The poet did not face his first problem, which is to define the limits of his personality and to objectify its moral implications in an appropriate symbolism. Crane could only assert a quality of will against the world, and at each successive failure of the will he turned upon himself. In the failure of understanding—and understanding, for Dante, was a way of love—the romantic modern poet of the age of science attempts to impose his will upon experience and to possess the world.

It is this impulse of the modern period that has given us the greatest romantic poetry: Crane instinctively continued the conception of the will that was the deliberate discovery of Rimbaud. A poetry of the will is a poetry of sensation, for the poet surrenders to his sensations of the object in his effort to identify himself with it, and to own it. Some of Crane's finest lyrics—those written in the period of *The Bridge*— carry the modern impulse as far as you will find it anywhere in the French romantics. "Lachrymae Christi" and "Passage," though on the surface made up of pure images without philosophical meaning of the explicit sort in *The Bridge,* are the lyrical equivalents of the epic: the same kind of sensibility is at work. The implicit grasp of his material that we find in "Praise for an Urn," the poet has exchanged for an external, random symbol of which there is no possibility of realization. *The Bridge* is an irrational symbol of the will, of conquest, of blind achievement in space; its obverse is "Passage," whose lack of external symbolism exhibits the poetry of the will on the plane of sensation; and this is the self-destructive return of the will upon itself.

Criticism may well set about isolating the principle upon which Crane's poetry is organized. Powerful verse overwhelms its admirers, and betrays them into more than technical imitation. That is one of the arguments of Platonism against literature; it is the immediate quality of an art rather than its whole significance that sets up schools and traditions. Crane not only ends the romantic era in his own person; he ends it logically and morally. Beyond Crane no future poet can go. (This does not mean that the romantic impulse may not rise and flourish again.) The finest passages in his work are single moments in the stream of sensation; beyond the moment he goes at his peril; for beyond it lies the discrepancy between the sensuous fact, the perception, and its organizing symbol— a discrepancy that plunges him into sentimentality and chaos. But the "bridge" is empty and static, it has no inherent content, and the poet's attribution to it of the qualities of his own moral predicament is arbitrary. That explains the fragmentary and often unintelligible framework of the poem. There was neither complete action nor ordered symbolism in terms of which the distinct moments of perception could be clarified.

This was partly the problem of Rimbaud. But Crane's problem was nearer to the problem of Keats, and *The Bridge* is a failure in the sense that "Hyperion" is a failure, and with comparable magnificence. Crane's problem, being farther removed from the epic tradition, was actually more difficult than Keats's, and his treatment of it was doubtless the most satisfactory possible in our time. Beyond the quest of pure sensation and its ordering symbolism lies the total destruction of art. By attempting an extreme solution of the romantic problem Crane proved that it cannot be solved.

HART CRANE
General Aims and Theories

> Hart Crane's ambition to write the American epic catapulted him into the Romantic-Classicist arena. Romantic by nature and inclination, he nevertheless feared what he termed the "sentimental fallacy" of a complete break with the past and tradition. In the short essay that follows, Crane defends his own use of myth, illustrating from his own poems. The essay was written in 1925, a time when all poets felt obliged to take a stand for or against the newly established Classical aesthetic. Crane's essay is less of a compromise than it is a considered apology for his own Romanticism.

*W*hen I started writing Faustus & Helen it was my intention to embody in modern terms (words, symbols, metaphors) a contemporary approximation to an ancient human culture or mythology that seems to have been obscured rather than illumined with the frequency of poetic allusions made to it during the last century. The name of Helen, for instance, has become an all-too-easily employed crutch for evocation whenever a poet felt a stitch in his side. The real evocation of this (to me) very real and absolute conception of beauty seemed to consist in a reconstruction in these modern terms of the basic emotional attitude toward beauty that the Greeks had. And in so doing I found that I was really building a bridge between so-called classic experience and many divergent realities of our seething, confused cosmos of today, which has no formulated mythology yet for classic poetic reference or for religious exploitation.

So I found "Helen" sitting in a street car; the Dionysian revels of her court and her seduction were transferred to a Metropolitan roof garden with a jazz orchestra; and the *katharsis* of the fall of Troy I saw approximated in the recent World War. The importance of this scaffolding may easily be exaggerated, but it gave me a series of correspondences between two widely separated worlds on which to sound some major themes of human speculation—love, beauty, death, renascence. It was a kind of grafting process that I shall doubtless not be interested in repeating, but which is consistent with subsequent theories of mine on the relation of tradition to the contemporary creating imagination.

It is a terrific problem that faces the poet today—a world that is so in transition from a decayed culture toward a reorganization of human evaluations that there are few common terms, general denominators of speech that are solid enough or that ring with any vibration or spiritual conviction. The great mythologies of the past (including the Church) are deprived of enough façade to even launch good raillery against. Yet much of their traditions are operative still—in millions of chance combinations of related and unrelated detail, psychological reference, figures of speech, precepts, etc. These are all a part of our common experience and the terms, at least partially, of that very experience when it defines or extends itself.

The deliberate program, then, of a "break" with the past or tradition seems to me to be a sentimental fallacy. . . . The poet has a right to draw on whatever practical resources he finds in books or otherwise about him. He must tax his sensibility and his touchstone of experience for the proper selections of these themes and details, however,—and that is where he either stands, or falls into useless archeology.

I put no particular value on the simple objective of "modernity." The element of the temporal location of an artist's creation is of very secondary importance; it can be left to the impressionist or historian just as well. It seems to me that a poet will accidentally define his time well enough simply by reacting honestly and to the full extent of his sensibilities to the states of passion, experience and rumination that fate forces on him, first hand. He must, of course, have a sufficiently universal basis of experience to make his imagination selective and valuable. His picture of the "period," then, will simply be a by-product of his curiosity and the relation of his experience to a postulated "eternity."

I am concerned with the future of America, but not because I think that America has any so-called par value as a state or as a group of people. . . . It is only because I feel persuaded that here are destined to be discovered certain as yet undefined spiritual quantities, perhaps a new hierarchy of faith not to be developed so completely elsewhere. And in this process I like to feel myself as a potential factor; certainly I must speak in its terms and what discoveries I may make are situated in its experience.

But to fool one's self that definitions are being reached by merely referring frequently to skyscrapers, radio antennae, steam whistles, or other surface phenomena of our time is merely to paint a photograph. I think that what is interesting and significant will emerge only under the conditions of our submission to, and examination and assimilation of the organic effects on us of these and other fundamental factors of our experience. It can certainly not be an organic expression otherwise. And the expression of such values may often be as well accomplished with the vocabulary and blank verse of the Elizabethans as with the calligraphic tricks and slang used so brilliantly at times by an impressionist like Cummings.

It may not be possible to say that there is, strictly speaking, any "absolute" experience. But it seems evident that certain aesthetic experience (and this may for a time engross the total faculties of the spectator) can be called absolute, inasmuch as it approximates a formally convincing statement of a conception or apprehension of life that gains our unquestioning assent, and under the conditions of which our imagination is unable to suggest a further detail consistent with the design of the aesthetic whole.

I have been called an "absolutist" in poetry, and if I am to welcome such a label it should be under the terms of the above definition. It is really only a *modus operandi*, however, and as such has been used organically before by at least a dozen poets such as Donne, Blake, Baudelaire, Rimbaud, etc. I may succeed in defining it better by contrasting it with the impressionistic method. The impressionist is interesting as far as he goes—but his goal has been reached when he has succeeded in projecting certain selected factual details into his reader's consciousness. He is really not interested in the *causes* (metaphysical) of his materials, their emotional derivations or their utmost spiritual consequences. A kind of retinal registration is enough, along with a certain psychological stimulation. And this is also true of your realist (of the Zola type), and to a certain extent of the classicist, like Horace, Ovid, Pope, etc.

Blake meant these differences when he wrote:

> We are led to believe in a lie
> When we see *with* not *through* the eye.

The impressionist creates only with the eye and for the readiest surface of the consciousness, at least relatively so. If the effect has been harmonious or even stimulating, he can stop there, relinquishing entirely to his audience the problematic synthesis of the details into terms of their own personal consciousness.

It is my hope to go *through* the combined materials of the poem, using our "real" world somewhat as a spring-board, and to give the poem *as a whole* an orbit or predetermined direction of its own. I would like to establish it as free from my own personality as from any chance evaluation on the reader's part. (This is, of course, an impossibility, but it is a characteristic worth mentioning.) Such a poem is at least a stab at a truth, and to such an extent may be differentiated from other kinds of poetry and called "absolute." Its evocation will not be toward decoration or amusement, but rather toward a state of consciousness, an "innocence" (Blake) or absolute beauty. In this condition there may be discoverable under new forms certain spiritual illuminations, shining with a morality essentialized from experience directly, and not from previous precepts or preconceptions. It is as though a poem gave the reader as he left it a single, new *word*, never before spoken and impossible to actually enunciate, but self-evident as an active principle in the reader's consciousness henceforward.

As to technical considerations: the motivation of the poem must be derived from the implicit emotional dynamics of the materials used, and the terms of expression employed are often selected less for their logical (literal) significance than for their associational meanings. Via this and their metaphorical inter-relationships, the entire construction of the poem is raised on the organic principle of a "logic of metaphor," which antedates our so-called pure logic, and which is the genetic basis of all speech, hence consciousness and thought-extension.

These dynamics often result, I'm told, in certain initial difficulties in understanding my poems. But on the other hand I find them at times the only means possible for expressing certain concepts in any forceful or direct way whatever. To cite two examples:—when, in Voyages (II), I speak of "adagios of islands," the reference is to the motion of a boat through islands clustered thickly, the rhythm of the motion, etc. And it seems a much more direct and creative statement than any more logical employment of words such as "coasting slowly through the islands," besides ushering in a whole world of music. Similarly in Faustus and Helen (III) the speed and tense altitude of an aeroplane are much better suggested by the idea of "nimble blue plateaus"—*implying* the aeroplane and its speed against a contrast of stationary elevated earth. Although the statement is pseudo in relation to formal logic—it *is* completely logical in relation to the truth of the imagination, and there is expressed a concept of speed and space that could not be handled so well in other terms.

In manipulating the more imponderable phenomena of psychic motives, pure emotional crystallizations, etc. I have had to rely even more on these dynamics of inferential mention, and I am doubtless still very unconscious of having committed myself to what seems nothing but obscurities to some minds. A poem like Possessions really cannot be technically explained. It must rely (even to a large extent with myself) on its organic impact on the imagination to successfully imply its meaning. This seems to me to present an exceptionally difficult problem, however, considering the real clarity and consistent logic of many of the other poems.

I know that I run the risk of much criticism by defending such theories as I have, but as it is part of a poet's business to risk not only criticism—but folly—in the conquest of consciousness I can only say that I attach no intrinsic value to what means I use beyond their practical service in giving form to the living stuff of the imagination.

New conditions of life germinate new forms of spiritual articulation. And while I feel that my work includes a more consistent extension of traditional literary elements than many contemporary poets are capable of appraising, I realize that I am utilizing the gifts of the past as instruments principally; and that the voice of the present, if it is to be known, must be caught at the risk of speaking in idioms and circumlo-

cutions sometimes shocking to the scholar and historians of logic.
Language has built towers and bridges, but itself is inevitably as fluid
as always.

D. H. LAWRENCE

Edgar Allan Poe

The most articulate enemy of modern Classicism and everything
it stands for is D. H. Lawrence. The "Moderns" (Classicists) never
tire of attacking Lawrence's views about religion, government, and
society. Eliot has been foremost in undermining Lawrence's
authority in literature and in social philosophy. Yet Lawrence's
authority in literature in the nineteen-sixties is so pervasive that it
amounts to something like a religion. All experimental, visionary,
anti-Establishment poetry of our time bears a close resemblance to
the theories and writings of Lawrence.

The two essays that follow are Lawrence's analysis of Poe, the
figurehead of modern Classicism, and Whitman, the great Romantic. The reader should bear in mind that Poe is frequently
regarded as a chief member of the Romantic movement in a de-
generating phase. Poe is commonly called a "gothic" Romantic,
the inventor of the modern detective story and of the psychological
approach to literature. Once again classification gets in the way of
understanding.

Lawrence's views are desperate and extreme, yet his loathing for
Poe and his homage to Whitman represent two of the central positions of modern literary thought.

*P*oe has no truck with Indians or Nature. He makes no bones
about Red Brothers and Wigwams.

He is absolutely concerned with the disintegration-processes of his
own psyche. As we have said, the rhythm of American art-activity is dual.

1. A disintegrating and sloughing of the old consciousness.

2. The forming of a new consciousness underneath.

Fenimore Cooper has the two vibrations going on together. Poe has
only one, only the disintegrative vibration. This makes him almost more
a scientist than an artist.

Moralists have always wondered helplessly why Poe's "morbid" tales
need have been written. They need to be written because old things
need to die and disintegrate, because the old white psyche has to be
gradually broken down before anything else can come to pass.

Man must be stripped even of himself. And it is a painful, sometimes a ghastly process.

Poe had a pretty bitter doom. Doomed to seethe down his soul in a great continuous convulsion of disintegration, and doomed to register the process. And then doomed to be abused for it, when he had performed some of the bitterest tasks of human experience, that can be asked of a man. Necessary tasks, too. For the human soul must suffer its own disintegration, *consciously,* if ever it is to survive.

But Poe is rather a scientist than an artist. He is reducing his own self as a scientist reduces a salt in a crucible. It is an almost chemical analysis of the soul and consciousness. Whereas in true art there is always the double rhythm of creating and destroying.

This is why Poe calls his things "tales." They are a concatenation of cause and effect.

His best pieces, however, are not tales. They are more. They are ghastly stories of the human soul in its disruptive throes.

Moreover, they are "love" stories.

Ligeia and *The Fall of the House of Usher* are really love stories.

Love is the mysterious vital attraction which draws things together, closer, closer together. For this reason sex is the actual crisis of love. For in sex the two blood-systems, in the male and female, concentrate and come into contact, the merest film intervening. Yet if the intervening film breaks down, it is death.

So there you are. There is a limit to everything. There is a limit to love.

The central law of all organic life is that each organism is intrinsically isolate and single in itself.

The moment its isolation breaks down, and there comes an actual mixing and confusion, death sets in.

This is true of every individual organism, from man to amœba.

But the secondary law of all organic life is that each organism only lives through contact with other matter, assimilation, and contact with other life, which means assimilation of new vibrations, nonmaterial. Each individual organism is vivified by intimate contact with fellow organisms: up to a certain point.

So man. He breathes the air into him, he swallows food and water. But more than this. He takes into him the life of his fellow men, with whom he comes into contact, and he gives back life to them. This contact draws nearer and nearer, as the intimacy increases. When it is a whole contact, we call it love. Men live by food, but die if they eat too much. Men live by love, but die, or cause death, if they love too much.

There are two loves: sacred and profane, spiritual and sensual.

In sensual love, it is the two blood-systems, the man's and the woman's, which sweep up into pure contact, and *almost* fuse. Almost mingle. Never quite. There is always the finest imaginable wall between the two blood-waves, through which pass unknown vibrations, forces, but through which the blood itself must never break, or it means bleeding.

In spiritual love, the contact is purely nervous. The nerves in the lovers are set vibrating in unison like two instruments. The pitch can rise higher and higher. But carry this too far, and the nerves begin to break, to bleed, as it were, and a form of death sets in.

The trouble about man is that he insists on being master of his own fate, and he insists on *oneness*. For instance, having discovered the ecstasy of spiritual love, he insists that he shall have this all the time, and nothing but this, for this is life. It is what he calls "heightening" life. He wants his nerves to be set vibrating in the intense and exhilarating unison with the nerves of another being, and by this means he acquires an ecstasy of vision, he finds himself in glowing unison with all the universe.

But as a matter of fact this glowing unison is only a temporary thing, because the first law of life is that each organism is isolate in itself, it must return to its own isolation.

Yet man has tried the glow of unison, called love, and he *likes* it. It gives him his highest gratification. He wants it. He wants it all the time. He wants it and he will have it. He doesn't want to return to his own isolation. Or if he must, it is only as a prowling beast returns to its lair to rest and set out again.

This brings us to Edgar Allan Poe. The clue to him lies in the motto he chose for *Ligeia*, a quotation from the mystic Joseph Glanville: "And the will therein lieth, which dieth not. Who knoweth the mysteries of the will, with its vigour? For God is but a great Will pervading all things by nature of its intentness. Man doth not yield himself to the angels, nor unto death utterly, save only through the weakness of his feeble will."

It is a profound saying: and a deadly one.

Because if God is a great will, then the universe is but an instrument.

I don't know what God is. But He is not simply a will. That is too simple. Too anthropomorphic. Because a man wants his own will, and nothing but his will, he needn't say that God is the same will, magnified *ad infinitum*.

For me, there may be one God, but He is nameless and unknowable.

For me, there are also many gods, that come into me and leave me again. And they have very various wills, I must say.

But the point is Poe.

Poe had experienced the ecstasies of extreme spiritual love. And he wanted those ecstasies and nothing but those ecstasies. He wanted that great gratification, the sense of flowing, the sense of unison, the sense of heightening of life. He had experienced this gratification. He was told on every hand that this ecstasy of spiritual, nervous love was the greatest thing in life, was life itself. And he had tried it for himself, he knew that for him it *was* life itself. So he wanted it. And he *would have* it. He set up his will against the whole of the limitations of nature.

This is a brave man, acting on his own belief, and his own experience. But it is also an arrogant man, and a fool.

Poe was going to get the ecstasy and the heightening, cost what it might. He went on in a frenzy, as characteristic American women nowadays go on in a frenzy, after the very same thing: the heightening, the flow, the ecstasy. Poe tried alcohol, and any drug he could lay his hand on. He also tried any human being he could lay his hands on.

His grand attempt and achievement was with his wife; his cousin, a girl with a singing voice. With her he went in for the intensest flow, the heightening, the prismatic shades of ecstasy. It was the intensest nervous vibration of unison, pressed higher and higher in pitch, till the blood vessels of the girl broke, and the blood began to flow out loose. It was love. If you call it love.

Love can be terribly obscene.

It is love that causes the neuroticism of the day. It is love that is the prime cause of tuberculosis.

The nerves that vibrate most intensely in spiritual unisons are the sympathetic ganglia of the breast, of the throat, and the hind brain. Drive this vibration over-intensely, and you weaken the sympathetic tissues of the chest—the lungs—or of the throat, or of the lower brain, and the tubercles are given a ripe field.

But Poe drove the vibrations beyond any human pitch of endurance. Being his cousin, she was more easily keyed to him.

Ligeia is the chief story. Ligeia! A mental-derived name. To him the woman, his wife, was not Lucy. She was Ligeia. No doubt she even preferred it thus.

Ligeia is Poe's love-story, and its very fantasy makes it more truly his own story.

It is a tale of love pushed over a verge. And love pushed to extremes is a battle of wills between the lovers.

Love is become a battle of wills.

Which shall first destroy the other, of the lovers? Which can hold out longest, against the other?

Ligeia is still the old-fashioned woman. Her will is still to submit. She wills to submit to the vampire of her husband's consciousness. Even death.

"In stature she was tall, somewhat slender, and, in her later days, even emaciated. I would in vain attempt to portray the majesty, the quiet ease, of her demeanour, or the incomprehensible lightness and elasticity of her footfall. I was never made aware of her entrance into my closed study save by the dear music of her low, sweet voice as she placed her marble hand on my shoulder."

Poe has been so praised for his style. But it seems to me a meretricious affair. "Her marble hand" and "the elasticity of her footfall" seem more like chair-springs and mantel-pieces than a human creature. She never was quite a human creature to him. She was an instrument, from which he got his extremes of sensation. His *machine à plaisir*, as somebody says.

All Poe's style, moreover, has this mechanical quality, as his poetry has a mechanical rhythm. He never sees anything in terms of life, almost always in terms of matter, jewels, marble, etc.—or in terms of force, scientific. And his cadences are all managed mechanically. This is what is called "having a style."

What he wants to do with Ligeia is to analyse her, till he knows all her component parts, till he has got her all in his consciousness. She is some strange chemical salt which he must analyse out in the test-tubes of his brain, and then—when he's finished the analysis—*E finita la commedia!*

But she won't be quite analysed out. There is something, something he can't get. Writing of her eyes, he says: "They were, I must believe, far larger than the ordinary eyes of our race"—as if anybody would want eyes "far larger" than other folks'. "They were even fuller than the fullest of the gazelle eyes of the tribe of Nourjahad—" Which is blarney. "The hue of the orbs was the most brilliant of black and, far over them, hung jetty lashes of great length."—Suggests a whiplash. "The brows, slightly irregular in outline, had the same tint. The *strangeness,* which I found in the eyes was of a nature distinct from the formation, or the colour, or the brilliancy of the features, and must, after all, be referred to as the *expression.*"—Sounds like an anatomist anatomizing a cat.—"Ah, word of no meaning! behind whose vast latitude of sound we intrench our ignorance of so much of the spiritual. The expression of the eyes of Ligeia! How for long hours have I pondered upon it! How have I, through the whole of a midsummer night, struggled to fathom it! What was it—that something more profound than the well of Democritus—which lay far within the pupils of my beloved? What *was* it? I was possessed with a passion to discover. . . ."

It is easy to see why each man kills the thing he loves. To *know* a living thing is to kill it. You have to kill a thing to know it satisfactorily. For this reason, the desirous consciousness, the SPIRIT, is a vampire.

One should be sufficiently intelligent and interested to know a good deal *about* any person one comes into close contact with. *About* her. Or *about* him.

But to try to *know* any living being is to try to suck the life out of that being.

Above all things, with the woman one loves. Every sacred instinct teaches one that one must leave her unknown. You know your woman darkly, in the blood. To try to *know* her mentally is to try to kill her. Beware, oh woman, of the man who wants to *find out what you are.* And, oh men, beware a thousand times more of the woman who wants to *know* you, or *get* you, what you are.

It is the temptation of a vampire fiend, is this knowledge.

Man does so horribly want to master the secret of life and of individuality *with his mind.* It is like the analysis of protoplasm. You can only analyse *dead* protoplasm, and know its constituents. It is a death process.

Keep KNOWLEDGE for the world of matter, force, and function. It has got nothing to do with being.

But Poe wanted to know—wanted to know what was the strangeness in the eyes of Ligeia. She might have told him it was horror at his probing, horror at being vamped by his consciousness.

But she wanted to be vamped. She wanted to be probed by his consciousness, to be KNOWN. She paid for wanting it, too.

Nowadays it is usually the man who wants to be vamped, to be KNOWN.

Edgar Allan probed and probed. So often he seemed on the verge. But she went over the verge of death before he came over the verge of knowledge. And it is always so.

He decided, therefore, that the clue to the strangeness lay in the mystery of will. "And the will therein lieth, which dieth not . . ."

Ligeia had a "gigantic volition." . . . "An intensity in thought, action, or speech was possibly, in her, a result, or at least an index" (he really meant indication) "of that gigantic volition which, during our long intercourse, failed to give other and more immediate evidence of its existence."

I should have thought her long submission to him was chief and ample "other evidence."

"Of all the women whom I have ever known, she, the outwardly calm, the ever-placid Ligeia, was the most violently a prey to the tumultuous vultures of stern passion. And of such passion I could form no estimate, save by the miraculous expansion of those eyes which at once so delighted and appalled me—by the almost magical melody, modulation, distinctness, and placidity of her very low voice—and by the fierce energy (rendered doubly effective by contrast with her manner of utterance) of the wild words which she habitually uttered."

Poor Poe, he had caught a bird of the same feather as himself. One of those terrible cravers, who crave the further sensation. Crave to madness or death. "Vultures of stern passion" indeed! Condors.

But having recognized that the clue was in her gigantic volition, he should have realized that the process of this loving, this craving, this knowing, was a struggle of wills. But Ligeia, true to the great tradition and mode of womanly love, by her will kept herself submissive, recipient. She is the passive body who is explored and analyzed into death. And yet, at times, her great female will must have revolted. "Vultures of stern passion!" With a convulsion of desire she desired his further probing and exploring. To any lengths. But then, "tumultuous vultures of stern passion." She had to fight with herself.

But Ligeia wanted to go on and on with the craving, with the love, with the sensation, with the probing, with the knowing, on and on to the end.

There is no end. There is only the rupture of death. That's where men, and women, are "had." Man is always sold, in his search for final KNOWLEDGE.

"That she loved me I should not have doubted; and I might have been easily aware that, in a bosom such as hers, love would have reigned no ordinary passion. But in death only was I fully impressed with the strength of her affection. For long hours, detaining my hand, would she pour out before me the overflowing of a heart whose more than passionate devotion amounted to idolatry." (Oh, the indecency of all this endless intimate talk!) "How had I deserved to be blessed by such confessions?" (Another man would have felt himself cursed.) "How had I deserved to be cursed with the removal of my beloved in the hour of her making them? But upon this subject I cannot bear to dilate. Let me say only that in Ligeia's more than womanly abandonment to a love, alas! unmerited, all unworthily bestowed, I at length recognized the principle of her longing with so wildly earnest a desire for the life which was fleeing so rapidly away. It is this wild longing—it is this vehement desire for life—but for life—that I have no power to portray—no utterance capable of expressing."

Well, that is ghastly enough, in all conscience.

"And from them that have not shall be taken away even that which they have."

"To him that hath life shall be given life, and from him that hath not life shall be taken away even that life which he hath."

Or her either.

These terribly conscious birds like Poe and his Ligeia deny the very life that is in them, they want to turn it all into talk, into *knowing*. And so life, which will *not* be known, leaves them.

But poor Ligeia, how could she help it. It was her doom. All the centuries of the SPIRIT, all the years of American rebellion against the Holy Ghost, had done it to her.

She dies, when she would rather do anything than die. And when she dies the clue, which he only lived to grasp, dies with her.

Foiled!

Foiled!

No wonder she shrieks with her last breath.

On the last day Ligeia dictates to her husband a poem. As poems go, it is rather false, meretricious. But put yourself in Ligeia's place, and it is real enough, and ghastly beyond bearing.

> "Out, out are all the lights—out all!
>   And over each quivering form
> The curtain, a funeral pall,
>   Comes down with the rush of a storm,
> And the angels, all pallid and wan,
>   Uprising, unveiling, affirm
> That the play is the tragedy 'Man,'
>   And its hero the Conqueror Worm."

Which is the American equivalent for a William Blake poem. For Blake, too, was one of these ghastly, obscene "Knowers."

" 'O God!' half shrieked Ligeia, leaping to her feet and extending her arms aloft with a spasmodic movement, as I made an end of these lines. 'O God! O Divine Father!—shall these things be undeviatingly so?

Shall this conqueror be not once conquered? Are we not part and parcel in Thee? Who—who knoweth the mysteries of the angels, *nor unto death utterly*, save only through the weakness of his feeble will.' "

So Ligeia dies. And yields to death at least partly. *Anche troppo.*

As for her cry to God—has not God said that those who sin against the Holy Ghost shall not be forgiven?

And the Holy Ghost is within us. It is the thing that prompts us to be real, not to push our own cravings too far, not to submit to stunts and high falutin, above all not to be too egoistic and wilful in our conscious self, but to change as the spirit inside us bids us change, and leave off when it bids us leave off, and laugh when we must laugh, particularly at ourselves, for in deadly earnestness there is always something a bit ridiculous. The Holy Ghost bids us never be too deadly in our earnestness, always to laugh in time, at ourselves and everything. Particularly at our sublimities. Everything has its hour of ridicule—everything.

Now Poe and Ligeia, alas, couldn't laugh. They were frenziedly earnest. And frenziedly they pushed on this vibration of consciousness and unison in consciousness. They sinned against the Holy Ghost that bids us all laugh and forget, bids us know our own limits. And they weren't forgiven.

Ligeia needn't blame God. She had only her own will, her "gigantic volition" to thank, lusting after more consciousness, more beastly KNOW-ING.

Ligeia dies. The husband goes to England, vulgarly buys or rents a gloomy, grand old abbey, puts it into some sort of repair, and furnishes it with exotic, mysterious, theatrical splendour. Never anything open and real. This theatrical "volition" of his. The bad taste of sensationalism.

Then he marries the fair-haired, blue-eyed Lady Rowena Trevanion, of Tremaine. That is, she would be a sort of Saxon-Cornish blue-blood damsel. Poor Poe!

"In halls such as these—in a bridal chamber such as this—I passed, with the Lady of Tremaine, the unhallowed hours of the first month of our marriage—passed them with but little disquietude. That my wife dreaded the fierce moodiness of my temper—that she shunned and loved me but little—I could not help perceiving, but it gave me rather pleasure than otherwise. I loathed her with a hatred belonging rather to a demon than a man. My memory flew back (Oh, with what intensity of regret!) to Ligeia, the beloved, the august, the entombed. I revelled in recollections of her purity . . ." etc.

Now the vampire lust is consciously such.

In the second month of the marriage the Lady Rowena fell ill. It is the shadow of Ligeia hangs over her. It is the ghostly Ligeia who pours poison into Rowena's cup. It is the spirit of Ligeia, leagued with the spirit of the husband, that now lusts in the slow destruction of Rowena. The two vampires, dead wife and living husband.

For Ligeia has not yielded unto death *utterly*. Her fixed, frustrated will comes back in vindictiveness. She could not have her way in life. So she, too, will find victims in life. And the husband, all the time, only uses Rowena as a living body on which to wreak his vengeance for his being thwarted with Ligeia. Thwarted from the final KNOWING her.

And at last from the corpse of Rowena, Ligeia rises. Out of her death, through the door of a corpse they have destroyed between them, reappears Ligeia, still trying to have her will, to have more love and knowledge, the final gratification which is never final, with her husband.

For it is true, as William James and Conan Doyle and the rest allow, that a spirit can persist in the after-death. Persist by its own volition. But usually, the evil persistence of a thwarted will, returning for vengeance on life. Lemures, vampires.

It is a ghastly story of the assertion of the human will, the will-to-love and the will-to-consciousness, asserted against death itself. The pride of human conceit in KNOWLEDGE.

There are terrible spirits, ghosts, in the air of America.

Eleanora, the next story, is a fantasy revealing the sensational delights of the man in his early marriage with the young and tender bride. They dwelt, he, his cousin and her mother, in the sequestered Valley of Many-coloured Grass, the valley of prismatic sensation, where everything seems spectrum-coloured. They looked down at their *own images* in the River of Silence, and drew the god Eros from that wave: out of their own self-consciousness, that is. This is a description of the life of introspection and of the love which is begotten by the self in the self, the self-made love. The trees are like serpents worshipping the sun. That is, they represent the phallic passion in its poisonous or mental activity. Everything runs to consciousness: serpents worshipping the sun. The embrace of love, which should bring darkness and oblivion, would with these lovers be a daytime thing bringing more heightened consciousness, visions, spectrum-visions, prismatic. The evil thing that daytime love-making is, and all sex-palaver.

In *Berenice* the man must go down to the sepulchre of his beloved and pull out her thirty-two small white teeth, which he carries in a box with him. It is repulsive and gloating. The teeth are the instruments of biting, of resistance, of antagonism. They often become symbols of opposition, little instruments or entities of crushing and destroying. Hence the dragon's teeth in the myth. Hence the man in *Berenice* must take possession of the irreducible part of his mistress. *"Toutes ses dents étaient des idées,*" he says. Then they are little fixed ideas of mordant hate, of which he possesses himself.

The other great story linking up with this group is *The Fall of the House of Usher*. Here the love is between brother and sister. When the self is broken, and the mystery of the recognition of *otherness* fails, then the longing for identification with the beloved becomes a lust. And it is this longing for identification, utter merging, which is at the base of the incest problem. In psychoanalysis almost every trouble in the psyche is traced to an incest-desire. But it won't do. Incest-desire is only one of the modes by which men strive to get their gratification of the intensest vibration of the spiritual nerves, without any resistance. In the family, the natural vibration is most nearly in unison. With a stranger, there is greater resistance. Incest is the getting of gratification and the avoiding of resistance.

The root of all evil is that we all want this spiritual gratification, this flow, this apparent heightening of life, this knowledge, this valley of many-coloured grass, even grass and light prismatically decomposed, giving ecstasy. We want all this *without resistance*. We want it continually. And this is the root of all evil in us.

We ought to pray to be resisted and resisted to the bitter end. We ought to decide to have done at last with craving.

The motto to *The Fall of the House of Usher* is a couple of lines from Béranger.

> "Son coeur est un luth suspendu;
> Sitôt qu'on le touche il résonne." *

We have all the trappings of Poe's rather overdone, vulgar fantasy. "I reined my horse to the precipitous brink of a black and lurid tarn that lay in unruffled lustre by the dwelling, and gazed down—but with a shudder even more thrilling than before—upon the remodelled and inverted images of the grey sedge, and the ghastly tree-stems, and the vacant and eye-like windows." The House of Usher, both dwelling and family, was very old. Minute fungi overspread the exterior of the house, hanging in festoons from the eaves. Gothic archways, a valet of stealthy step, sombre tapestries, ebon black floors, a profusion of tattered and antique furniture, feeble gleams of encrimsoned light through latticed panes, and over all "an air of stern, deep, irredeemable gloom"—this makes up the interior.

The inmates of the house, Roderick and Madeline Usher, are the last remnants of their incomparably ancient and decayed race. Roderick has the same large, luminous eye, the same slightly arched nose of delicate Hebrew model, as characterized Ligeia. He is ill with the nervous malady of his family. It is he whose nerves are so strung that they vibrate to the unknown quiverings of the ether. He, too, has lost his self, his living soul, and become a sensitized instrument of the external influences; his nerves are verily like an æolian harp which must vibrate. He lives in "some struggle with the grim phantasm, Fear," for he is only the physical, post-mortem reality of a living being.

It is a question how much, once the true centrality of the self is broken, the instrumental consciousness of man can register. When man becomes self-less, wafting instrumental like a harp in an open window, how much can his elemental consciousness express? The blood as it runs has its own sympathies and responses to the material world, quite apart

---

* ["His heart is a hanging lute;
If one but touches it, it sounds."—Ed.]

from seeing. And the nerves we know vibrate all the while to unseen presences, unseen forces. So Roderick Usher quivers on the edge of material existence.

It is this mechanical consciousness which gives "the fervid facility of his impromptus." It is the same thing that gives Poe his extraordinary facility in versification. The absence of real central or impulsive being in himself leaves him inordinately mechanically sensitive to sounds and effects, associations of sounds, associations of rhyme, for example— mechanical, facile, having no root in any passion. It is all a secondary, meretricious process. So we get Roderick Usher's poem, *The Haunted Palace*, with its swift yet mechanical subtleties of rhyme and rhythm, its vulgarity of epithet. It is all a sort of dream-process, where the association between parts is mechanical, accidental as far as passional meaning goes.

Usher thought that all vegetable things had sentience. Surely all material things have a *form* of sentience, even the inorganic: surely they all exist in some subtle and complicated tension of vibration which makes them sensitive to external influence and causes them to have an influence on other external objects, irrespective of contact. It is of this vibration or inorganic consciousness that Poe is master: the sleep-consciousness. Thus Roderick Usher was convinced that his whole surroundings, the stones of the house, the fungi, the water in the tarn, the very reflected image of the whole, was woven into a physical oneness with the family, condensed, as it were, into one atmosphere—the special atmosphere in which alone the Ushers could live. And it was this atmosphere which had moulded the destinies of his family.

But while ever the soul remains alive, it is the moulder and not the moulded. It is the souls of living men that subtly impregnate stones, houses, mountains, continents, and give these their subtlest form. People only become subject to stones after having lost their integral souls.

In the human realm, Roderick had one connection: his sister Madeline. She, too, was dying of a mysterious disorder, nervous, cataleptic. The brother and sister loved each other passionately and exclusively. They were twins, almost identical in looks. It was the same absorbing love between them, this process of unison in nerve-vibration, resulting in more and more extreme exaltation and a sort of consciousness, and a gradual break-down into depth. The exquisitely sensitive Roderick, vibrating without resistance with his sister Madeline, more and more exquisitely, and gradually devouring her, sucking her life like a vampire in his anguish of extreme love. And she asking to be sucked.

Madeline died and was carried down by her brother into the deep vaults of the house. But she was not dead. Her brother roamed about in incipient madness—a madness of unspeakable terror and guilt. After eight days they were suddenly startled by a clash of metal, then a distinct, hollow metallic, and clangorous, yet apparently muffled, reverberation. Then Roderick Usher, gibbering, began to express himself: "We *have put her living into the tomb!* Said I not that my senses were acute? I *now* tell you that I heard her first feeble movements in the hollow coffin. I heard them—many, many days ago—yet I dared not—I *dared not speak.*"

It is the same old theme of "each man kills the thing he loves." He knew his love had killed her. He knew she died at last, like Ligeia, unwilling and unappeased. So, she rose again upon him. "But then without those doors there *did* stand the lofty and enshrouded figure of the Lady Madeline of Usher. There was blood upon her white robes, and the evidence of some bitter struggle upon every portion of her emaciated frame. For a moment she remained trembling and reeling to and fro upon the threshold, then, with a low moaning cry, fell heavily inward upon the person of her brother, and in her violent and now final death-agonies bore him to the floor a corpse, and a victim to the terrors he had anticipated."

It is lurid and melodramatic, but it is true. It is a ghastly psychological truth of what happens in the last stages of this beloved love, which cannot be separate, cannot be isolate, cannot listen in isolation to the isolate Holy Ghost. For it is the Holy Ghost we must live by. The next era is the era of the Holy Ghost. And the Holy Ghost speaks individually inside each individual: always, for ever a ghost. There is no manifestation to the general world. Each isolate individual listening in isolation to the Holy Ghost within him.

The Ushers, brother and sister, betrayed the Holy Ghost in themselves. They would love, love, love, without resistance. They would love, they would merge, they would be as one thing. So they dragged each other down into death. For the Holy Ghost says you must *not* be as one thing with another being. Each must abide by itself, and correspond only within certain limits.

The best tales all have the same burden. Hate is as inordinate as love, and as slowly consuming, as secret, as underground, as subtle. All this underground vault business in Poe symbolizes that which takes place *beneath* the consciousness. On top, all is fair-spoken. Beneath, there is awful murderous extremity of burying alive. Fortunato, in *The Cask of Amontillado,* is buried alive out of perfect hatred, as the Lady Madeline of Usher is buried alive out of love. The lust of hate is the inordinate desire to consume and unspeakably possess the soul of the hated one, just as the lust of love is the desire to possess, or to be possessed by, the beloved, utterly. But in either case the result is the dissolution of both souls, each losing itself in transgressing its own bounds.

The lust of Montresor is to devour utterly the soul of Fortunato. It would be no use killing him outright. If a man is killed outright his soul remains integral, free to return into the bosom of some beloved, where it can enact itself. In walling-up his enemy in the vault, Montresor seeks to bring about the indescribable capitulation of the man's soul, so that he, the victor, can possess himself of the very being of the vanquished. Perhaps this can actually be done. Perhaps, in the attempt, the victor breaks the bonds of his own identity, and collapses into nothingness, or into the infinite. Becomes a monster.

What holds good for inordinate hate holds good for inordinate love. The motto, *Nemo me impune lacessit,* might just as well be *Nemo me impune amat.*

In *William Wilson* we are given a rather unsubtle account of the attempt of a man to kill his own soul. William Wilson, the mechanical, lustful ego succeeds in killing William Wilson, the living self. The lustful ego lives on, gradually reducing itself towards the dust of the infinite.

In the *Murders in the Rue Morgue* and *The Gold Bug* we have those mechanical tales where the interest lies in the following out of a subtle chain of cause and effect. The interest is scientific rather than artistic, a study in psychologic reactions.

The fascination of murder itself is curious. Murder is not just killing. Murder is a lust to get at the very quick of life itself, and kill it—hence the stealth and the frequent morbid dismemberment of the corpse, the attempt to get at the very quick of the murdered being, to find the quick and to possess it. It is curious that the two men fascinated by the art of murder, though in different ways, should have been De Quincey and Poe, men so different in ways of life, yet perhaps not so widely different in nature. In each of them is traceable that strange lust for extreme love and extreme hate, possession by mystic violence of the other soul, or violent deathly surrender of the soul in the self: an absence of manly virtue, which stands alone and accepts limits.

Inquisition and torture are akin to murder: the same lust. It is a combat between inquisitor and victim as to whether the inquisitor shall get at the quick of life itself, and pierce it. Pierce the very quick of the soul. The evil will of man tries to do this. The brave soul of man refuses to have the life-quick pierced in him. It is strange: but just as the thwarted will can persist evilly, after death, so can the brave spirit preserve, even through torture and death, the quick of life and truth. Nowadays society is evil. It finds subtle ways of torture, to destroy the life-quick, to get at the life-quick in a man. Every possible form. And still a man can hold out, if he can laugh and listen to the Holy Ghost. —But society is evil, evil, and love is evil. And evil breeds evil, more and more.

So the mystery goes on. La Bruyère says that all our human unhappinesses *viennent de ne pouvoir être seuls.* As long as man lives he will be subject to the yearning of love or the burning of hate, which is only inverted love.

But he is subject to something more than this. If we do not live to eat, we do not live to love either.

We live to stand alone, and listen to the Holy Ghost. The Holy Ghost, who is inside us, and who is many gods. Many gods come and go, some say one thing and some say another, and we have to obey the

God of the innermost hour. It is the multiplicity of gods within us make up the Holy Ghost.

But Poe knew only love, love, love, intense vibrations and heightened consciousness. Drugs, women, self-destruction, but anyhow the prismatic ecstasy of heightened consciousness and sense of love, of flow. The human soul in him was beside itself. But it was not lost. He told us plainly how it was, so that we should know.

He was an adventurer into vaults and cellars and horrible underground passages of the human soul. He sounded the horror and the warning of his own doom.

Doomed he was. He died wanting more love, and love killed him. A ghastly disease, love. Poe telling us of his disease: trying even to make his disease fair and attractive. Even succeeding.

Which is the inevitable falseness, duplicity of art, American Art in particular.

D. H. LAWRENCE

Whitman

*P*ost mortem effects?

But what of Walt Whitman?

The "good grey poet."

Was he a ghost, with all his physicality?

The good grey poet.

Post mortem effects. Ghosts.

A certain ghoulish insistency. A certain horrible pottage of human parts. A certain stridency and portentousness. A luridness about his beatitudes.

DEMOCRACY! THESE STATES! EIDOLONS! LOVERS, ENDLESS LOVERS!

ONE IDENTITY!

ONE IDENTITY!

I AM HE THAT ACHES WITH AMOROUS LOVE.

Do you believe me, when I say post mortem effects?

When the *Pequod* went down, she left many a rank and dirty steamboat still fussing in the seas. The *Pequod* sinks with all her souls, but their bodies rise again to man innumerable tramp steamers, and ocean-crossing liners. Corpses.

What we mean is that people may go on, keep on, and rush on, without souls. They have their ego and their will, that is enough to keep them going.

So that you see, the sinking of the *Pequod* was only a metaphysical tragedy after all. The world goes on just the same. The ship of the *soul* is sunk. But the machine-manipulating body works just the same: digests, chews gum, admires Botticelli and aches with amorous love.

I AM HE THAT ACHES WITH AMOROUS LOVE.

What do you make of that? I AM HE THAT ACHES. First generalization. First uncomfortable universalization. WITH AMOROUS LOVE! Oh, God! Better a bellyache. A bellyache is at least specific. But the ACHE OF AMOROUS LOVE!

Think of having that under your skin. All that!

I AM HE THAT ACHES WITH AMOROUS LOVE.

Walter, leave off. You are not HE. You are just a limited Walter. And your ache doesn't include all Amorous Love, by any means. If you ache you only ache with a small bit of amorous love, and there's so much more stays outside the cover of your ache, that you might be a bit milder about it.

I AM HE THAT ACHES WITH AMOROUS LOVE.

CHUFF! CHUFF! CHUFF!

CHU-CHU-CHU-CHU-CHUFF!

Reminds one of a steam-engine. A locomotive. They're the only things that seem to me to ache with amorous love. All that steam inside them. Forty million foot-pounds pressure. The ache of AMOROUS LOVE. Steam-pressure. CHUFF!

An ordinary man aches with love for Belinda, or his Native Land, or the Ocean, or the Stars, or the Oversoul: if he feels that an ache is in the fashion.

It takes a steam-engine to ache with AMOROUS LOVE. All of it.

Walt was really too superhuman. The danger of the superman is that he is mechanical.

They talk of his "splendid animality." Well, he'd got it on the brain, if that's the place for animality.

I am he that aches with amorous love:
Does the earth gravitate, does not all matter, aching, attract all matter?
So the body of me to all I meet or know.

What can be more mechanical? The difference between life and matter is that life, living things, living creatures, have the instinct of turning right away from *some* matter, and of blissfully ignoring the bulk of most matter, and of turning towards only some certain bits of specially selected matter. As for living creatures all helplessly hurtling together into one great snowball, why, most very living creatures spend the greater part of their time getting out of the sight, smell or sound of the rest of living creatures. Even bees only cluster on their own queen. And that is sickening enough. Fancy all white humanity clustering on one another like a lump of bees.

No, Walt, you give yourself away. Matter *does* gravitate, helplessly. But men are tricky-tricksy, and they shy all sorts of ways.

Matter gravitates because it *is* helpless and mechanical.

And if you gravitate the same, if the body of you gravitates to all you meet or know, why, something must have gone seriously wrong with you. You must have broken your mainspring.

You must have fallen also into mechanization.

Your Moby Dick must be really dead. That lonely phallic monster of the individual you. Dead mentalized.

I only know that my body doesn't by any means gravitate to all I meet or know. I find I can shake hands with a few people. But most I wouldn't touch with a long prop.

Your mainspring is broken, Walt Whitman. The mainspring of your own individuality. And so you run down with a great whirr, merging with everything.

You have killed your isolate Moby Dick. You have mentalized your deep sensual body, and that's the death of it.

I am everything and everything is me and so we're all One in One Identity, like the Mundane Egg, which has been addled quite a while.

"Whoever you are, to endless announcements—"
"And of these one and all I weave the song of myself."

Do you? Well, then, it just shows you haven't *got* any self. It's a mush, not a woven thing. A hotch-potch, not a tissue. Your self.

Oh, Walter, Walter, what have you done with it? What have you done with yourself? With your own individual self? For it sounds as if it had all leaked out of you, leaked into the universe.

Post mortem effects. The individuality had leaked out of him.

No, no, don't lay this down to poetry. These are post mortem effects. And Walt's great poems are really huge fat tomb-plants, great rank graveyard growths.

All that false exuberance. All those lists of things boiled in one pudding-cloth! No, no!

I don't want all those things inside me, thank you.

"I reject nothing," says Walt.

If that is so, one must be a pipe open at both ends, so everything runs through.

Post mortem effects.

"I embrace ALL," says Whitman. "I weave all things into myself."

Do you really! There can't be much left of *you* when you've done. When you've cooked the awful pudding of One Identity.

"And whoever walks a furlong without sympathy walks to his own funeral dressed in his own shroud."

Take off your hat then, my funeral procession of one is passing. This awful Whitman. This post mortem poet. This poet with the private soul leaking out of him all the time. All his privacy leaking out in a sort of dribble, oozing into the universe.

Walt becomes in his own person the whole world, the whole universe, the whole eternity of time. As far as his rather sketchy knowledge of history will carry him, that is. Because to *be* a thing he had to know it. In order to assume the identity of a thing, he had to know that thing. He was not able to assume one identity with Charlie Chaplin, for example, because Walt didn't know Charlie. What a pity! He'd have done poems, pæans and what not, Chants. Songs of Cinematernity.

"Oh, Charlie, my Charlie, another film is done—"

As soon as Walt *knew* a thing, he assumed a One Identity with it. If he knew that an Esquimo sat in a kyak, immediately there was Walt being little and yellow and greasy, sitting in a kyak.

Now will you tell me exactly what a kyak is?

Who is he that demands petty definition? Let him behold me *sitting in a kyak*.

I behold no such thing. I behold a rather fat old man full of a rather senile, self-conscious sensuosity.

DEMOCRACY. EN MASSE. ONE IDENTITY.

The universe, in short, adds up to ONE.

ONE.

1.

Which is Walt.

His poems, *Democracy, En Masse, One Identity,* they are long sums in addition and multiplication, of which the answer is invariably MYSELF.

He reaches the state of ALLNESS.

And what then? It's all empty. Just an empty Allness. An addled egg.

Walt wasn't an esquimo. A little, yellow, sly, cunning, greasy little Esquimo. And when Walt blandly assumed Allness, including Esquimo-ness, unto himself, he was just sucking the wind out of a blown egg-shell, no more. Esquimos are not minor little Walts. They are something that I am not. I know that. Outside the egg of my Allness chuckles the greasy little Esquimo. Outside the egg of Whitman's Allness too.

But Walt wouldn't have it. He was everything and everything was in him. He drove an automobile with a very fierce headlight, along the track of a fixed idea, through the darkness of this world. And he saw Everything that way. Just as a motorist does in the night.

I, who happen to be asleep under the bushes in the dark, hoping a snake won't crawl into my neck; I, seeing Walt go by in his great fierce poetic machine, think to myself: What a funny world that fellow sees!

ONE DIRECTION! toots Walt in the car, whizzing along it.

Whereas they are myriads of ways in the dark, not to mention trackless wildernesses. As anyone will know who cares to come off the road, even the Open Road.

ONE DIRECTION! whoops America, and sets off also in an automobile.

ALLNESS! shrieks Walt at a cross-road, going whizz over an unwary Red Indian.

ONE IDENTITY! chants democratic En Masse, pelting behind in motorcars, oblivious of the corpses under the wheels.

God save me. I feel like creeping down a rabbit-hole, to get away from all these automobiles rushing down the ONE IDENTITY track to the goal of ALLNESS.

"A woman waits for me——"

He might as well have said: "The femaleness waits for my maleness." Oh, beautiful generalization and abstraction! Oh, biological function. "Athletic mothers of these States——" Muscles and wombs. They needn't have had faces at all.

"As I see myself reflected in Nature,
As I see through a mist, One with inexpressible completeness, sanity, beauty,
See the bent head, and arms folded over the breast, the Female I see."

Everything was female to him: even himself. Nature just one great function.

"This is the nucleus—after the child is born of woman, man is born of woman,
This is the bath of birth, the merge of small and large, and the outlet again——"

"The Female I see——"

If I'd been one of his women, I'd have given him Female. With a flea in his ear.

Always wanting to merge himself into the womb of something or other.

"The Female I see——"

Anything, so long as he could merge himself.

Just a horror. A sort of white flux.

Post mortem effects.

He found, like all men find, that you can't really merge in a woman, though you may go a long way. You can't manage the last bit. So you have to give it up, and try elsewhere. If you *insist* on merging.

In *Calamus* he changes his tune. He doesn't shout and thump and exult any more. He begins to hesitate, reluctant, wistful.

The strange calamus has its pink-tinged root by the pond, and it sends up its leaves of comradeship, comrades from one root, without the intervention of woman, the female.

So he sings of the mystery of manly love, the love of comrades. Over and over he says the same thing: the new world will be built on the love of comrades, the new great dynamic of life will be manly love. Out of this manly love will come the inspiration for the future.

Will it though? Will it?

Comradeship! Comrades! This is to be the new Democracy: of Com-

rades. This is the new cohering principle in the world: Comradeship.
Is it? Are you sure?

It is the cohering principle of true soldiery, we are told in *Drum Taps*.
It is the cohering principle in the new unison for creative activity. And
it is extreme and alone, touching the confines of death. Something
terrible to bear, terrible to be responsible for. Even Walt Whitman felt
it. The soul's last and most poignant responsibility, the responsibility of
comradeship, of manly love.

"Yet you are beautiful to me, you faint-tinged roots, you make me think
of death.
Death is beautiful from you (what indeed is finally beautiful except
death and love?)
I think it is not for life I am chanting here my chant of lovers, I think it
must be for death,
For how calm, how solemn it grows to ascend to the atmosphere of
lovers,
Death or life, I am then indifferent, my soul declines to prefer
(I am not sure but the high soul of lovers welcomes death most)
Indeed, O death, I think now these leaves mean precisely the same as
you mean——"

This is strange, from the exultant Walt.
Death!
Death is now his chant! Death!
Merging! And Death! Which is the final merge.
The great merge into the womb. Woman.
And after that, the merge of comrades: man-for-man love.
And almost immediately with this, death, the final merge of death.

There you have the progression of merging. For the great mergers,
woman at last becomes inadequate. For those who love to extremes.
Woman is inadequate for the last merging. So the next step is the merging of the man-for-man love. And this is on the brink of death. It slides
over into death.

David and Jonathan. And the death of Jonathan.
It always slides into death.
The love of comrades.
Merging.
So that if the new Democracy is to be based on the love of comrades,
it will be based on death too. It will slip so soon into death.

The last merging. The last Democracy. The last love. The love of
comrades.
Fatality. And fatality.
Whitman would not have been the great poet he is if he had not
taken the last steps and looked over into death. Death, the last merging,
that was the goal of his manhood.

To the mergers, there remains the brief love of comrades, and then
Death.

"Whereto answering, the sea
Delaying not, hurrying not
Whispered me through the night, very plainly before daybreak,
Lisp'd to me the low and delicious word death,
And again death, death, death, death.
Hissing melodions, neither like the bird nor like my arous'd child's heart,
But edging near as privately for me rustling at my feet,
Creeping thence steadily up to my ears and laving me softly all over
Death, death, death, death, death——"

Whitman is a very great poet, of the end of life. A very great post mortem poet, of the transitions of the soul as it loses its integrity. The poet of the soul's last shout and shriek, on the confines of death. *Après moi le déluge.*

But we have all got to die, and disintegrate.

We have got to die in life, too, and disintegrate while we live.

But even then the goal is not death.

Something else will come.

"Out of the cradle endlessly rocking."

We've got to die first, anyhow. And disintegrate while we still live.

Only we know this much. Death is not the *goal*. And Love, and merging, are now only part of the death-process. Comradeship—part of the death-process. Democracy—part of the death-process. The new Democracy—the brink of death. One Identity—death itself.

We have died, and we are still disintegrating.

But IT IS FINISHED.

Consummatum est.

Whitman, the great poet, has meant so much to me. Whitman, the one man breaking a way ahead. Whitman, the one pioneer. And only Whitman. No English pioneers, no French. No European pioneer-poets. In Europe the would-be pioneers are mere innovators. The same in America. Ahead of Whitman, nothing. Ahead of all poets, pioneering into the wilderness of unopened life, Whitman. Beyond him, none. His wide, strange camp at the end of the great high-road. And lots of new little poets camping on Whitman's camping ground now. But none going really beyond. Because Whitman's camp is at the end of the road, and on the edge of a great precipice. Over the precipice, blue distances, and the blue hollow of the future. But there is no way down. It is a dead end.

Pisgah. Pisgah sights. And Death. Whitman like a strange, modern, American Moses. Fearfully mistaken. And yet the great leader.

The essential function of art is moral. Not æsthetic, not decorative, not pastime and recreation. But moral. The essential function of art is moral.

But a passionate, implicit morality, not didactic. A morality which changes the blood, rather than the mind. Changes the blood first. The mind follows later, in the wake.

Now Whitman was a great moralist. He was a great leader. He was a great changer of the blood in the veins of men.

Surely it is especially true of American art, that it is all essentially moral. Hawthorne, Poe, Longfellow, Emerson, Melville: it is the moral issue which engages them. They all feel uneasy about the old morality. Sensuously, passionally, they all attack the old morality. But they know nothing better, mentally. Therefore they give tight mental allegiance to a morality which all their passion goes to destroy. Hence the duplicity which is the fatal flaw in them: most fatal in the most perfect American work of art, *The Scarlet Letter*. Tight mental allegiance given to a morality which the passional self repudiates.

Whitman was the first to break the mental allegiance. He was the first to smash the old moral conception, that the soul of man is something "superior" and "above" the flesh. Even Emerson still maintained this tiresome "superiority" of the soul. Even Melville could not get over it. Whitman was the first heroic seer to seize the soul by the scruff of her neck and plant her down among the potsherds.

"There!" he said to the soul. "Stay there!"

Stay there. Stay in the flesh. Stay in the limbs and lips and in the belly. Stay in the breast and womb. Stay there, O Soul, where you belong.

Stay in the dark limbs of negroes. Stay in the body of the prostitute. Stay in the sick flesh of the syphilitic. Stay in the marsh where the calamus grows. Stay there, Soul, where you belong.

The Open Road. The great home of the Soul is the open road. Not heaven, not paradise. Not "above." Not even "within." The soul is neither "above" nor "within." It is a wayfarer down the open road.

Not by meditating. Not by fasting. Not by exploring heaven after heaven, inwardly, in the manner of the great mystics. Not by exaltation. Not by ecstasy. Not by any of these ways does the soul come into her own.

Only by taking the open road.

Not through charity. Not through sacrifice. Not even through love. Not through good works. Not through these does the soul accomplish herself.

Only through the journey down the open road.

The journey itself, down the open road. Exposed to full contact. On two slow feet. Meeting whatever comes down the open road. In company with those that drift in the same measure along the same way. Towards no goal. Always the open road.

Having no known direction, even. Only the soul remaining true to herself in her going.

Meeting all the other wayfarers along the road. And how? How meet them, and how pass? With sympathy, says Whitman. Sympathy. He does not say love. He says sympathy. Feeling with. Feel with them as they feel with themselves. Catching the vibration of their soul and flesh as we pass.

It is a new great doctrine. A doctrine of life. A new great morality.

A morality of actual living, not of salvation. Europe has never got beyond the morality of salvation. America to this day is deathly sick with saviourism. But Whitman, the greatest and the first and the only American teacher, was no Saviour. His morality was no morality of salvation. His was a morality of the soul living her life, not saving herself. Accepting the contact with other souls along the open way, as they lived their lives. Never trying to save them. As leave try to arrest them and throw them in gaol. The soul living her life along the incarnate mystery of the open road.

This was Whitman. And the true rhythm of the American continent speaking out in him. He is the first white aboriginal.

"In my Father's house are many mansions."

"No," said Whitman. "Keep out of mansions. A mansion may be heaven on earth, but you might as well be dead. Strictly avoid mansions. The soul is herself when she is going on foot down the open road."

It is the American heroic message. The soul is not to pile up defenses round herself. She is not to withdraw and seek her heavens inwardly, in mystical ecstasies. She is not to cry to some God beyond, for salvation. She is to go down the open road, as the road opens, into the unknown, keeping company with those whose soul draws them near to her, accomplishing nothing save the journey, and the works incident to the journey, in the long life-travel into the unknown, the soul in her subtle sympathies accomplishing herself by the way.

This is Whitman's essential message. The heroic message of the American future. It is the inspiration of thousands of Americans today, the best souls of today, men and women. And it is a message that only in America can be fully understood, finally accepted.

Then Whitman's mistake. The mistake of his interpretation of his watchword: Sympathy. The mystery of SYMPATHY. He still confounded it with Jesus' LOVE, and with Paul's CHARITY. Whitman, like all the rest of us, was at the end of the great emotional highway of Love. And because he couldn't help himself, he carried on his Open Road as a prolongation of the emotional highway of Love, beyond Calvary. The highway of Love ends at the foot of the Cross. There is no beyond. It was a hopeless attempt, to prolong the highway of Love.

He didn't follow his Sympathy. Try as he might, he kept on automatically interpreting it as Love, as Charity. Merging.

This merging, en masse, One Identity, Myself monomania was a carry-over from the old Love idea. It was carrying the idea of Love to its logical physical conclusion. Like Flaubert and the leper. The decree of unqualified Charity, as the soul's one means of salvation, still in force.

Now Whitman wanted his soul to save itself, *he* didn't want to save it. Therefore he did not need the great Christian receipt for saving the soul. He needed to supersede the Christian Charity, the Christian Love, within himself, in order to give his Soul her last freedom. The highroad of Love is no Open Road. It is a narrow, tight way, where the soul walks hemmed in between compulsions.

Whitman wanted to take his Soul down the open road. And he failed in so far as he failed to get out of the old rut of Salvation. He forced his Soul to the edge of a cliff, and he looked down into death. And there he camped, powerless. He had carried out his Sympathy as an extension of Love and Charity. And it had brought him almost to madness and soul-death. It gave him his forced, unhealthy, post-mortem quality.

His message was really the opposite of Henley's rant:

I am the master of my fate.
I am the captain of my soul.

Whitman's essential message was the Open Road. The leaving of the soul free unto herself, the leaving of his fate to her and to the loom of the open road. Which is the bravest doctrine man has ever proposed to himself.

Alas, he didn't quite carry it out. He couldn't quite break the old maddening bond of the love-compulsion, he couldn't quite get out of the rut of the charity habit. For Love and Charity have degenerated now into habit: a bad habit.

Whitman said Sympathy. If only he had stuck to it! Because Sympathy means feeling with, not feeling for. He kept on having a passionate feeling *for* the negro slave, or the prostitute, or the syphilitic. Which is merging. A sinking of Walt Whitman's soul in the souls of these others.

He wasn't keeping to his open road. He was forcing his soul down an old rut. He wasn't leaving her free. He was forcing her into other peoples' circumstances.

Supposing he had felt true sympathy with the negro slave? He would have felt *with* the negro slave. Sympathy—compassion—which is partaking of the passion which was in the soul of the negro slave.

What was the feeling in the negro's soul?

"Ah, I am a slave! Ah, it is bad to be a slave! I must free myself. My soul will die unless she frees herself. My soul says I must free myself."

Whitman came along, and saw the slave, and said to himself: "That negro slave is a man like myself. We share the same identity. And he is bleeding with wounds. Oh, oh, is it not myself who am also bleeding with wounds?"

This was not *sympathy*. It was merging and self-sacrifice. "Bear ye one another's burdens."—"Love thy neighbour as thyself."—"Whatsoever ye do unto him, ye do unto me."

If Whitman had truly *sympathised*, he would have said: "That negro slave suffers from slavery. He wants to free himself. His soul wants to free him. He has wounds, but they are the price of freedom. The soul has a long journey from slavery to freedom. If I can help him I will: I will not take over his wounds and his slavery to myself. But I will help him fight the power that enslaves him when he wants to be free, if he wants my help. Since I see in his face that he needs to be free. But even when he is free, his soul has many journeys down the open road, before it is a free soul."

And of the prostitute Whitman would have said:

"Look at that prostitute! Her nature has turned evil under her mental lust for prostitution. She has lost her soul. She knows it herself. She likes to make men lose their souls. If she tried to make me lose my soul, I would kill her. I wish she may die."

But of another prostitute he would have said:

"Look! She is fascinated by the Priapic mysteries. Look, she will soon be worn to death by the Priapic usage. It is the way of her soul. She wishes it so."

Of the syphilitic he would say:

"Look! She wants to infect all men with syphilis. We ought to kill her."

And of another syphilitic:

"Look! She has a horror of her syphilis. If she looks my way I will help her to get cured."

This is sympathy. The soul judging for herself, and preserving her own integrity.

But when, in Flaubert, the man takes the leper to his naked body; when Bubi de Montparnasse takes the girl because he knows she's got syphilis; when Whitman embraces an evil prostitute: that is not sympathy. The evil prostitute has no desire to be embraced with love; so if you sympathise with her, you won't try to embrace her with love. The leper loathes his leprosy, so if you sympathise with him, you'll loathe it too. The evil woman who wishes to infect all men with her syphilis hates you if you haven't got syphilis. If you sympathise, you'll feel her hatred, and you'll hate too, you'll hate her. Her feeling is hate, and you'll share it. Only your soul will choose the direction of its own hatred.

The soul is a very perfect judge of her own motions, if your mind doesn't dictate to her. Because the mind says Charity! Charity! you don't have to force your soul into kissing lepers or embracing syphilitics. Your lips are the lips of your soul, your body is the body of your soul; your own single, individual soul. That is Whitman's message. And your soul hates syphilis and leprosy. Because it *is* a soul, it hates these things which are against the soul. And therefore to force the body of your soul into contact with uncleanness is a great violation of your soul. The soul wishes to keep clean and whole. The soul's deepest will is to preserve its own integrity, against the mind and the whole mass of disintegrating forces.

Soul sympathises with soul. And that which tries to kill my soul, my soul hates. My soul and my body are one. Soul and body wish to keep clean and whole. Only the mind is capable of great perversion. Only the mind tries to drive my soul and body into uncleanness and unwholesomeness.

What my soul loves, I love.

What my soul hates, I hate.

When my soul is stirred with compassion, I am compassionate.

What my soul turns away from, I turn away from.

That is the *true* interpretation of Whitman's creed: the true revelation of his Sympathy.

And my soul takes the open road. She meets the souls that are passing, she goes along with the souls that are going her way. And for one and all, she has sympathy. The sympathy of love, the sympathy of hate, the sympathy of simple proximity: all the subtle sympathisings of the incalculable soul, from the bitterest hate to the passionate love.

It is not I who guide my soul to heaven. It is I who am guided by my own soul along the open road, where all men tread. Therefore, I must accept her deep motions of love, or hate, or compassion, or dislike, or indifference. And I must go where she takes me. For my feet and my lips and my body are my soul. It is I who must submit to her.

This is Whitman's message of American democracy.

The true democracy, where soul meets soul, in the open road. Democracy. American democracy where all journey down the open road. And where a soul is known at once in its going. Not by its clothes or appearance. Whitman did away with that. Not by its family name. Not even by its reputation. Whitman and Melville both discounted that. Not by a progression of piety, or by works of Charity. Not by works at all. Not by anything but just itself. The soul passing unenhanced, passing on foot and being no more than itself. And recognized, and passed by or greeted according to the soul's dictate. If it be a great soul, it will be worshipped in the road.

The love of man and woman: a recognition of souls, and a communion of worship. The love of comrades: a recognition of souls, and a communion of worship. Democracy: a recognition of souls, all down the open road, and a great soul seen in its greatness, as it travels on foot among the rest, down the common way of the living. A glad recognition of souls, and a gladder worship of great and greater souls, because they are the only riches.

Love, and Merging, brought Whitman to the Edge of Death! Death! Death!

But the exultance of his message still remains. Purified of MERGING, purified of MYSELF, the exultant message of American Democracy, of souls in the Open Road, full of glad recognition, full of fierce readiness, full of joy of worship, when one soul sees a greater soul.

The only riches, the great souls.

APPENDIX

A Chronological Guide to Modern Poetry*

1817. CRITICISM: Coleridge, *Biographia Literaria.*

1827. POETRY: Poe, *Tamerlane.*

1840. POETRY: Browning, *Sordello.* PROSE: Poe, *Tales of the Grotesque and Arabesque.*

1846. CRITICISM: Poe, "The Philosophy of Composition." EVENTS: Poe translated by Baudelaire (1846–65).

1850. CRITICISM: Poe, "The Poetic Principle."

1851. CRITICISM: Sainte-Beuve, *Les Causeries de lundi* (1851–62). OTHER PROSE: Melville, *Moby Dick.*

1852. POETRY: Gautier, *Emaux et Camées.*

1854. PROSE: Thoreau, *Walden.*

1855. POETRY: Whitman, *Leaves of Grass.*

1857. POETRY: Baudelaire, *Les Fleurs du mal.* PROSE: Flaubert, *Madame Bovary.*

1865. PROSE: Carroll, *Alice's Adventures in Wonderland.*

1866. POETRY: *Le Parnasse contemporain* (anthology).

1867. PROSE: Marx, *Das Kapital.* EVENTS: Death of Baudelaire.

1868. POETRY: Browning, *The Ring and the Book.*

1869. CRITICISM: Arnold, *Culture and Anarchy.*

1871. PROSE: Darwin, *The Descent of Man.*

1872. CRITICISM: Nietzsche, *The Birth of Tragedy.*

1873. POETRY: Rimbaud, *Une Saison en enfer;* Corbière, *Les Amours jaunes.* CRITICISM: Pater, *Studies in the History of the Renaissance.*

1874. POETRY: Verlaine, *Romance sans paroles.*

1876. POETRY: Mallarmé, "L'Après-midi d'une faune."

1877. PROSE: Blavatsky, *Isis Unveiled.*

1879. PROSE: Ibsen, *A Doll's House.*

1880. "Decadents" (1880–90).

* The editor wishes to thank Ronald A. Mohl for assisting in the preparation of this guide.

1881. PROSE: Ibsen, *Ghosts*; Flaubert, *Le Bouvard et pécuchet* (posthumous).

1883. Death of Wagner.

1884. CRITICISM: Verlaine, *Les Poètes maudits*. OTHER PROSE: Huysmans, *A Rebours*.

1885. POETRY: Laforgue, *Les Complaintes*.

1886. Symbolist Manifesto.

1887. POETRY: Rimbaud, *Les illuminations*; Mallarmé, *Poésies complètes*. PROSE: Lang, *Myth, Ritual, and Religion*. EVENTS: Death of Laforgue.

1890. POETRY: Laforgue, *Les derniers vers* (posthumous). PROSE: Frazer, *The Golden Bough* (1890–1915).

1891. Death of Rimbaud.

1892. CRITICISM: Wilde, "The Decay of Lying." EVENTS: Death of Tennyson.

1893. POETRY: Thompson, *Poems*.

1894. *The Yellow Book* (1894–97).

1896. POETRY: Housman, *A Shropshire Lad*; Robinson, *The Torrent and the Night Before*; Dowson, *Non Sum Qualis Eram*. . . . EVENTS: Austin made Laureate; death of Verlaine.

1897. POETRY: Mallarmé, "Un Coup de Dés."

1898. POETRY: Wilde, "Ballad of Reading Gaol"; Hardy, *Wessex Poems*. CRITICISM: Tolstoy, *What Is Art?* EVENTS: Death of Mallarmé.

1899. POETRY: Yeats, *The Wind Among the Reeds*. CRITICISM: Symons, *The Symbolist Movement in Literature*. EVENTS: Irish National Theater.

1900. Death of Stephen Crane.

1901. POETRY: Hardy, *Poems of the Past and the Present*. EVENTS: Death of Victoria; reign of Edward VII.

1902. POETRY: Rilke, *Das Buch der Bilder*; Laforgue, *Oeuvres Complètes* (posthumous).

1904. POETRY: Hardy, *The Dynasts* (1904–8). EVENTS: Abbey Theater.

1905. PROSE: Synge, *Riders to the Sea*.

1906. POETRY: Yeats, *The Poetical Works* (1906–7).

1907. PROSE: Synge, *Playboy of the Western World*.

1908. POETRY: Nerval, *Choix de poésies*.

1909. POETRY: Pound, *Personae* and *Exultations*. EVENTS: *Nouvelle Revue Française*; Futurist Manifesto.

1910. POETRY: Aldington, *Images*. CRITICISM: Pound, *The Spirit of Romance*. EVENTS: Death of Tolstoy; reign of George V.

1911. PROSE: Lawrence, *The White Peacock*.

1912. POETRY: Amy Lowell, *A Dome of Many-Colored Glass*; Pound, *Ripostes*; *Georgian Poetry* (anthology, 1912–23). EVENTS: Founding of *Poetry*; Futurist Exhibition, Paris.

1913. POETRY: Lawrence, *Love Poems*; Frost, *A Boy's Will*; Lindsay, *General William Booth . . .*; · Apollinaire, *Alcools*. PROSE: Proust, *A la recherche du temps perdu* (1913–27); Harrison, *Ancient Art and Ritual*; Lawrence, *Sons and Lovers*. EVENTS: Bridges made Laureate.

1914. POETRY: Dickinson, *The Single Hound* (posthumous); Frost, *North of Boston*; Lindsay, *The Congo*; Pound, *Des Imagistes* (anthology). PROSE: Joyce, *Dubliners*; Stein, *Tender Buttons*. EVENTS: Vorticist Manifesto; *Blast*; *The Little Review* (1914–29).

1915. POETRY: Masters, *Spoon River Anthology*; Pound, *Cathay*; Fletcher, *Irradiations*. PROSE: Lawrence, *The Rainbow*. EVENTS: *Some Imagist Poets* (annual anthology, 1915–17); death of Brooke.

1916. POETRY: Sandburg, *Chicago Poems*; Robinson, *The Man Against the Sky*. CRITICISM: Freud, *Leonardo da Vinci*. OTHER PROSE: Jung, *Psychology of the Unconscious*. EVENTS: Dadaism (1916–22).

1917. POETRY: Monroe and Henderson, eds., *The New Poetry* (anthology); Eliot, *Prufrock*; Millay, *Renascence*; Valéry, "La Jeune Parc"; W. C. Williams, *Al Que Quiere!* EVENTS: First *Canto* published in *Poetry*.

1918. POETRY: Lawrence, *New Poems*; Brooke, *Collected Poems* (posthumous); Sassoon, *Counter-Attack*; Hopkins, *Poems* (posthumous); Apollinaire, *Calligrammes*. CRITICISM: Pound, "A Retrospect"; EVENTS: Founding of *The Dial* (1918–29); death of Owen.

1919. POETRY: Yeats, *The Wild Swans at Coole*; Waley (translator), *170 Chinese Poems*.

1920. POETRY: Hardy, *Collected Poems*; Owen, *Poems* (posthumous); Valéry, "Le Cimetière Marin"; W. C. Williams, *Kora in Hell*; Eliot, *Poems*; Pound, *Hugh Selwyn Mauberley*. CRITICISM: Eliot, *The Sacred Wood*. OTHER PROSE: Fenollosa, "The Chinese Written Character"; Uspenskii, *Tertium Organum*.

1921. POETRY: M. Moore, *Poems*. CRITICISM: Eliot, "The Metaphysical Poets."

1922. POETRY: Eliot, *The Waste Land*; Yeats, *Later Poems*; Sitwell, *Façade*; Housman, *Last Poems*; Laforgue, *Derniers vers* (posthumous). PROSE: Joyce, *Ulysses*; Cummings, *The Enormous Room*; Lawrence, *Fantasia of the Unconscious*. EVENTS: Founding of *Criterion* (1922–39).

1923. POETRY: Stevens, *Harmonium*; Rilke, *Duineser Elegien* and *Sonette an Orpheus*; Cummings, *Tulips and Chimneys*; Lawrence, *Birds,*

Beasts, and Flowers. CRITICISM: Eliot, "'Ulysses,' Order, and Myth"; Lawrence, *Studies in Classical American Literature.* OTHER PROSE: Ogden and Richards, *The Meaning of Meaning*; E. Jones, *Essays in Applied Psychoanalysis*; Jung, *Psychological Types.*

1924. POETRY: M. Moore, *Observations*; Dickinson, *Complete Poems* (posthumous); Ransom, *Chills and Fever.* CRITICISM: T. E. Hulme, *Speculations.* OTHER PROSE: O'Neill, *Complete Works.* EVENTS: Surrealist Manifesto.

1925. POETRY: Jeffers, *Tamar and Other Poems* and *Roan Stallion . . .*; H. D., *Collected Poems*; Pound, *A Draft of XVI Cantos*; Hardy, *Collected Poems.* PROSE: W. C. Williams, *In the American Grain*; Yeats, *A Vision.*

1926. POETRY: Hart Crane, *White Buildings.* PROSE: Spengler, *Decline of the West.*

1927. POETRY: Jeffers, *The Women at Point Sur.* CRITICISM: J. L. Lowes, *The Road to Xanadu.* EVENTS: Founding of *Transition* (1927–38).

1928. POETRY: Pound, *Selected Poems*; Stephen Benét, *John Brown's Body*; Lawrence, *Collected Poems.* EVENTS: *Lady Chatterley* arrested; death of Hardy.

1929. POETRY: Bridges, *The Testament of Beauty*; Day Lewis, *Transitional Poem*; Wylie, *Angels and Earthly Creatures*; Yeats, *The Winding Stair.* PROSE: Lawrence, *The Man Who Died.*

1930. POETRY: Hart Crane, *The Bridge*; Stephen Crane, *Collected Poems* (posthumous); Auden, *Poems*; Frost, *Collected Poems*; Sitwell, *Collected Poems*; Eliot, *Ash Wednesday*; Perse, *Anabase* (translated by Eliot). CRITICISM: Parrington, *Main Currents in American Thought*; Empson, *Seven Types of Ambiguity.* OTHER PROSE: Kafka, *The Castle* (translated); Joyce, *Anna Livia Plurabelle.* EVENTS: Death of Lawrence; Masefield made Laureate; death of Mayakovsky.

1931. CRITICISM: Wilson, *Axel's Castle.*

1932. POETRY: Auden, *The Orators*; MacLeish, *Conquistador.* CRITICISM: Eliot, *Selected Essays.* OTHER PROSE: Dos Passos, *1919.* EVENTS: Death of Hart Crane.

1933. POETRY: Hart Crane, *Collected Poems* (posthumous); Spender, *Poems*; Geoffrey Grigson, ed., *New Verse* (anthology, 1933–39); Yeats, *Collected Poems.* CRITICISM: Housman, *The Name and the Nature of Poetry*; Praz, *The Romantic Agony.*

1934. POETRY: Auden, *Poems*; Dylan Thomas, *Poems* (18). CRITICISM: Pound, *The ABC of Reading.* OTHER PROSE: Henry Miller, *Tropic of Cancer.* EVENTS: *Ulysses* unbound; founding of *Partisan Review.*

1935. POETRY: MacNeice, *Poems*; Stevens, *Ideas of Order*; M. Moore, *Selected Poems.* CRITICISM: Pound, *Make It New*; Spender, *The De-*

structive Element; Empson, *Some Versions of Pastoral*. OTHER PROSE: Pound, *Jefferson and/or Mussolini*.

1936. POETRY: Dylan Thomas, *25 Poems*; Sandburg, *The People, Yes*; Rilke, *Sonnets to Orpheus* (translated). CRITICISM: Tate, *Reactionary Essays*. OTHER PROSE: Henry Miller, *Black Spring*. EVENTS: Founding of New Directions.

1937. PROSE: Kafka, *The Trial* (translated).

1938. POETRY: Cummings, *Collected Poems*.

1939. POETRY: Dylan Thomas, *The World I Breathe*; Lorca, *Poems* (translated); Rilke, *Duino Elegies* (translated); Dujardin, *We'll to the Woods No More* (translation of *Les Lauriers sont coupés*, 1888). PROSE: Pound, *The ABC of Economics*; Brooks and Warren, *Understanding Poetry*; Joyce, *Finnegans Wake*; Henry Miller, *Tropic of Capricorn*. EVENTS: Death of Yeats; founding of *Kenyon Review*.

1940. PROSE: Eliot, *Idea of a Christian Society*.

1941. CRITICISM: Ransom, *The New Criticism*.

1942. PROSE: Sartre, *Les Mouches*; Camus, *Le Mythe de Sisyphe* and *L'Etranger*.

1943. POETRY: Eliot, *Four Quartets*. PROSE: Sartre, *L'Etre et le Néant*.

1944. POETRY: Shapiro, *V-Letter and Other Poems*.

1945. POETRY: Auden, *The Collected Poetry*. PROSE: Salinger, *The Catcher in the Rye*; Tennessee Williams, *The Glass Menagerie*; Reich, *Character Analysis*. EVENTS: Death of Valéry; Pound imprisoned.

1946. POETRY: R. Lowell, *Lord Weary's Castle*; W. C. Williams, *Paterson*; Pasternak, *Selected Poems*. PROSE: Henry Miller, *The Time of the Assassins*. EVENTS: Death of Stein.

1947. POETRY: Auden, *The Age of Anxiety*; Melville, *Collected Poems* (posthumous). PROSE: Pound, *The Unwobbling Pivot*; Sartre, "Existentialism."

1948. POETRY: Tate, *Poems 1922–47*; Pound, *The Pisan Cantos*; Roethke, *The Lost Son*. CRITICISM: Hyman, *The Armed Vision*. OTHER PROSE: Mailer, *The Naked and the Dead*; Norman, *The Case of Ezra Pound*; Graves, *The White Goddess*; Tennessee Williams, *Summer and Smoke*.

1949. PROSE: Orwell, *1984*. EVENTS: Bollingen Prize for *Pisan Cantos*.

1950. POETRY: Eliot, *The Cocktail Party*; Fry, *The Lady's Not for Burning*. CRITICISM: Auden, *The Enchafed Flood*.

1951. PROSE: Pound, *Confucian Analects*.

1952. POETRY: Cavafy, *Poems* (translated).

1953. POETRY: Dylan Thomas, *Under Milk Wood*. CRITICISM: Jarrell, *Poetry and the Age*. OTHER PROSE: Tennessee Williams, *Camino Real*. EVENTS: Death of Dylan Thomas; death of O'Neill.

1954. POETRY: Jeffers, *Hungerfield and Other Poems*; Cummings, *Poems.* EVENTS: Death of Bodenheim.

1955. Death of Stevens.

1956. POETRY: Ginsberg, *Howl.*

1957. CRITICISM: James E. Miller, *A Critical Guide to "Leaves of Grass."* OTHER PROSE: Kerouac, *On the Road.*

1958. PROSE: Pasternak, *Doctor Zhivago*; Norman, *The Magic-Maker.* EVENTS: Pound released.

1959. POETRY: Pound, *Thrones*; Pasternak, *Poems.* PROSE: Tate, *Collected Essays.* EVENTS: *Lady Chatterley* released.

1960. POETRY: Donald M. Allen, ed., *The New American Poetry 1945–1960* (anthology). PROSE: Pound, *Impact.* EVENTS: Death of Camus.

INDEX

257